The Cost
of Being
Female

THE COST
OF BEING
FEMALE

Sue Headlee and Margery Elfin

PRAEGER

Library of Congress Cataloging-in-Publication Data

Headlee, Sue E. (Sue Eleanor), 1943–
    The cost of being female / Sue Headlee, Margery Elfin.
        p.   cm.
    Includes bibliographical references and index.
    ISBN 0–275–95536–2 (alk. paper). — ISBN 0–275–95688–1 (pbk. :
alk. paper)
    1. Sex discrimination against women.   2. Women—Social conditions.
3. Women—Economic conditions.   I. Elfin, Margery.   II. Title.
HQ1237.H43   1996
305.42—dc20   96–15324

British Library Cataloguing in Publication Data is available.

Library of Congress Catalog Card Number: 96–15324
ISBN: 0–275–95536–2
        0–275–95688–1 (pbk.)

First published in 1996

Praeger Publishers, 88 Post Road West, Westport, CT 06881
An imprint of Greenwood Publishing Group, Inc.

Printed in the United States of America

The paper used in this book complies with the
Permanent Paper Standard issued by the National
Information Standards Organization (Z39.48–1984).

10 9 8 7 6 5 4 3 2 1

To the memory of
Harriet Taylor
and
John Stuart Mill

CONTENTS

TABLES

PREFACE

This book is dedicated to the memory of Harriet Taylor and John Stuart Mill whose marriage we admire as a partnership of equals and a meeting of the minds. They were feminists and progressive social reformers whose ideas on marriage, divorce, and society are startlingly modern.

Romance and reform meet in a quiet cemetery in the south of France, for it is there that two kindred souls are buried—Mill, the renowned nineteenth-century British philosopher, and Harriet Taylor, the wife of his later years.

It was an overcast day in April when we made a pilgrimage to Avignon to pay our respects at the tomb of this remarkable couple. We found St. Veran Cemetery on Avenue John Stuart Mill and bought some roses to lay on their grave. We stood in silence and read the loving inscription that Mill had written for his wife:

HER GREAT AND LOVING HEART
HER NOBLE SOUL
HER CLEAR POWERFUL ORIGINAL AND
COMPREHENSIVE INTELLECT
MADE HER THE GUIDE AND SUPPORT
THE INSTRUCTOR IN WISDOM
AND THE EXAMPLE IN GOODNESS
AS SHE WAS THE SOLE EARTHLY DELIGHT

TO THOSE WHO HAD THE HAPPINESS TO BELONG TO HER
AS EARNEST FOR THE PUBLIC GOOD
AS SHE WAS GENEROUS AND DEVOTED
TO ALL WHO SURROUNDED HER
HER INFLUENCE HAS BEEN FELT
IN MANY OF THE GREATEST
IMPROVEMENTS OF THE AGE
AND WILL BE IN THOSE STILL TO COME
WERE THERE BUT A FEW HEARTS AND INTELLECTS
LIKE HERS
THIS EARTH WOULD ALREADY BECOME
THE HOPED-FOR-HEAVEN.

Both authors acknowledge their collaboration as a tremendous learning experience and intellectual awakening. We are happy that after sitting shoulder to shoulder in front of the word processor nearly every Friday for five years, we emerge with a fair and equal relationship and a respect for each other's abilities. We thank Marcy Weiner, Economics Editor for Praeger, for appreciating our vision.

Both authors have a special place in their hearts for France and thank their many French friends and the government officials who helped them with their book.

Margery Elfin thanks the wonderful people of Norway who gave her such a warm welcome and the family of Anna Maripuu in Sweden who shared their experiences so generously.

Sue Headlee thanks all the generous people who hosted her in China in May of 1993 and introduced her to the other half of the world.

Sue Headlee wishes to thank mentors Nancy Barrett, Barbara Bergmann, Cynthia Taft Morris, Nancy Gordon, Heidi Hartmann, Nancy Folbre, and Harriet Harper; and friends Mary Redwine, Cheryl Powell-Williams, Agnes Denalane, Isabel Gandibleu, Birgitta Bjorkman, Wang Haiyan, Tian Ling, Edie Rasell, her sister, Ann Headlee, and her parents, Eleanor and Raymond Headlee. Special thanks to her dear husband, Jeffrey Reiman, for lowering the cost of being female for her.

Margery Elfin thanks the generations of women who made this book possible and whose histories she has tried to preserve. She thanks especially those who have made her life happy, interesting, and productive—her husband, Mel, who provided invaluable research assistance, her son and daughter, David and Dana, their spouses, and the grandchildren who will grow up in an age of equality. She is grateful to her mother, father, and sisters for their lifelong support and encouragement. She especially appreciates the many devoted friends from college days and later years whose honesty and willingness to share have made them her best sources of material.

INTRODUCTION: THE COST OF BEING FEMALE INDEX

Standing around at a cocktail party after an academic conference, a group of women were exchanging stories about discrimination they had experienced in their careers. The idea of the cost of being female came up when we discussed a recent case at the university where a woman had been paid less than her male counterparts. Another woman professor, interested in exploring such potential inequities on campus, pressured the university to undertake a study of faculty salaries. The study revealed that many women in the same rank were paid substantially less than men.

As a result of this study, the university gave raises to those women who had been underpaid. One of these women was Alice Brick, a forty-year-old college professor, who had never been elected to the rank and tenure committee of her department, although she was granted tenure—the only woman ever to be tenured in her department (Personal Interview, Spring 1991). She did not receive the course reductions (important to faculty involved in research) that her male colleagues did, despite a much better publications record. She had to wait longer for decisions from committees who hand them down for male professors quickly. All along she had felt outside the process and isolated from the decisions that tend to make academic life smoother or more difficult. She was clearly not regarded as "one of the boys," and this forced her into a series of confrontations about fairness. One male colleague told her she was too accomplished and too good; therefore she was threatening!

Alice Brick's case was settled by awarding her a 10 percent increase in salary. Thus the cost of being female for her was judged to be 10 percent of a male professor's salary!

> *Thinking about this cost to one woman and the ensuing settlement, the authors were reminded of the government's Cost of Living Adjustment index (COLA), which is calculated annually to compensate for inflation. Starting in 1973 when inflation was accelerating, the Nixon administration instituted a cost of living adjustment for social security recipients to help them maintain their standard of living in the face of that inflation.*
>
> *The idea of the COLA stimulated us to try to come up with an index to measure the cost of discrimination against women: the Cost of Being Female index (COBF). We think that the cost of being female should be calculated annually to compensate for discrimination. Some universities are now carrying out these studies on an annual basis for faculty salaries.*

Professor Brick's is a true story, although we have changed her name to protect her privacy. This is the method we have used throughout the book. We have used the experiences of more than seventy such women to test our hypothesis that it costs to be female. We have listed and described these women in the appendix. Most of the narratives that we have set apart in the text are based on interviews with particular women, but some are composite profiles.

It costs to be female in the United States in the 1990s. We are excluded from many good jobs. We are discriminated against in pay. More and more of us are supporting ourselves and our children with or without a husband's help. If we try to climb the corporate ladder, we bump our heads on a "glass ceiling," beyond which we cannot climb. The glass ceiling metaphor for subtle gender discrimination in the corporate world was first used in *The Wall Street Journal* in 1986. While we are moving into the professions, we are stalled in the lower-paying positions. Politically, we are vastly underrepresented in the legislative, executive, and judicial branches of federal, state, and local government. The same is true for female representation in key diplomatic positions.

We have observed changes in the cost of being female across the generations. The one area where the cost of being female has declined is in obtaining a college education. On the other hand, in the area of health, the cost of being female now includes an increasing incidence of rape, breast cancer, and new limits on our rights to abortion. In family life, we are still responsible for child care, husband care, and elder care. And now that the majority of women work, many work a double shift. After work for pay, we come home and cook and clean the house.

Certainly, there are benefits to being female. Some of us are still supported by men. There is less pressure for us to maximize our earnings, the traditional role of the husband. Thus we may have the opportunity to choose an interesting job for less pay. We tend to have physically easier jobs. Perhaps our jobs are of the less stressful type because we may have less responsibility. In the area of education, we are freer to study subjects that we find interesting but that the market does not reward highly.

We live longer than men. But since much of this time is spent in widowhood and poor health, this benefit is ambiguous. We have the benefit of bearing children. This is one of the real joys of being female. We usually get to know our children better than our husbands do. We exercise our caring capacity as we care for children, husbands, and parents. Women generally organize family and social activities. Some women enjoy homemaking and the autonomy of not working for pay. They find that work in the home is more fulfilling than working for pay.

On balance, however, we believe that the costs of being female outweigh the benefits. These costs are unnecessary and damaging constraints on women who represent more than half of the population. For this reason, we recommend public policies that reduce these constraints.

Table 1 summarizes the costs and benefits of being female, and our policy recommendations to reduce the costs. These claims will be defended in greater detail in the chapters that follow.

THE POLICIES WE RECOMMEND

We argue for these public policies, not just to loosen the constraints on women and not just to provide benefits for women. There are other reasons why men and women should support these policies. First, we want to live in a fair society. It is unjust to have systematic gender bias in employment, in political life, in the home, in the factories and offices of this country. Women are rational beings and as such have moral as well as legal rights to fair and equal treatment. This idea goes back a long way in history— to Mary Wollstonecraft in 1792 in England when she wrote *A Vindication of the Rights of Women*. For years gender bias was unquestioned, being as much a part of the political landscape as free elections. It took years and the trauma of two world wars to raise public consciousness. It took the weakening of the nuclear family to get people to realize that women, who are often the primary support of their households, must receive fair compensation.

Second, we want to maintain the standard of living that we have achieved in this country. In order to compete in the world today, we have to get rid of the inefficiency of discrimination. Discrimination means that women's talents are not being used where they will be most effective. It has been estimated that our gross domestic product (GDP) would be 15 percent greater if we could eliminate gender and racial discrimination. The new wealth that would begin to flow could finance the public policy programs that we recommend. Moreover, from now until well into the next century, the net additions to the workforce will be almost exclusively women and minorities. If our economy is to grow, we have to rid the workplace and the labor market of gender and racial discrimination.

Some feminists think that we should give up on the quest for equal rights

Table 1
Costs and Benefits of Being Female, and Public Policy Responses

	Costs	Benefits	Policy
Economic	Occupational segregation	Being supported if married	Mandate financing for rigorous enforcement of equal employment opportunity laws
	Hiring discrimination	Physically easier jobs	
	Promotion discrimination	Less stress	
	Earnings discrimination	Less responsibility	
	Less on-the-job training	Don't have to maximize earnings	Federal and local finance of quality child care
	Sexual harassment	Can go for the interesting job	
			Paid parental and family leave
Business and the professions	"Glass ceiling" limits advancement		Government incentives for corporate benefit policies reflective of women's needs
Political	Exclusion from political life	More time to do volunteer community service	Fund raising for women candidates
			Reduced cost of campaigning
Education	Girls not encouraged to study math and science	Can study disciplines that don't pay much but are interesting	Encourage girls to study science, math, technical areas
Health	NIH research underrepresents female health concerns	Women live longer	Women's Health Equity Act
	Rape	Women can bear children	Make rape a hate crime, a violation of women's civil rights
	Breast cancer		
	Limits on rights to abortion		Freedom of Choice Act

Table 1 (continued)

	Costs	Benefits	Policy
Social life	Husband care Child care Elder care Kin work	Women care about children's development Women get to know their children better Women get to manage the family's social life	Encourage men to take family leave Public finance of child care and elder care centers National health insurance for long-term care Enforcement of child support
Housekeeping	Cooking Cleaning Double shift	Women may enjoy homemaking for family Autonomy	Bureau of Labor Statistics to collect data on hours spent in housework Include housework in the GNP

and equal opportunities. In a 1991 cover story in *U.S. News and World Report,* neo-feminists (Camille Paglia, Suzanne Gordon, Elizabeth Fox-Genovese) rejected the attempt of women to break through the glass ceiling because it is impossible to achieve equality in a male corporate world. To be sure, the professions are dominated by a male style of aggressiveness that women should not emulate. But our answer is not to give up, but to work to get into the professions, and then change the rules to reflect women's attitudes and preferences—to reach consensus over combat, if that is what women want. If women want to drop out of the paid labor force and have children, fine. If men want parental leave, so be it. In Sweden, men have the right to six months of paid parental leave. The work world should accommodate those who take time out to raise the next generation of workers and citizens. But this is no reason to give up on the struggle for equal opportunity for the majority of women who now work. We reject the idea that rights are a male idea.

We also fear a backlash against women for the gains they have made. Several decisions of the Supreme Court in 1989 have made it more difficult for women and minorities to win in discrimination suits. Moreover, we can see the backlash in our popular culture. All the press and television news programs talk about women giving up paid work and staying home with babies; this sounds like "Feminine Mystique II" to us. Just as Rosie the Riveter had to be pressured back into the home after World War II so that the men could have their jobs back, now conservatives argue that women's quest for equality has destroyed the family. This mind-set leads to articles and programs about women giving up careers on the fast track and staying home with the children. On Mother's Day 1992 in the *Washington Post,* a male writer lamented how hard it is to be a mother in this day and age of working women. The answer is not to give up on the world of work, unless that is the woman's true choice. Rather, the failure is in the lack of private and public policies to meet the needs of working women. Since the late 1970s, the majority of women, including mothers of small children, have joined the labor force.

We also believe that the "Mommy Track" can be chosen by women and men who want to balance paid work and home life. Some women and men prefer slower career advancement and flexible work schedules so that they can take care of a sick child or other responsibilities. Until the gender revolution is achieved in the personal lives of men and women, we can use our market economy and our government to provide the services that women used to provide before they worked for pay. We advocate new policies for corporations to accommodate the changing workforce: "flextime" and day-care are two obvious examples. Let's create a "Human Track" for men and women with a better balance between work and family.

THE WOMEN WHOSE EXPERIENCES WE RECOUNT

Some feminists stress the differences, not the similarities, between men and women. When it comes to public life, public policy, the goals of a fair society and competitive economy, we call for stressing the similarities between men and women. Stressing the differences will encourage stereotypes of men and women. We want a world in which it is possible to have aggressive women and caring men, and vice versa.

We also disagree with the radical feminists in academia who want to throw out all theory and knowledge generated by white men in Western civilization. We do agree that not enough attention has been paid to gender, class, and race. The women's movement has been accused of being limited to white, middle-class women. In this book, we are concerned about the cost of being female for working-class women, especially since the deindustrialization of the United States that began in the 1970s. Some of the closing of the earnings gap between men and women has occurred not because of the success of women, but rather because blue-collar men have failed to sustain the real wages they were earning before 1973. We are also concerned about the cost of being female for women of color in this country. We will look at the progress of middle-class black women and the deteriorating condition of underclass black women.

We are interested in Freud's question, "What do women want?"

Therefore, we have interviewed many women asking them this very question. We also wanted to know how their lives are different from their mothers' lives. And we asked women what they wanted for their children. Thus we look at the cost of being female across the generations from post–World War II to our own day.

One of the women we will meet is a white midwestern woman who graduated from college before World War II and married soon after. Dorothy supported her husband through medical school by working as an interior decorator, but she never considered this as more than stopgap employment (Personal Interview, Spring 1992). Once her husband's career was launched, she became a full-time housewife and mother. Apparently, there was no conflict in her decision to remain at home, and they experienced no economic hardship in living as a one-income family. Her time outside the home was happily spent in volunteer work for her church and community.

Another woman whose life we will follow is a woman of the 1950s who earned a B.A. degree at a liberal arts college. Barbara had never received any guidance about careers; in fact, the college was rather contemptuous of "vocational" education and did not even offer a major in education, although teaching was one of the few fields then entirely open to women (Personal Interview, Fall 1991). This meant that many of her classmates found themselves unqualified to teach in any public school system and had to accept low-paying jobs in private schools. Only a few of her classmates went on to medical school or law school. Most married within a year of graduation and began a period of putting their husbands through graduate school by working at low-level jobs.

This transitional generation did not live happily ever after. It seems rather to have experienced a very high level of frustration, sublimated perhaps into an attempt to have the perfect marriage, perfect family, and perfect house and garden. Often, the marriages ended, and many women returned to graduate school and began careers.

A 1960s woman whom we are following, Nancy, proved to be far more independent than her 1950s sister (Personal Interview, Fall 1991). Influenced by the "social revolution" of the 1960s, she felt far less pressure to marry. Nancy did ultimately marry but did not stay in her first marriage. Nor did she have children. When she married a second time, she married a man who was receptive to a marriage on equal terms. She felt liberated and anxious to prove she could make it on her own. Now most schools and professions were open to her, and marriage and family were no longer the icons they had been. Social arrangements were a lot looser. Yet in the job market she was still not on a level playing field.

By the 1970s the effects of the social revolution began to be widely apparent. Consciousness had been raised for many people as a result of the founding of important women's rights organizations, the campaign for the

Equal Rights Amendment (ERA), and the abortion issue. The media focused an enormous amount of attention on women's issues, and laws were now in place guaranteeing equal opportunity. Our 1970s woman is career-minded and marries late, if at all. If she has children, she has them later. As greater numbers of women enter the professions, she finds herself more easily accepted in workplaces where ten years before she had been an oddity. A survey of Wellesley graduates from 1939 to 1989 found that the class of 1979 was the first in which there were more lawyers in the class than lawyer spouses! Only later when questions of promotion arise will these women find that discrimination still exists.

For a woman coming of age in the 1980s, the number of choices open to her often became confusing. The pressure to succeed at a career, to work as hard as men and compete on equal terms, was strong. The idea of marriage as a postgraduate career was considered anachronistic. The world was open to women, and they were expected to take advantage of it—to become investment bankers or truck drivers—to be pathbreakers in fields previously closed to women. Jennifer, a 1980s woman, began work at a nonprofit organization after graduating from a coed university, but it soon became apparent that it was more a job than a career (Personal Interview, Spring 1992). Jennifer realized that if she did not marry, she would need to work the rest of her life and that she needed better credentials to have the most rewarding life she could. She chose to return to school and earn a law degree.

As we glimpse these women in all the complexity and richness of their lives, we will see how gender has affected them. The world is changing for everyone, requiring new skills and new family arrangements. If discrimination continues to exist, we will all suffer the costs.

Our approach is to use the narratives of women's lives and experiences to demonstrate the costs of being female. We also use statistical analysis to see how the stories of the women we interview fit into the larger picture of gender and discrimination.

In the fifty years since World War II, almost half of the full-time homemakers in the United States have joined the paid labor force. This has been called "the economic emergence of women." Many costs were associated with this transition. As these women moved into paid work, they found occupational segregation with clear demarcation lines between men's jobs and women's jobs. Because the women's jobs paid less, there was an earnings gap. And because family members did not take up the slack, women found that, when they got home from work, they still had the same domestic responsibilities that they had when they were full-time homemakers.

On the benefit side, women enjoyed new opportunities, responsibilities, and privileges by being out in the world. Some achieved economic independence, intellectual growth, and self-confidence.

THE COBF INDEX

What was the net effect of the costs and benefits of this dramatic change in the activities of American women? What is the net cost of being female in 1995 compared to the cost of being female in 1945?

By the COBF, we mean the costs of discrimination against women in American society. In employment, when two people, one a man and one a woman, do the same work and get paid different amounts, the man earning more than the woman, we suspect discrimination. Of course, most women do not do the same work as men because of occupational segregation.

In developing our COBF index, we have defined the cost of being female as the unexplained difference in earnings between people doing work of the same productivity. In the case of Alice Brick, a clear example of unequal pay, we can look at the components of salary as the university does. We compare her credentials to those of males. If we find that she is equal to males in her graduate degrees, her teaching experience, and her publications record, and she is still earning less than they, we conclude that the resulting gap is evidence of discrimination. Hence, we arrive at a cost index. Dr. Brick, equal or superior in every component the university considers, is paid less. This difference constitutes a cost to her—the cost of being female.

Economists argue that people are paid according to how productive they are for the employer. Education makes an employee productive. If men have more education than women, on average, they will be more productive, and we will expect them to earn more. That would be pay equity. Educational differences may have been the case in the past, but now American women have made great strides in education. In fact, the situation is now reversed: more women than men are graduating from high school and college. We will test the hypothesis that the earnings gap can no longer be explained by the education gap.

Economists also argue that experience makes employees more productive. If men have more experience than women, then they will be more productive and we will expect them to earn more. We will estimate the experience gap. In 1950, only about one in three women worked outside the home. Since women did not have the work experience of men in 1950, it might be equitable then for men to earn more money than women. We would, however, expect this difference to decline over our time period, because of the massive movement of women into the paid labor force. By around 1990, more than 50 percent of women in the United States were in the paid labor force.

In the case of college and university teachers like Alice Brick, individuals of the same rank are paid differently according to gender. In one of the earliest studies, Nancy Gordon and her co-workers found that male full professors earned on average $5,000 more than women professors; male associate professors earned on average over $2,000 more than female ones;

and male assistant professors earned on average over $1,000 more than women of this rank.

Do men really make more than women in America today? Yes. In 1992, for every dollar a man earned, a woman earned, on average, 71 cents according to the Women's Bureau of the U.S. Department of Labor. (Apparently, this difference has been around for a long time. In Leviticus [27:1–4], the Bible says that women should be paid two-thirds of what men are paid.) Let us say that the COBF in the workplace in America in 1992 was 29 cents per dollar earned by a male. This number is for full-time employees, so the fact that women work fewer hours than men means that they earn even less than our measure implies. Some of this 29 cent difference is due to women having less experience and may be considered legitimate. We will argue that 29 cents is an unnecessary and damaging cost to women and to everyone in American society (and has been from biblical times).

The COBF is more than the wage gap. However, wage data are collected and easy to understand. It is convenient to talk of the COBF as the percentage gap between men and women's earnings. Furthermore, the COBF in the workplace is actually the unfair part of the gap, the part that is discrimination in the labor market. This is rarely measured and is difficult to calculate. Again, for convenience, we say that the COBF in the workplace is the wage gap.

A large part of the COBF is due to the fact that men and women work at different occupations and men's occupations pay more than women's. It has been estimated that over a third of the COBF is due to occupational segregation. Assuming that women do not *choose* jobs that pay poorly (a proposition that we will defend later in this book), we can conclude that this is employment discrimination and economic inequity.

In addition to discrimination resulting from occupational segregation, there is direct discrimination in pay, among men and women in the same occupation. It has been estimated that one-half of the earnings gap is due to direct discrimination in the labor market, as opposed to subtler forms of discrimination in education, in society, in the family and home, and so on.

The earnings gap then is made up of several components: occupational segregation, pay discrimination per se, and educational and social discrimination, and thus is a good indicator of the overall cost of being female.

Advocates of women's rights could argue that women are owed reparations for this discrimination. Our government could tax everyone with progressive taxes and then pay women what they would be earning in a gender-fair society, or what they would be earning if they were men. The COBF index could be computed each year and paid out as Cost of Living Adjustments (COLAs). Beneficiaries of government transfer payments and union employees receive COLAs to compensate for the erosion of their real earning power due to inflation.

Another use of the COBF index would be to monitor and measure our success in reducing gender discrimination in our society. If the COBF was 29 cents in 1992, then our goal could be to reduce the cost to 19 cents in 2002, to 9 cents in 2012, and to zero in 2022.

According to the Women's Bureau, in 1955 the COBF was 36 cents for each male dollar earned. In 37 years, the COBF has been reduced by 7 cents. That is approximately 1 cent for every five years. At that rate, assuming that there is no retrogression, it would take more than a century to eliminate the COBF. That is not fast enough. When we add the political, educational, social, and health COBF, we hypothesize that the net costs are greater today than they were in 1955.

This study asks the question: How has the COBF changed since World War II when the majority of women went from being full-time homemakers to women working in the marketplace? Are the benefits of paid work greater than the costs in America today for women? We hypothesize that the COBF is greater today than it was before World War II because adaptation to the economic emergence of women has not been completed. While economic opportunity for women has increased, new economic and social costs have emerged.

Moreover, progress is not necessarily continuous: often we take two steps forward and one step back. In this study we will ask: how did the COBF in the 1970s, the active decade of the modern women's movement, compare with the COBF in the 1980s, the era of the so-called backlash against women's achievements? Were the 1980s an economic plateau for women? Was the situation still improving, even if more slowly? Was a moderation or correction taking place? What are the prospects for the 1990s?

This dramatic change in American society occurred in just two generations. Our major interest is in measuring (exploring, understanding, explaining) the COBF in 1945 when the majority of women in America were full-time homemakers and comparing that to the COBF in 1995 when the majority of women were working outside the home.

In probing the transition between these two points, we measure the COBF for a 1950s woman, who deals with the transition by being a full-time homemaker for the key ten years when her children are young, but for the rest of her life has a career. Then we measure the COBF for a 1960s woman, who deals with the transition by not having children and working for pay her whole life. Studies have shown that the COBF, if one does not have children, is 10 cents per male dollar earned. Thus children constitute a major element in the COBF. For example, economist June O'Neill finds that the ratio of female-to-male hourly earning ratios of workers with children is 72 percent, whereas without children the ratio is 90.7 percent.

The COBF varies by marital and parental status. The COBF is greater if a woman marries; unmarried women make 15 cents more than married women. The COBF increases after divorce, whereas men maintain their incomes after divorce. It costs even more if a woman has children and no husband (divorced or never married). We will estimate the COBF for women who are full-time homemakers married to working men, women in dual-earner families, and women who are single heads of household.

The COBF varies by class. As a proxy for class, we look at occupations and educational levels. One-fourth of all working women are professionals or in management, which requires a college degree. The COBF for professional women (doctor, lawyer, college teacher) is 29 cents for each male dollar earned.

If you have a high school diploma, you could be a clerical worker along with one-third of all working women in the United States. Thus, if you are a secretary, the COBF is 31 cents per male dollar earned. If you do not have a high school diploma, then you would be among the 20 percent of working women in the service sector, 7 percent in sales, or 13 percent in blue-collar jobs. If you are in the service sector, the COBF is 31 cents, and if you are a blue-collar worker, the COBF is 34 cents.

The COBF varies by race in the United States. The COBF for black women is 40 cents for each dollar earned by a white male compared to 33 cents for white women. Class and race affect the COBF enormously.

How does the American woman compare to other women in the world? The COBF in Sweden is 10 cents per male dollar earned. We have something to learn from Sweden, and we will investigate how this low COBF was achieved. The COBF in Japan is 46 cents. This is worse than the biblical one-third. We do know that only 29 percent of university students in Japan are female. The battle against discrimination has given us a comparative advantage over Japan in this area. The COBF in France is 29 cents if you work in a big firm with five hundred or more employees, but only 16 cents if you work in a small firm of ten to fourteen employees. We will examine the COBF in China where more women are in the workplace and where there is less occupational segregation.

Now that we have explained our concept of the COBF, using the simple proxy of the earnings gap, we move to refine it. We talk as if the COBF is the earnings gap, but it is a proxy and it is just one aspect, the economic aspect of the COBF. Just as economists have been criticized for depending too much on GDP per capita as a measure of a society's well-being, we would not want to make the mistake of thinking that unequal pay is the only issue in the cost of being female. Equal pay itself does not answer our desire for justice. The United Nations has developed a Human Development Index which adds indicators of health and education to the GNP in order to judge a nation's well-being. Later, the United Nations added a measure of political development. We propose to add measures of education, health, and political equity to our estimation of the earnings gap. To complete our COBF index, we will also include the social costs of being female, following the lead of the Population Crisis Committee.

In the first five chapters, we analyze five aspects of the COBF: the economic COBF in the labor market and workplace, the COBF in political life, the COBF in social life, the COBF in education, and the COBF in health care. In these five chapters we discuss these costs for contemporary American women. In the next three chapters, we use the index to estimate the COBF in Sweden and Norway, in France, and in China. In Chapter 9, we look at the impact of the Industrial Revolution on the COBF in England, France, and the United States in the nineteenth century. In Chapter 10, we compare the COBF across the generations from World War II to the present. Finally, in the conclusion, we present the COBF index, all five aspects, for all time periods and for all countries studied.

1

THE COST OF BEING FEMALE IN THE WORKPLACE

Caroline landed a position to train to become a compositor-typesetter in a large manufacturing firm in the Middle West. In the old days, the printing needs of this manufacturing corporation were met by unionized, male workers who did the hot, dirty, and heavy work of typesetting. The computer revolution turned this occupation into "women's work," clean and cool in an office. Recently, Caroline's title has been changed from typesetter to desktop publishing operator (Personal Interview, May 24, 1992). To place Caroline in perspective, note that in 1970, 17 percent of typesetters were female; in 1980, 75 percent were female. Along with this dramatic change, note that the pay is no longer that of a skilled craft worker, but that of a clerical worker.[1]

Shantel is a mail carrier. She likes working outdoors on this job. She says that "if you are independent and efficient, your fellow workers will help you. If you don't use feminism, and with the help of God, then men treat you all right. There is discrimination at work, but if you want to, you can overcome it. For example, the men claim that it is too hard to push the big mail bags around. I said, let me try, and I did." However, Shantel does feel that her employer discriminates. "If men want overtime, they can get it. If no men wanted it, then it was forced on me, a woman" (Personal Interview, April 10, 1992). Recently, Shantel was elected shop steward of her local chapter of the Letter Carriers Union. After the results of the election were announced, a male co-worker went to his desk and started to grind his teeth (Personal Interview, October 20, 1995). To understand the context for Shantel, note

*that in 1975 less than 9 percent of mail carriers were women, in 1984, only
17 percent were, and by 1992, nearly 28 percent were.*[2]

Now that the majority of women in the United States work for pay, they
have found independence, feelings of self-worth, and autonomy. But the
price they pay for these benefits is high. They have discovered the great
economic costs of being female in the labor market and in the workplace:
the gender pay gap and occupational segregation by gender. These costs
are unnecessary constraints on the welfare of women and the standard of
living of their families. In addition, the economic costs to women harm
men and our economy.

In the first section of this chapter, we document the claim that the majority of women in the United States today are working for pay. In the
second section, we discuss the gender pay gap, the fact that women make
less money than men. And in the third section, we explore the most important reason why women make less money than men, the fact that they
are excluded from high-paying "men's jobs" and are crowded into low-
paying "women's jobs."

THE 1970s: AN ECONOMIC WATERSHED FOR WOMEN

While the number and percentage of women who work for pay have
been increasing for over a hundred years, this phenomenon accelerated
greatly after World War II. By the end of the 1970s, a majority of women
were in the workplace. Economists at the Urban Institute such as Ralph
Smith, Nancy Barrett,[3] and Nancy Gordon[4] called this the "subtle revolution: women at work" in their 1979 book of that name.[5] Barbara Bergmann, professor of economics, has called this "the economic emergence of
women" in her 1985 book of that name.[6]

In the 1970s, working women went from being a minority to a majority
of women. In 1970, 42 percent of women worked for pay; in 1980, 51
percent of women were in the labor force.[7] As of 1978, 35 million women
were in the labor force, or over 50 percent of women in the population.[8]
As of 1991, 57 million American women were in the labor force, or 57
percent of all women of working age.[9] This rate of participation is expected
to continue to grow into the next century.

Why Did Women Go to Work?

There are several reasons for the entry of women into the workforce.
Some of these reasons are economic. (1) The main reason, according to
Barbara Bergmann, is that real wages rose because of industrialization, and
it became more valuable for women to work for a wage than to stay home
and serve the family. This is an important fact to note because politicians

and the media tend to obfuscate the underlying economics of women's behavior in favor of cultural and psychological explanations. (2) Women went to work because they needed money: either they had no husband, an unemployed husband, or a low-wage earner husband. (3) The growth of white-collar and service jobs that did not require brute strength made more jobs available to women. (4) Women had more education by the end of the 1970s and better career prospects.

Certain social changes also explain women's entry into the paid workforce. (1) Women were having fewer children by the 1970s and so needed to spend less time at home. (2) It had become more socially acceptable to combine motherhood and work. Six million women went to work during World War II, even mothers of preschool children. This gave legitimacy to married women working.[10] (3) Many women wanted to maintain the identity that they had established outside the house. (4) There were rising family aspirations to join the middle class.

Single Women Work

In the past, it was not uncommon for single women to work for pay, especially if they were poor, black, or immigrants. Many would stop working when they got married. This custom of single women working was even stronger among the foreign born. In 1890, over 70 percent of single foreign-born women worked; by 1930, the figure was 74 percent. In the 1940s, 46 percent of all single women worked for pay.[11]

Mary Lou's mother migrated from Ireland to Boston early in this century. She worked as a domestic servant in the home of a wealthy family. When she married, she left the labor force, but did hard home production: baking bread and doing heavy laundry. Mary Lou moved to Washington, D.C. during World War II. She found a job as a secretary to her Congressman. She loved working in the 1940s and the 1950s. Eventually, she retired when she married and had one child. But she misses the old days of work and being in the world. (Personal Interviews, 1992–1995)

Married Women Work

The crucial change in women's participation in the labor force is that most married women now work. The change from minority status to majority status of married women working for pay came in the 1970s. In 1970, 40 percent of married women worked, and in 1980, 50 percent did.[12] By 1992, 59 percent of married women with a husband present worked for pay.[13]

Working Mothers

Dorothy quit working in the early 1940s when she had her first child, and never returned to the workplace. Barbara quit working in the 1960s for ten years to raise her family and then went back to work. Sheila, a 1980s woman, returned to work after she physically recovered from bearing each of her two children. (Personal Interviews, 1992)

By 1978, women commonly went back to work after their last child graduated from high school—66 percent of them according to the Urban Institute study.[14] Mothers of school-age children (ages six to fourteen) had a participation rate of 58 percent.[15] The majority of women with children under the age of six did not work for pay; only 42 percent did.[16] By 1992, however, 55 percent of mothers of preschool children did work for pay.[17] These rates of working for pay are for married women with the husband present. The rates are even higher for divorced women, as we will see below. Even mothers of children under the age of three went to work in the 1980s. In 1980, 41 percent of married women with husband present and children under the age of three were in the labor force; by 1990, it was 56 percent.[18]

Why do mothers work for pay? In a study prepared by the Joint Economic Committee, 71 percent of working mothers with children at home reported that they worked to support the family, 4 percent said it was to support themselves, 9 percent wanted extra money, 5 percent said it was interesting, and 11 percent said it was a combination of motives.[19] Thus magazine articles about women giving up their jobs to take care of the children are describing the exceptions, not the rule. The fact is that these days, most families cannot survive without the wife's paycheck. If it had not been for wives going to work, the standard of living of most working Americans would have declined. Wives went to work and continue to work to maintain the standard of living for their families. This remains true in the 1990s.

Women Who Maintain Families

Women maintain families either because they are divorced or because they never married. Divorced women with young children started working for pay long before married women with young children did. In 1970, 73 percent of divorced mothers were in the labor force.[20] The rates of divorced mothers of children under six and those with children under three were only slightly lower. Most notable is the fact that in 1978, 60 percent of divorced women with preschool children were working for pay, whereas only a minority of married women with young children worked for pay.[21] In 1992, 80 percent of divorced women with children under eighteen, 85 percent with their youngest child in the range of fourteen to seventeen, 86 percent with children in the six to thirteen range, and 66 percent with children under six worked for pay.[22]

In 1950, only 9 percent of families were headed by women: in 1989, 17 percent were.[23] Contrary to the widely held opinion that these are all welfare mothers, the majority of never-married mothers were in the labor force in 1980, although not a majority of those with children under the age of six or under three.[24] The welfare system was designed in the 1930s when the majority of mothers did not work outside the home. In 1992, 53 percent of never-married women with children under eighteen were in the workforce; 76 percent with no children under fourteen to seventeen; and 65 percent with no children under age six worked for pay.[25]

THE GENDER PAY GAP

The economic cost of being female is that women, on average, earn less than men do. To be precise, that part of the gender pay gap that cannot be explained by relevant factors is the economic COBF. Since the economic COBF is difficult to measure and is rarely measured, we use the whole gap as a proxy for the unfair part of the gap. A large part of the difference is due to discrimination against women in the labor market and in the workplace. Labor market discrimination occurs when an individual's employment or pay is based on arbitrary factors irrelevant to job performance.

Two forms of discrimination should be distinguished: *Statistical discrimination,* like prejudice, is judging an individual on the basis of the average characteristics of the group to which the individual belongs. An employer refuses to train a woman worker because, on average, women workers drop out of the labor force to have children, and thus the employer will not get a return on his investment. But many women today do not have children (28 percent according to Victor Fuchs), and thus are being discriminated against statistically.[26]

Taste discrimination occurs when members of one group simply do not like members of another group.[27] Employers may not like women and will refuse to hire them unless they can pay them less. Employers can save money by underemploying women, that is, by not promoting them. The other employees may not like to have women around and certainly not as supervisors; so they may demand a wage premium to work with women. Customers may not want to buy machinery and equipment from women, and they let their suppliers know. Or customers may not want to buy cars from women. This theory sees discrimination as personal prejudice, not as a structural problem. Economist Gary Becker wrote *The Economics of Discrimination,* the first treatise on this form of discrimination, and claims that this form of discrimination—taste discrimination—is all that exists. It is a theory of the economics of discrimination. We believe, however, that this theory is only a partial explanation of discrimination. For us, gender discrimination is more complex and not merely a personal prejudice. It is a systematic part of our economy and society.

How do we know when discrimination has occurred? How do we measure it? One way to measure discrimination in earnings is to try to explain as much of the gender gap in pay as one possibly can, using characteristics of people that make them productive, and thus worthy of earning pay. And then what cannot be explained is called discrimination in the labor market. If we took the earnings of all the men and the earnings of all the women in America and averaged each of them, we would find the gender gap. The Women's Bureau reports that in 1992 the median earnings of a year-round, full-time woman worker was $21,440 and for a man worker it was $30,358.[28] Thus women, on average, make about 71 percent of what men make. If men are more educated, more experienced, and have more tenure with their current employer, then it is legitimate for them to make more than women because they are likely to be more productive. That is what we pay for in our market economy. This is called the human capital theory and is a view widely held by economists. The reasons why men are more educated, experienced, and so on, may be illegitimate, but that would be due to socialization, not discrimination in the marketplace.

Through standard statistical techniques, we can control for the years of education, experience, job tenure, and other factors that are relevant to productivity. If, after we do this, we still find a gender gap in earnings, then many economists claim that this residual in the gap is due to discrimination: women are paid less simply because they are women.

A classic study by Mary Corcoran and Greg Duncan shows that less than half of the gender gap can be explained by factors relevant to productivity, and this suggests the existence of discrimination.[29] Francine Blau and Andrea Beller, in their study on the gender earnings gap, find that "men's jobs" pay more than "women's jobs"; they define a "male job" as one that contains 70 percent or more male employees, and they consider jobs with 41 to 69 percent males as integrated jobs.[30] Occupational segregation is the most important cause of the gender gap in pay.

Why do "women's jobs" pay less than "men's jobs?" Barbara Bergmann proposes a "crowding theory" to explain why. She argues that men and women don't really compete in the same labor market. There is a market for men's labor, where the high-paying jobs are. Women are excluded from this market, leaving a scarcity of labor and thus high wages for men. The market for women's labor is low-paying and overcrowded because all the women are segregated there.

Blau and Beller also found gender pay differentials by marital and parental status. Married men make more money than unmarried men, all else being equal. They earn a wage to support a family. Fathers make more money than men without children. However, the reverse is true for women:

they make less if they have children. Men are rewarded and women pe-
nalized for having children. One reason for this difference is that, unlike
some countries, such as Sweden, the United States does not give extensive
paid maternity leave. Sweden and other Western European countries do
give paid time off for infant care, whereas American women are forced to
choose between high-paying jobs and motherhood. It has been estimated
that 30 percent of the gender earnings gap can be explained by the marital
status of men, as employers may promote them to help them support their
families. But women earn less because they often give up their careers to
have children, and they never catch up again with men.

June O'Neill finds discrimination against childless women. All else equal,
childless female workers earn 10 cents less for each male dollar earned by
childless male workers.[31] However, the discrimination against working
mothers is even greater. The cost of being female if one has children is 33
cents for each dollar a man earns.[32] This appears to be a case of discrimination against mothers, a sort of generalized "Mommy Track" bias. Adelman found that among a large sample of people in their thirties, men earned
on average $25,000 in 1985, women with no children made $19,000, and
women with children $15,000.[33]

Alan Blinder has developed another technique for estimating discrimination.[34] This technique looks at the returns to productivity characteristics
and, again, is based on the human capital model of earnings. Yes, men may
earn more because they have more years of education; but are women being
rewarded for each year of education at the same rate as men? Is there
gender discrimination in the rewards to education, experience, tenure, and
the like?

In a 1991 study for the Urban Institute, Elaine Sorensen found that the
returns to men for most of the productivity characteristics were greater than
those for women.[35] Men make more for a year of education, for a year of
training, for a year of experience, for a year of tenure with the current
employer, than women do. In another study for the U.S. Department of
Education, Adelman found that women in their thirties actually have more
education than men in that age group, and still are paid less. Maybe the
labor market is not rewarding productivity after all. Adelman suggests that
perhaps men are better able to exploit the political and social systems to
reach positions of power.

Another cause of the gender gap, according to O'Neill, is women's higher
turnover rate than men. Women leave the paid labor force when they have
children. This may harm their productivity. It also harms the women: Economist Heidi Hartmann, founder and director of the Institute for Women's
Policy Research, has estimated that, "taken together, women who have
babies but do not have the right to return to their jobs lose 607 million
more dollars annually than those women who have babies and return to
their former jobs."[36] Sorensen shows that women who work continuously

earn 50 percent more than women who work intermittently. It has been estimated that one-quarter to one-half of the gender pay gap is due to women's intermittent work patterns. Over the life cycle, women are more likely to drop out to rear children. They also are absent from work to care for sick children, spouses, or parents.

Women take time out from paid labor for two reasons: for childbearing and for childrearing. We hear complaints from employers that it is too expensive and bothersome for them to take the women back after childbirth or after a longer period of childrearing. Is this really true? Does it harm productivity to take the women workers back? If the woman is in a career position, her human capital may get rusty, and she could be less productive when she returns after a few years. Employers do not want the expense of paid leave to keep a skilled woman employee. If the woman is in an unskilled job, she may be easy to replace. We believe that employers do not like the government to tell them to take the women back, but that in reality, maternity leave and even longer family leave is not really very burdensome to business. Women are good workers. It takes a great deal of time and effort to replace good workers, so why not save their place for them? Moreover, if society wants women to bear and rear children, for future workers and citizens, then society should help with paid parental leave and subsidized child care.

Many economists find benign explanations for the gender gap. Gary Becker argues that women are tired after doing housework and caring for children, and do not put as much energy or intensity into their work. Therefore it is appropriate to pay them less. Becker does believe that a few employers, a few male employees, and a few customers have taste discrimination against women. But he believes they will be competed out of business in a market economy. However, social forces may be stronger than market forces in this case. It may be that human prejudices outweigh the forces of the market.

Linda worked for her state's Occupational Safety and Health Administration in the construction workers division. When her supervisor retired, she applied for and obtained his position. She was tough in her evaluation of four men that she supervised. They went over her head to complain and subsequently she was demoted from her supervisory position. She lost some of her duties. She now supervises women clerical workers, and computer-support staff. She makes less money. (Personal Interview, December 27, 1995)

So much for Becker's theory that taste discrimination will be competed away. Some men employees don't have the taste for women supervisors. Sexism may be stronger than market forces. According to the Women's

Bureau, only 1.9 percent of people in the construction trades were women, and only 4.7 percent of construction inspectors were women in 1993.[37]

Victor Fuchs argues that the conflict between career and family is stronger in women than in men.[38] On average, women feel a stronger desire for children than men do and a greater concern for their welfare after they are born. Fuchs does not think it is a matter of employer discrimination or the exploitation of women. Rather, women have their minds on family, not career.

Other economists use the human capital theory to explain the difference between men and women's occupations and pay. People invest in themselves in the form of education and training because the investment in "human capital" is expected to pay off in the workplace in the form of higher pay and promotions. Employers also invest in training some workers in the interests of productivity. The longer an employee works over his or her lifetime, the more the payoff to the employee and the employer. Since women drop out of the workplace to have children or take a day off to care for a sick child, the payoff time for investments in human capital, both for the woman and for her employer, is shorter. Therefore employers feel justified in training and paying women less than men. But as we have seen, younger women have more education than men and still earn less. Moreover, we see that the returns to education and experience are not the same for men and for women. Other economists believe that women have less bargaining power than men. They can't argue for a job or a raise as a man does because the employer can say, "Oh, you are a woman, your husband can support you."

If there is no discrimination, then we should be able to explain more than half of the wage gap with productivity factors. But we can't. There is no reason for a gender difference in the rewards for productivity characteristics; this must be due to discrimination. In her book *The Economic Emergence of Women,* Bergmann gives detailed evidence of employer discrimination from court cases brought by women under Title VII of the Civil Rights Act of 1964. Many other studies detail discrimination; notable among them is Heidi Hartmann's study of promotion policies in a large insurance firm.[39] Finally, the authors of the present volume have interviewed many women and heard their experiences of discrimination. Not all women have experienced discrimination, but enough have to suggest a pattern of unfair treatment. We conclude that it is incontrovertible that gender discrimination exists in the labor market and in the workplace today. It is structural, and while it may or may not be intentional, it is caused by powerful, fundamental forces of our society and economy.

Women earn about 71 cents for each dollar a man earns. The economic cost of being female is the unfair part of the 29 cents for every dollar a man earns, which for a day's work, a week's work, a month's work, a year's work, and a lifetime really adds up.

OCCUPATIONAL SEGREGATION

The major reason for the pay gap is that women are concentrated in low-paying "women's work" and are excluded from high-paying "men's work." In the 1970s, a working woman had a 33 percent chance of being a secretary and a 25 percent chance of being a nurse, teacher, maid, or waitress.[40] By this time, the most extreme form of occupational segregation—where the man is the breadwinner and the woman the homemaker—was disappearing, but the majority of women were still doing "women's work." Women were nurses, not doctors. Women were school teachers, not college professors.

Even today, occupations and jobs are divided into "women's work" and "men's work," due to sex stereotyping, defined as "attributing behaviors, abilities, interests, values, and roles to a person or a group of persons on the basis of their sex."[41] Jobs are a badge of gender, writes Barbara Bergmann.

"Men's jobs" include (1) executives, managers, and administrators, where they are protected by a "glass ceiling"; (2) professional specialties, guarded by professional associations; and (3) skilled blue-collar jobs, protected by a "steel door," guarded by unions.

"Women's jobs" include (1) clerical work in offices; (2) service work in health, education, and personal services; and (3) sales clerk work in stores and shops. Women are kept down in these low-paying jobs by "the sticky floor."

In the 1970s, there was some decrease in occupational segregation, compared to the 1960s. Most of the change was due to women making inroads into male occupations. Most occupations, however, remained sex-stereotyped: men in craft jobs and women in clerical jobs. Barbara Reskin and Patricia Roos organized a study of some of the occupations that became women's jobs in the 1970s, one of which was typesetting, Caroline's job.[42]

The Glass Ceiling

Stephanie H. had always been interested in business. During high school she had worked in retailing. She went on to college and majored in business administration, then worked for several years in midlevel positions, but felt she had dead-ended so returned to school and earned an M.B.A. Out in the corporate world, armed with her new degree, she landed a good job in a major corporation. After five years, despite a good performance record, she was passed over for higher executive-level positions and became increasingly discouraged. What had gone wrong? Why wasn't her career advancing at the same pace as the men she had started with?

Barbara B. Grogan, Jeanine S. Hettinga, Marta E. Maxwell, and Carol L. Ball are four women on the Board of Directors of the U.S. Chamber of Commerce.[43] *So some women are breaking through the "glass ceiling," mainly by starting their own businesses.*

Debbie, a high school graduate, works in the print shop of a large manufacturing firm. When her male boss retired, she got his managerial position. She has successfully run the department for five years. (Personal Interview, 1994)

The glass ceiling prevents women from making it to the top executive ranks. As they climb up the corporate ladder, women hit their heads on a hard transparent barrier. They can see to the top, but they can't reach it.

The first major step toward cracking the glass ceiling was taken by Elizabeth Dole when she was secretary of labor in 1989.[44] Part of her responsibility as secretary was to make sure that big firms that had contracts with the federal government didn't discriminate against women. The Office of Federal Contract Compliance had been set up in 1965 in the Labor Department to enforce the executive order against discrimination by race. Then in 1968 President Lyndon Johnson extended federal protection to women in firms that do business with the federal government. In carrying out her duties, Dole found that seventy-four large companies with federal contracts had very few women in high-level management positions.

In 1989, Dole commissioned a study of senior executives in nine Fortune 500 firms. The study found no women in this category. Dole then suggested that they look lower in the management hierarchy to find some women. In 1991, the Report on the Glass Ceiling Initiative was published. Among its findings were that of 31,000 managers, only 17 percent were women. Of 4,500 executive-level managers (assistant vice presidents or higher), only 7 percent were women. Only three of one hundred top executives were women, where executive jobs are defined as assistant vice president and higher.

There are 6 million women in management positions. Increasing numbers of women have entered business in recent years. Since 1978, there has been a rapid rise in the percentage of managers who are women (from 27 percent in 1978 to 39 percent in 1988). Despite their increasing numbers, women are still relegated to traditionally female areas like personnel (now called human resource development), community relations, or public relations. They are excluded from financial analysis and manufacturing. Women are placed in staff positions, and men are placed in line positions. Staff positions do not have much chance of promotion, whereas line positions lead to higher ranks. Before women hit their heads against the glass ceiling, they face glass walls that keep them from moving laterally and getting the broad experience they need to move up later.

When corporations are faced with charges of gender discrimination, they usually give several reasons for treating women differently than men. Basically, corporations think that women will drop out and raise children; therefore, they don't put them into training programs for top positions. They also say that women can't travel overseas due to family responsibilities, and this hurts their advancement. It's the old story that women put family before work and thus don't give their all to the company. Perhaps this was true in the past, but with women marrying later, having fewer children, and obtaining more MBAs, this is an outdated stereotype.

Although discrimination against women in employment was outlawed in 1964 through Title VII of the Civil Rights Act, big business must be discriminating against women in management or their numbers would be greater. There are subtle means of excluding women from executive positions. It is the job of the Equal Employment Opportunity Commission to oversee compliance with Title VII.

Women are at a disadvantage from the beginning of their corporate careers. In recruitment, the "old-boy network" leads to men hiring men. Firms that have contracts with the federal government try to hire women managers to comply with the executive order, but they often hire them at the lower end of management. Another roadblock for women on the corporate route is the lack of mentoring. Men tend to mentor men. Since mentoring by senior management is one way to the top, women lose. Corporate managers pick their successors and train them. Again, men tend to pick men, and thus women are denied this training.

In the study, *Empowering Women in Business,* Eleanor Smeal's Feminist Majority Foundation argues that it is discrimination against women, not their family responsibilities, that keeps women down. The study quotes a survey in which 50 percent of women managers said that discrimination against women was a barrier; only 3 percent said that family responsibility was. Sixty-one percent of women managers had had the experience of being mistaken for a secretary at a business meeting.[45]

Women managers make less money than men managers. The median income of women managers was $21,874 in 1987, or 60 percent of the median income of men managers at $36,155, according to the Women's Bureau. This is a serious gender gap. In a study funded by the Women's Bureau, it was found that men and women MBAs start out at the same salary, but that after ten years, the woman is earning only 80 percent of what the man earns.

Dr. Terri Scandura undertook a project for the Women's Bureau on "Breaking the Glass Ceiling," in which she studied women who had shattered the glass ceiling to see how they did it. She found that the women who made it into executive management held strong beliefs about the equality of men and women. Many female and male executives still have trouble accepting women in roles outside the home. The more the women believed in gender equality, as measured by a twenty-question test, the higher their earnings were.

Dr. Scandura also found that the women who move up are those who had gotten into line positions rather than staff positions. Those line positions are rigidly structured in that they do not allow women to take time off from working during the childbearing years. She found that men exercised authority over larger budgets than women. Men had more people directly reporting to them than women.

Why are women in staff rather than line positions? *The Wall Street Journal* says that many men still feel uncomfortable dealing with women, and many doubt that a woman can balance career and family. Moreover, women are stereotyped as people who can provide support, and thus they are put in staff positions, not line positions.

Women who get ahead in business have mentors, where mentor is defined by Dr. Scandura as "an influential individual in your work environment who has advanced experience and knowledge and who is committed to providing upward mobility and support in your career."

It is interesting to note that 70 percent of the people in Dr. Scandura's random, national sample of executive managers had college educations. Only 20 percent of the women executives had changed jobs because of their partners' career changes. Female executives with children under eighteen, living at home, reported more stress, less expectation of promotion, and increased thoughts of quitting.

Go to Wellesley! Wellesley College has more female alumni who have become directors of Fortune 500 companies and senior executives than any other college or university in the United States.[46] Two women in business policy who graduated from Wellesley are Alicia Munnell, former top Treasury Department official and current member of the Council of Economic Advisors, and Margaret Yeo, senior vice president of the Federal Reserve Bank of New York. Of course, Smith College can claim Laura D'Andre Tyson, former chair of the Council of Economic Advisors, now director of the White House's National Economic Council. Economics Professor Carolyn Shaw Bell (who taught from 1950 until her retirement in 1989) revealed Wellesley's secret: "It was a personal value that any woman should be able to support herself and her children, whether or not she has to. Wellesley produced women who were responsible for themselves."

The Exclusion of Women from the Professions

It seems like good news that there are 6.8 million women professionals compared to 7.2 million men professionals, but within the general category of professions, there are "men's professions" and "women's professions."

Women are clustered into typically "caring" professions. For example, the majority of preschool and kindergarten teachers (98 percent) are female. The majority of registered nurses (95 percent) are women. The majority of elementary school teachers (89 percent) are female. The majority of librarians (87 percent) are women. The majority of social workers (68 percent) are women. These are the lower status and lower paying professions.[47]

The majority of the clergy are male—only 8 percent are women—although this pattern is changing, especially in the Protestant and Jewish religions. The majority of dentists are male; only 9 percent are women. The majority of physicians are male; only 18 percent are women. The majority of lawyers are male; only 22 percent are women. The majority of college and university teachers are male; 39 percent are women. These are the higher status and higher paying professions.

Women fare better in the following professions: 41 percent of economists are female; 49 percent of editors and reporters are female; 55 percent of secondary school teachers are women; and 54 percent of psychologists are women.[48]

Once women make it into a "male" profession, they often encounter the glass ceiling. Women doctors are less likely to become surgeons and more likely to be pediatricians. Women lawyers are less likely to become partners in large corporate law firms and more likely to be in small firms practicing family law. Women professors are rarely full professors, and if they are it is in the humanities. Moreover, within college and university teaching: the majority of full professors are male, only 13 percent of full professors are women; the majority of associate professors are male, 26 percent of associate professors are female; 40 percent of assistant professors are male.[49] We see that 60 percent of assistant professors—the lowest position on the college level—are female.

The COBF in the American Medical Profession

In the 1970s, there was a great surge in the number of women entering the medical field. In the academic year 1991–1992, 39 percent of first-year medical students were women, up 500 percent from 1969–1970.

In the United States today, 104,000 women physicians are practicing medicine. This accounts for 18 percent of the nation's doctors. The American Medical Association (AMA) predicts that by the year 2010, 30 percent of all doctors will be women. In 1994, a historic milestone was reached in the top three-ranked medical schools—Harvard, Yale, and Johns Hopkins: all three enrolled more women than men that year. We've come a long way since 1849 when the first women in the United States graduated from medical school.[50]

The COBF in the medical profession is due to segregation by specialty. Women are crowded in five fields: (1) internal medicine; (2) pediatrics (half of all pediatric residents today are female); (3) family practice; (4) psychiatry and child psychiatry (where half of all the residents today are women); and (5) obstetrics/gynecology.

Meg worked as a family practitioner in a federally funded clinic for low-income people in the West. No patient ever rejected her as a woman doctor, and most of the nurses liked it. However, it was a different story in med school. She recalls that during slide shows, the professors would periodically show slides of naked women to wake the students up. (Personal Interview, August 8, 1992)

Women in Psychiatry

Gloria is a ninety-two-year-old retired psychiatrist. In 1930, she was told that psychology was no place for women. In 1932 she entered medical school at the University of Chicago. It was during the Depression. She experienced no discrimination against women. She graduated from medical school in 1938. In 1951, at age fifty, she began her practice as a psychiatrist. Her patients had gender-related problems. She encouraged them to have a life of their own rather than to depend on their husband's. Many of her male colleagues referred women patients to her to get rid of them and their attentions. (Personal Interview, 1992)

Kathryn Chizek Bemman is a psychiatrist and has just been elected the president of the American Medical Women's Association, a support group for women in "a conservative profession dominated by men," especially in specialties such as surgery and urology. Dr. Bemman says that men in the medical profession have outnumbered, overpowered, and silenced women physicians. Dr. Bemman went to medical school in the late 1950s and was one of three women out of eighty-five students in her class. She works for the county mental health clinic. Her agenda for the year is the treatment and prevention of violence against women. Doctors need to recognize the possibility of this violence. Women's input as caregivers (as well as researchers) is important, she says.[51]

Women in Surgery

Bernadine Healy, the first female director of the National Institutes of Health (NIH), is a cardiologist and is married to a prominent heart surgeon. She says that "certain qualities, like toughness, decisiveness and confidence are probably needed in surgery, no matter what the doctor's gender is." She started the Women's Health Initiative.

Frances Conley is now a famous woman brain surgeon because she resigned from her professorship at Stanford Medical Center to protest the impending appointment of a man as chief of neurosurgery which, she argued, would "condone and perpetuate sexism in my work environment." The system re-inforces men's ideas that they are superior beings, she says in her L.A. Times article, *"Why I'm Leaving Stanford: I Wanted My Dignity Back" (1991). She was tired of being treated as less than an equal person.*

Frances Conley was called "hon" by her male colleagues. Her differences of opinion were put down as caused by PMS or being "on the rag." Her ideas were not taken as seriously as those of the men she worked with. Women put up with this sort of thing to get ahead. She did so for twenty-four years. This form of sexism is "extremely pervasive and debilitating." In an article for the New England Journal of Medicine, *Conley argued that sex stereotyping has been instrumental in maintaining a glass ceiling for women in medicine. When men are confident and aggressive, we like it, but if a woman acts this way, we say she is abrasive. Men are tenacious, but women are stubborn; men are self-sufficient, but women are strident; men are pow-erful, but women are emasculating; men get promoted, but women get passed over and held in contempt.*

Frances Conley has returned to Stanford. The objectionable appointment was withdrawn.

Kathryn Anderson, age fifty-three, was denied promotion to chairman and chief of staff of surgery at a children's hospital because she was "aggressive and abrasive." She is suing the hospital on the grounds that these are not proper job criteria. In 1989, in the Price Waterhouse case, the Supreme Court said that it was illegal to use sexual stereotypes in employment decisions, when a woman was denied partnership in the accounting firm for not defer-ring to men. Kathryn Anderson is suing on the grounds that she was denied the promotion for behavior that if done by a man is acceptable, while if done by a woman is not. Kathryn Anderson, meanwhile, is chief of surgery in a hospital in L.A., one of three women in the United States to be chiefs of surgery.

Women in Urology

Carol graduated from Georgetown Medical School in 1991. During medical school she changed her mind several times about what her specialty would be, but finally settled on urology. It was at this point she found herself treated as "invisible." When in clinical training, making rounds with a leading urol-ogist, she was overlooked and ultimately discouraged from this specialty.

Female medical students are turned away from urology rotation at university hospitals because the male professors say that their male patients would feel uncomfortable in the presence of a woman. There is never any question about male students observing female patients on obstetrics rotation.[52]

According to the American Board of Medical Specialties, today only 138 out of 8,874 certified urologists are women. The fourth woman to be certified in 1981 says that the lack of referrals from male physicians has been a major barrier to women entering this male-dominated field.

The economic cost of being female in American medicine is 18 cents. That is, female physicians earn 82 percent of what male physicians earn.[53]

The Steel Door

Rosie the Riveter could rivet during World War II, but when the troops came home, she lost her job.

Cindy is a forklift driver at a manufacturing plant. She is married and has two children, ages ten and nine. In a company newsletter, it says that Cindy can operate the Hussler Crane, the Crown Life, and the Raymond Paller picker. She reaches thirty feet without fluttering an eyelash. "Keep up the good work girls," says her employer to her and another forklift worker. (Personal Interview, 1992)

Berdie operates a machine that is bigger than a house. She runs a press that turns a mass of petrochemicals into telephones in Baltimore for Western Electric. (Personal Interview, 1992)

Joyce Miller, International vice president of the Amalgamated Clothing and Textile Workers Union; Lenore Miller, president of the Retail, Wholesale, and Department Store Workers Union; and Dee Maki, president of the Flight Attendants Union are members of the Executive Board of the AFL-CIO.[54]

Whereas women face a glass ceiling in business and the professions, they face a steel door in blue-collar occupations. There it is the unions that exclude, instead of professional associations. Most women, without union protection, lose out on both training and premium wages. The steel door is firmly shut to women, blocking their advancement and ability to make a living wage.

There are very few women in the skilled crafts, the most elite and highest paid of blue-collar workers. Over 90 percent of skilled blue-collar workers are men.[55] Almost 14 million men have these high-paying jobs, compared to 1.2 million women.[56] Some crafts are harder for women to get into than others. For example, only 3.1 percent of mechanics and only 8 percent of electricians are women.[57]

Men dominate the blue-collar jobs of transportation and moving materials. The majority of forklift drivers are men. Only 400,000 women in the United States are in transportation and material moving, compared to 4.2 million men—8 percent of these jobs go to women.[58]

When it comes to machine operators and assembly-line workers, the steel door has opened a little. In fact, machine operator has become the fourteenth leading occupation of women, so that 30 percent of machine operators are now women. Over 90 percent of textile sewing machine operators are women.[59] Making textiles and clothing has always been considered "women's work." Firms turn to women for these jobs because they can pay women less. Many female assembly-line workers are employed in the electronics industry because of their smaller fingers and supposed greater tolerance of boredom.

> *Juanita and her husband started together at a large manufacturing plant in the Midwest when they were just out of high school. He was placed in trucking, and she was placed "on the line" doing piece work. Juanita explains that piece work is for women because they have dexterity in their fingers and because they can take the boredom. Actually, she says she had her best ideas while working on the line. Juanita has been working for twenty-nine years. Her husband worked his way up from being an hourly worker to a salaried worker and earns much more than she does. Juanita's mother had eleven children and worked in the home baking bread and preserving food. She could never understand why her daughter wanted to work in a factory. Juanita says it gave her more equality in her marriage than her poor mother had, trapped by the eleven children. Juanita has one daughter in college and is getting divorced. (Personal Interview, December 26, 1995)*

The Sticky Floor

The majority of the 55 million working women today are stuck in low-paying occupations at the bottom of the job ladder. This has been called "the sticky floor." It includes clerical workers and service workers.

Of the top 5 occupations of women (secretary, cashier, nurse, manager, and bookkeeper), two are clerical: 3.5 million women are secretaries and 1.6 million women are bookkeepers. In fact, one-third of all working women are some kind of office worker.[60]

Clerical work usually requires a high school degree but does not pay very well. A secretary makes much less than her boss, the manager.

Over 80 percent of clerical jobs are held by women.[61] Within the category of clerical work, there are "men's jobs" and "women's jobs." Men's white-collar jobs are the higher status and higher paying ones. Women's white-collar jobs, known as "pink-collar jobs," are more often of the sticky floor variety.

Men's clerical jobs include post office mail carrier—only 22 percent of mail carriers in the postal service are women; shipping and receiving—only 27 percent of this occupation is female; stock clerk, and storekeeper.[62]

Women's clerical jobs include secretary: 99 percent of secretaries are women;[63] typist; telephone operator; bank teller (a man's job before World War II); and bookkeeper.

The majority of service jobs (60 percent) are held by women, that is, nearly 9 million women.[64] It was the growth of this sector that made it easier for women to move into the labor force. It is much easier for women to get into the service sector than into industrial jobs like mining, manufacturing, or construction.

And yet there is great occupational segregation within the service sector. Here, too, there are "men's jobs" and "women's jobs." One type of service job that is "men's work" is that of security. So, for example, most police officers are men; only 12 percent of police officers are female.[65] Rose is a police officer and has a shotgun. She says "It's hard to get the men's trust" (Personal Interview, 1994).

Garbage collection is the most male of all male jobs. No occupation has a higher percentage of men in it. Why is this so? Is it their upper body strength or is it male bonding?

Being a pilot is a "man's job." However, under pressure, during wartime, the armed services have used women to fly freight airplanes, as they did in World War II and the Gulf War. Amelia Earhart was a pioneer and mentor for many women.

Captain Dianne L. Wade is a pilot of a large regional airline. The flight attendant told the passengers over the microphone that Captain Dianne Wade welcomed them aboard. Later a male voice told how high the flight was and how long it would be. After a smooth landing, Captain Dianne Wade opened the cockpit door. Seeing two elderly women in need of aid walking, she personally escorted them, holding their arms, to the terminal. (Personal Interview, December 27, 1995)

As of 1993, 4 percent of airplane pilots and navigators were female—about 4,000 of them—but only 400 were captains.[66]

Women's service jobs include personal services like hairdresser, 90 percent of whom are women. Two million women are cashiers. Over a million women are waitresses. Almost a million women are child care workers. Ninety-six percent of child care workers are women. Over a million women are nursing aides, orderlies, or attendants. Almost a million women are cooks. Men are chefs, women are cooks.[67]

Many women are stuck in jobs as sales clerks. There are 1.3 million of them. Again, this kind of work does not require a high school diploma, so it pays very little. Forty-seven percent of sales jobs are held by women: 1.7 million men and 1.6 million women hold sales jobs. But it must be noted that women sell different things than men. Men sell expensive items, like cars, often on commission, whereas women sell everyday things like dishes for a salary. The good news is that the service sector of the economy is growing, and this means increasing employment opportunities for women. But the kinds of jobs that women get in the service sector are often temporary, part-time, and low paying. The new jobs are in health, child care, elder care—all the things that women have traditionally done. They are undervalued in our society, and thus when they become paid jobs, they pay very little.

Only two of the top five occupations of women are not a sticky floor occupation: 1.8 million managers, and 1.6 million registered nurses. Even when women do break through the barriers of occupational segregation, they earn less than their male counterparts. Male doctors earn more than female doctors: Adelman found that among his thirty year olds, men physicians made $39,000 and women physicians $31,000. Male lawyers earn more than female lawyers: $34,000 compared to $29,000 for female lawyers. Men economists earn $35,000, and women economists $34,000. The Women's Bureau reports that women police officers make 90 percent of what men police officers make; women electricians make 95 percent of what men electricians make.

Women earn less than men in "women's jobs" too. The Women's Bureau finds that, although 84 percent of elementary school teachers are women, they earn only 90 percent of what a male elementary school teacher makes. While 67 percent of social workers are women, they earn 85 percent of what male social workers earn. Bergmann reports that women secretaries make less than men secretaries: $278 a week versus $365.

In sum, women now account for nearly half the labor force, but they still are not paid fairly, and they are kept out of the high-paying, high-status occupations and jobs.

The majority of women work in lower-level jobs. The bad news is that a woman like Linda lost her job as inspector of construction sites in the city for her state OSHA and was reassigned to manage female clerical workers in the office. The good news is that many women are making inroads into formerly "male" occupations. We met Debbie who broke the glass ceiling and landed a managerial position even though she has no college education. We met three women who squeezed through the steel door normally closed to women: Berdie worked as a machine operator, Juanita worked on the assembly line, and Cindy drove a forklift. Three women got off the sticky floor: Rose became a police officer, Shantel became a letter carrier, and Dianne became an airline pilot. We celebrate these women as pioneers in lowering the cost of being female.

We have documented our claim that it costs to be female in the workplace and in the labor market. We turn now to the cost of being female in political life.

NOTES

1. Barbara Reskin and Patricia Roos, *Job Queues, Gender Queues: Explaining Women's Inroads into Male Occupations* (Philadelphia: Temple University Press, 1990), p. 275.

2. Women's Research and Education Institute, *The American Woman 1994–*

95: Where We Stand, edited by Cynthia Costello and Anne J. Stone (New York: W. W. Norton, 1994), p. 298.

3. Nancy Barrett, "Women in the Job Market: Occupations, Earnings, and Career Opportunities," and "Women in the Job Market: Unemployment and Work Schedules," in Smith's *The Subtle Revolution.*

4. Nancy Gordon, "Institutional Responses: The Federal Income Tax System," and "Institutional Responses: The Social Security System," in Smith's *The Subtle Revolution.*

5. Ralph Smith, ed., *The Subtle Revolution: Women at Work* (Washington, D.C.: Urban Institute, 1979).

6. Barbara Bergmann, *The Economic Emergence of Women* (New York: Basic Books, 1986).

7. Claudia Goldin, *Understanding the Gender Gap: An Economic History of American Women* (New York: Oxford University Press, 1990), p. 17.

8. Women's Research and Education Institute, p. 283.

9. Women's Bureau, U.S. Department of Labor, *1993 Handbook on Women Workers: Trends and Issues* (Washington, D.C., 1993), p. 1.

10. William Chafe, *The Paradox of Change: American Women in the 20th Century* (New York: Oxford University Press, 1991), p. 233.

11. Goldin, p. 17.

12. Ibid.

13. Women's Bureau, p. 5.

14. Smith, p. 11.

15. Ibid.

16. Ibid.

17. Women's Bureau, p. 5.

18. Ibid., p. 12.

19. Ibid., p. 11.

20. Ibid., p. 12.

21. Smith, p. 11.

22. Women's Bureau, p. 5.

23. Francine Blau and Marianne Ferber, *The Economics of Women, Men and Work,* 2nd ed. (Englewood Cliffs, N.J.: Prentice-Hall, 1992), p. 285.

24. Women's Bureau, p. 12.

25. Blau and Ferber, p. 285.

26. Victor Fuchs, *Women's Quest for Economic Equality* (Cambridge, Mass.: Harvard University Press, 1988), p. 15.

27. Gary Becker, *Economics of Discrimination,* 2nd ed. (Chicago: University of Chicago Press, 1971).

28. Women's Bureau, p. 32.

29. Mary Corcoran and Greg J. Duncan, "Work History, Labor Force Attachment, and Earnings Differences between the Races and Sexes," *Journal of Human Resources* (Winter 1979).

30. Francine Blau and Andrea Beller, "Trends in Earning Differentials by Gender, 1971–1981," *Industrial and Labor Relations Review* 41, no. 4 (July 1988).

31. June O'Neill, "Women and Wages," *American Enterprise* (November–December 1990).

32. Walter Block and Michael A. Walker in their critique of the Abella Royal

Commission Report, "On Employment Equity," *Focus* 17 (1985), argue that there is no employer or labor market discrimination against women. Rather, they say, the difference in pay is due to the socialization of women and society assigning women the task of childrearing. They base their argument on a study of single women, which they said is the only appropriate unit of study. However, in the United States, O'Neill finds that single women earn only 90 percent of what single men earn. Moreover, because of statistical discrimination, single women are treated in the labor force and by employers as if they may have children one day, and thus even single women suffer from discrimination in employment.

33. Clifford Adelman, *Women at Thirtysomething: Paradoxes of Attainment,* 2nd ed. (Washington, D.C.: U.S. Department of Education, 1992).

34. Alan S. Blinder, "Wage Discrimination: Reduced Form and Structural Estimates," *Journal of Human Resources,* 8, no. 4 (1973).

35. Elaine Sorensen, *Exploring the Reasons Behind the Narrowing of the Gender Gap in Earnings* (Washington, D.C.: Urban Institute, 1991).

36. In Janet Shibley and Marilyn Essex, eds., *Parental Leave and Child Care* (Philadelphia: Temple University Press, 1991).

37. Women's Bureau, "Nontraditional Occupations for Women in 1993," Division of Statistical and Economic Analysis, February 1994. Nontraditional occupations are any in which women comprise 25 percent or less of the total employed.

38. Victor Fuchs, "Sex Differences in Economic Well-Being," *Science* (April 1986).

39. Heidi Hartmann, "Internal Labor Markets and Gender: A Case Study of Promotion," *Gender in the Workplace* (Washington, D.C.: Brookings Institution, 1987).

40. Smith, pp. 1–29.

41. Sharon Harlan and Ronnie Steinberg, eds., *Job Training for Women: The Promise and Limits of Public Policies* (Philadelphia: Temple University Press, 1989), p. 96.

42. Andrea H. Beller, "Changes in the Sex Composition of U.S. Occupations, 1960–1981," *Journal of Human Resources* 20, no. 2 (1985). See note 1 on Reskin and Roos.

43. Provided by the Briefing Center of the U.S. Chamber of Commerce in Washington, D.C. January 15, 1992.

44. U.S. Department of Labor, *A Report on the Glass Ceiling Initiative* (Washington, D.C.: 1991).

45. Feminist Majority Foundation, *Empowering Women in Business* (Washington, D.C.: 1991).

46. *New York Times,* October 29, 1995.

47. Blau and Ferber, p. 124.

48. Bergmann, Appendix.

49. Blau and Ferber, p. 125.

50. Elizabeth Blackwell, *Monthly Forum on Women in Higher Education* 1, no. 1 (October 1995).

51. *Journal of the American Psychiatric Association.*

52. *Washington Post,* Health Section, February 18, 1992.

53. Heidi Hartmann of the Institute of Women's Policy Research testifying at the House Education and Labor Committee, 1990.

54. Information from the Washington, D.C., headquarters of the AFL-CIO, 1992.

55. "Women in the Skilled Trades and Other Manual Occupations" (Washington, D.C.: Women's Bureau, 1991).

56. Ibid.

57. Ibid., pp. 5–7.

58. Ibid.

59. "Twenty Leading Occupations of Employed Women" (Washington, D.C.: Women's Bureau, 1994).

60. Ibid.

61. Women's Bureau, *1993 Handbook*, p. 19.

62. Ibid., p. 18.

63. Ibid., p. 17.

64. Ibid., p. 19.

65. Ibid.

66. Ibid.

67. Ibid.

2

THE COST OF BEING FEMALE
IN POLITICS

"The cost for me is one of time." That's what Congresswoman Constance B. Morella, a Republican, who represents the Seventh District in Maryland, says when she talks about her career. "I am probably ten years behind because I started late." (Personal Interview, September 13, 1991)

It wasn't that Ms. Morella was a late bloomer; quite the contrary, she had led an active life as a teacher and as a wife and mother. But when Connie got into politics in the 1970s, women were oddities in electoral politics. They were important backstage participants, but they had little credibility as candidates.

Connie Morella was elected to Congress in 1986 from wealthy, politically liberal Montgomery County, a bedroom community of Washington inside the Beltway. She is very much aware of the attitudes that keep women out of politics and the new determination of women to get in despite the difficulties.

"Women assume power differently; they're not as confrontational. Women are less threatening and pay more attention to detail. Men are used to having their secretaries do things for them. Women care about their constituents in a more personal way. They usually get into politics on the basis of issues."

Morella has worked hard to counter the belief that "women make phone calls and coffee; men make policy." Her career as a hard-working member of the House has earned her the respect of her colleagues. She is the first woman to chair the Arms Control and Foreign Policy Caucus. Connie sees this as both a breakthrough for women and a tribute to the men who are overcoming long-entrenched patterns of discrimination.

As for money, one of the factors that has kept women out of higher elective offices, Morella sees some heartening changes in women's ability both to give and to raise money. Along with developing these skills, women are also beginning to organize and run campaigns, tasks heretofore male dominated.

Morella's significant contribution to policy change is in the area of women's health equity where she has been a moving force in sponsoring legislation to require federal funds for health research to be spent equitably whereas in the past funds were targeted to male needs.

"In politics (once elected) there is equity in terms of salary, but not in terms of leadership. Women are excluded from many issue areas and commissions where they might serve."

Connie Morella has fought discrimination successfully in her own career and has helped insure that the costs for women now entering politics will be considerably reduced from the period when she began to run for office.

We usually define politics as running for or holding elective office, along with serving in appointed positions within government or within the party structure. Thus the category encompasses a wide range of local, state, and federal agencies, and legislative bodies. Of course, politics goes far beyond elective office and covers activities from lobbying to community service. For women especially, because they have been historically excluded from political careers as such, we expand our definition to include the large numbers of women who have been involved in politics as volunteers and in their communities from the time they first had an extra minute from their household duties. If we did not expand the definition, our history of women in politics would be extraordinarily brief, beginning two decades into the twentieth century when women got the vote.

The costs of political activity vary from level to level, whether they are economic, social, or psychological. For example, running for the U.S. Senate, which, after the 1992 election, is now 8 percent female,[1] and has never been higher, will require raising a lot more money than is needed for seeking lower office. Clearly, this is equally true for men, but men have more access to money. The fact is that women have no old-boy network to rely on. Although the argument is frequently advanced that women, generally referring to rich widows, control the wealth in this country, that is hardly true if their chief financial advisers are men.

Despite the fact that they have a necessarily limited record of elective office, which is the usual measure of male success in politics, women have a long and extensive record of volunteerism and activism which has prepared them very well for political careers. They have tended to enter the political arena for causes rather than career advancement. This does not necessarily imply a superior morality (although the luxury of pursuing causes might be considered a benefit of being female). Rather, it reflects the fact that since women did not vote or hold elective office until well into the twentieth century, there were no spoils for women to divide.

HOW WOMEN WERE EXCLUDED FROM POLITICS

Interestingly enough, it was the Industrial Revolution that freed middle-class women for politics in several respects. First, middle-class women were no longer as tied to domestic chores and had more leisure time. As a consequence, many women began to educate themselves or to be educated when the first women's colleges were founded in the last decades of the nineteenth century. As they looked outside the home and observed the plight of less fortunate women working in the mills and factories, they also became outraged over the abuses of child labor. These women provided the strong core of the Progressive movement and spearheaded many of its reforms. "The merger of suffragism with Progressivism—and the central role played by women reformers in both—offers a means of answering critical questions about both movements. William Chafe speculates that there may have been *two* progressive eras—one based on the cultural politics of men (business regulations and railroads), the other based on women's values—safety, hours of work, and child labor."[2] Yet, as money became the standard of success in a rapidly industrializing America, women were more and more excluded from power.

From the pre-suffrage days when women marched for the right to vote, they have been held up to ridicule in the public arena. As far back as 1837, when the Grimké sisters toured the South speaking for the abolitionist cause, their efforts were described in derogatory terms. Here is an excerpt from a letter that addresses the role of women, circulated by the General Association of the Congregational Clergy and meant to be read from pulpits as part of the Sunday service:

The power of woman is in her dependence, flowing from the consciousness of that weakness which God has given her for her protection. . . . But when she assumes the place and tone of a man as a public performer, . . . she yields the power which God has given her for protection, and her character becomes unnatural.[3]

The scorn that women experienced as a result of their activism endured even through the 1960s and the civil rights movement when women were shunted to the back of the protest marches and left to do the grunt work of the movement. Later, in the peace demonstrations, male leaders found it advantageous to place women in the front lines, thinking that police would be more restrained if there were "chicks up front." Men were still the strategists. Resistance to female participation crosses party, race, and class lines, and innumerable examples can be given of political exclusion through history to the time of this writing.

The experience of the suffrage movement is an interesting and paradoxical one. What possible reasons could there be to deny women the vote? It took a fair amount of imagination even in the nineteenth century to rationalize the ban against women voting when they were sharing the burdens and privations of the frontier with their menfolk. The arguments were very much weakened at the end of the Civil War when, even the most wrong-headed Northerners could not justify denying the newly emancipated slaves the rights and privileges of American citizenship. What then would be the effect on women if this group were enfranchised while women were still denied the vote?

The issue of the passage of the Fifteenth Amendment, which gave black males the franchise, split the woman suffrage movement badly. Some women acceded to the pleas of congressional Republicans not to confuse the issue of voting rights for blacks by insisting on their own rights, but others, feeling outraged and betrayed, refused to be quiet and wait their turn. That turn was a long time coming, fully fifty years after black males won the right to vote.

There were more subtle political reasons why many states continued to deny women the franchise. Most of these states were east of the Mississippi and had large immigrant, often Catholic, populations. By the end of the nineteenth and into the beginning of the twentieth centuries, these immigrants were voting in considerable numbers. Politicians were feeling the pressure from organized, but voteless, women on many social issues, but perhaps the one that was most disturbing to them was the prohibitionist stance. These urban politicos felt that giving women the vote would be tantamount to ushering in prohibition since so many women were increasingly vocal about the effect of alcohol on family life.

There's no way to substantiate this argument fully, but a contrary illustration from the frontier may illuminate the point. Wyoming, while still a territory in 1870, awarded women the vote. Why? Again the reason was pragmatic; it suited male purposes. As the speculation goes, the state was so sparsely populated that male settlers wanted to make it more attractive to women. The recorded sentiment of the territorial legislator who sponsored the measure, when asked to explain his action, is that he "felt it was just." No other explanation was given. Wyoming, achieving statehood in 1890, led the way for women with several "firsts"—the first woman justice of the peace, the first woman to serve on a jury, the first woman elected to a state legislature, and the first woman governor. Many in the soon-to-be state insisted that they would not enter the union if women could not vote: "We won't come in without our women."[4]

Wyoming was just one of several frontier states with seemingly progressive attitudes toward women. Montana, for example, elected the first woman to Congress, Jeannette Rankin, a Republican. This woman, serving terms widely separated, one during World War I and the next, just before the outbreak of World War II, had a consistent voting record. Having voted against entry into World War I, she was the only member of the House to vote against entering World War II. The First World War was the impetus for granting women the vote, because women had been so necessary to the war effort, much as, by 1971, the eighteen year olds serving in Vietnam could not likely be denied the franchise.

Women Get the Vote

Women have been voting for only seventy-odd years. They won the suffrage in 1920, and the first president they had a chance to vote for was Warren G. Harding, a political matinee idol. Their voting, minimal as might be expected for a first-time phenomenon, replicated the male vote. In the succeeding decades, most women in elective office of any importance were there by virtue of inheritance—their husbands had died, their name was still worth something, and they were able to keep the seat. Very often they were exploited by the political machines in this regard. An example is Lurleen Wallace in Alabama who became governor when her husband, Governor George Wallace, by law, could not succeed himself. There were enough women who filled vacancies left by their husbands to add to the glossary of political terms, the "over his dead body" phenomenon. For example, Muriel Humphrey (D-Minn.), Maurine Neuberger (D-Ore.), and Rose Long (D-La.) were all appointed to their husbands' seats.

As recently as 1991, when Governor Richard Snelling of Vermont died suddenly, his wife's name was the first possibility suggested to replace him. Another example is that of Teresa Heinz whose husband John, a Republican senator from Pennsylvania, died in a helicopter crash in 1991. Although she had no political experience, she was asked to run for the seat. (She wisely turned down the offer.) Perhaps this says more about a lack of professionalism in politics than it does about women as the eternal stand-ins.

It would be many elections before anything resembling a gender gap, that is, independent voting on the part of women, would appear. In a poll recorded by the National Commission on Working Women in 1988, strong differences between men and women emerged on gun control, aid to Nicaragua, nuclear power plant operations, and Reagan's performance as president.[5] Gender did seem to count in politics, and candidates were beginning to pay attention to the fact.

For decades after they won the vote, women remained second-class citizens in both major parties. When delegations were chosen for the party nominating conventions, women were always the alternates. When chairmen were elected, women were always the vice chairs. Not until internal reforms were forced on the Democratic party after the debacle of the 1968 convention were women given equal representation. Unions, traditionally the backbone of Democratic strength, have been resistant to women in leadership positions and undoubtedly acted as a brake on women gaining power in Democratic circles for many years. Now, with the erosion of union support for the Democrats, the situation has changed.

Today, as a result of a long campaign for minority representation, women may actually benefit in politics as decision makers take into account the facts that women comprise 53 percent of the electorate and 60 percent of the elderly vote, which has proved to be more influential as the twentieth century draws to a close.

WOMEN IN POLITICS TODAY

Women in State and Local Politics

Mary Boergers who is in her late forties is energetic and young looking. She was always interested in history and had family connections in Connecticut Democratic politics, but was never an activist. (Interview with Senator Mary Boergers, Maryland State Senate, April 20, 1993)

Both of her parents were from Minnesota where she went to college at her mother's alma mater, St. Catherine's in St. Paul. She had a completely Catholic education, but the nuns at St. Catherine's were very forward-looking and the intellectual content of her education was high. They encouraged leadership in women. They had a Phi Beta Kappa chapter.

The key factor in turning her on to politics was the Kennedy campaign. It had an incredible impact on her desire for public service. Both JFK and Bobby were heroes to her. She is clearly the Clinton generation of politics. She came to Washington in 1968 for graduate school. After she got a Master's in American history, she looked for a job on the Hill which was her career goal. Someone advised her not to learn to type because she would then be boxed in as a secretary the rest of her career. She landed a job with the National Education Association.

She married and got a job teaching at Rockville High School in Montgomery County. While there she found a liberal candidate for Congress who interested her and worked on his failed campaign. She was recruited by a friend who was the Montgomery County NOW director as legislative coordinator. She did that for one year and then became state legislative coordinator. By then she had had her second child.

She was becoming quite familiar with Annapolis (the state capital) and also with how to raise money in the state and who the best political contacts were. She grew to know both process and cast of characters, always allying herself with the most liberal elements. She and other NOW workers set up an ERA Commission to review Maryland laws to see how they would be affected by the ERA state amendment.

In 1981 she won over two other political factions who were fighting each other for a vacated seat. She seemed the best alternative when the two warring factions couldn't agree, and for $49.10 she won the nomination. That represented the cost of her xeroxing her resume and sending it to the Montgomery County Democratic Committee. Surprising everybody, she won the seat.

Once in the House she was appointed to the House Ways and Means Committee, the fourth woman on the committee. Her experience in the House was helped by the presence of a male Speaker who was fair in his treatment of women, unlike most of the men who were absolutely insensitive and stereotypically male chauvinist.

By 1990 Mary was ready to take on a long-term incumbent in her senate district. Choice was a major issue before the legislature, and her opponent was a right-to-life person. Although Mary is a Catholic, she is a strong feminist and has taken a firm pro-choice position which has gotten her into a lot of trouble with her alma mater and many Catholic voters. She won the election with 71 percent of the vote in the primary. The loser didn't know what hit him.

Women in Office

Mary says that there are two types of legislators and that this applies to both sexes. In Maryland where the Democratic party dominates, most legislators take their lead from the party. They are the ones who get financing, places on the ticket and committee assignments, but they lose their freedom to decide positions (if they ever had it). Coming from an affluent and independent suburban country, Mary was able to be more independent herself. Although her predecessor had followed the party line for twenty years, in the end, it didn't help him. He was an affable, typical politician who was not effective in the Senate. Many women also have kept their seats by keeping quiet.

Many women feel they owe their office to the party and don't feel confident enough that they can act on their own. When there was a key vote on sexual harassment charges against a male legislator, many women stayed with the old boy network, refusing to believe that he was guilty.

Mary tells the story of how committee assignments are handed out by the old boy network. Women have been traditionally assigned to the "soft" committees that deal with children, social issues and other matters the leadership regards as unimportant. The men get the money committees. One session, the leadership, without realizing it, had appointed thirteen women to the Environmental Committee. When they realized what they had done, they had to scurry around undoing it and begging committee chairs to take a few women on their committees to re-right the imbalance. That was a breakthrough in getting women represented on all committees.

Old entrenched attitudes prevail in Annapolis. The number of women in the legislature is fairly high (about 25 percent), but women are largely absent from leadership positions. This sets a catch-22 in motion because the media, which aren't terribly interested in state politics anyway, only call on those in leadership positions for interviews and comments. Since women are not in leadership positions, they are invisible in the media.

Business is done in the cloakroom in Annapolis, and women have traditionally been excluded. Attitudes are very slow to change. After a member's nomination for a judgeship was withdrawn because of accusations of sexual harassment, Mary was being interviewed by a male *Washington Post* reporter when a male senator passing by made a sexist comment to her in full hearing of the reporter who used it as his lead. Her colleague said to Mary (it was the end of the legislative session) that she must now be looking forward to her "conjugal visit."

Women in the Maryland legislature, although they have a caucus, are far from united. The group split on this issue of sexual harassment, doubting the testimony of women who made the accusations and generally repeating the Anita Hill divisions of opinion. Not supporting or trusting other women is characteristic of much female political behavior; this is disappointing to Boergers who tries to support all women when she can. She says one of the things women lack in politics is the ability to see questions impersonally. Never having played team sports, they don't realize that you don't have to like your teammates, but you do have to keep your eye on the shared goal of winning.

Boergers sees some change in that more black women are seeing the value of uniting with white women on gender discrimination where formerly they had not. Some of this she thinks is because these women are now more likely to be professional and won't take the sexism from their black male counterparts that their predecessors did. She is hopeful that the women's movement will lose its white upper-middle-class image. Many black women who have been the backbone of organizations have never received credit or visibility. As long as feminists concentrate on a pro-choice agenda, black women are not turned on. Economic discrimination is a better agenda.

From the social perspective, lower level elective office has some advantages for women in that the work is often part-time and it is possible to work much closer to home. Serving in the nation's capital will likely entail moving one's family, and there is traditionally more spouse resistance to this type of move when the officeholder is female. It is interesting to note that both women senators in the 102nd Congress were unmarried (one is divorced); they have been joined by six new female senators, three of whom have been married and divorced (although in two instances remarried). A significant number of the congressional delegation is also single, and few have young children. Pat Schroeder's (D-Colo.) husband actually made news when he moved with her to Washington. Imagine a newsworthy story in the other direction: "Wife moves to Washington with newly elected representative."

The psychological costs of running for office are high in that many of the characteristics necessary to a winning campaign—aggressiveness, humor, and toughness—are not regarded as feminine, and the voters often react negatively to behaviors that would be perfectly appropriate for men. Men in office are valued as performing public service, whereas women are often criticized for leaving their families to enter public life.

Many people run for office without suffering financial loss because they are self-employed or can leave what they're doing without harm to their employer and return with added value. This may change for women, but they are all too often employed as teachers, nurses, social workers, or in other fields where leaves are difficult to obtain. They tend to be employees more than employers and accordingly have less flexibility.

In the higher reaches of appointive office, women are still vastly underrepresented, which indicates that perhaps a glass ceiling mentality operates in politics as well as in business and the professions. Women do not appear often in the ranks of top presidential advisers, they do not come anywhere close to mirroring the population in the judiciary, and they are pitifully represented in the ambassadorial ranks. The Clinton administration has made a strong effort to remedy this situation with the appointment of Madeleine K. Albright, ambassador to the United Nations, Janet Reno, attorney general, and Ruth Bader Ginsburg to the Supreme Court. Until the 1970s, the U.S. Foreign Service was run on an extremely sexist basis, and women, despite more enlightened policies, have not yet caught up with men to serve at higher levels.

WOMEN'S ISSUES ON THE FRONT BURNER: EQUAL RIGHTS AND ABORTION

After the turbulence of the civil rights movement and the antiwar protests which drew many women into politics, the 1970s might have been expected to be a period of regrouping, but two key issues kept the pot boiling for women: the battle over the Equal Rights Amendment and the abortion controversy.

The fight for the ERA polarized women as it politicized them, sketching the outlines of class conflict and raising questions once more about women's proper role in the political arena. The ERA failed to pass because the opposition successfully put the question in ideological terms that made many women feel threatened. They were told they would lose their "protected" status; in fact, that they had everything to lose—alimony, child support, pensions—and nothing to gain. The right buttons were pushed to cause anxieties in an age when traditional values were seemingly at risk. But underneath the radical overlay were real issues relating directly to the theme of equality. Unfortunately, these issues, such as the costs of single-parent households, divorce, and spousal abuse, were smothered under the rhetoric of unisex toilets and women in combat, which won extensive media coverage.

Thanks to attitudinal research and the technology available for a mass media and direct mail campaign, the ERA opponents were able to turn the perception of an amendment that granted rights into one that subverted them.[6] The challenge for supporters was to get their message across that there was a problem of fairness in American public policy and that women had been denied, not just equal, but fair treatment. They were never able to make the case that the ERA was necessary for all women. It is interesting to note that men supported the ERA in numbers equal to women.

The arguments over "values" overwhelmed the arguments for fairness in the economic and social realms and created a backlash from which the women's movement still suffers long after the ERA died in 1982. The ERA was perceived as antifamily and elitist.

The strength of the fundamentalist churches in the politics of the 1980s became more apparent. Whether this strength would manifest itself in policy changes or whether it was simply the ability of evangelical fervor to capture headlines is uncertain, but many otherwise politically inactive women became involved as the "Stop ERA" campaign heated up. As fundamentalist Christians, these ERA opponents sincerely felt that ERA went counter to the teachings of the New Testament. "My religion strictly says that women should submit to their husbands."[7]

In her excellent study of the failure of the ERA in Illinois, Jane Mansbridge writes of the division of "us and them" that characterized opposing forces—the women in red with their hexagonal "Stop ERA" buttons and the women in green with their "ERA YES" buttons.

As a proponent, I found it impossible to sit in a legislative gallery, hear even a few legislators joke as they voted down equal rights for women, and not hate. And I have rarely seen such concentrated hate as I saw on the faces of some women in red when I stepped into an elevator in the state capitol on lobbying day wearing my green "ERA YES" button.[8]

Divisions exacerbated by the women's movement went far beyond the fight over the ERA. Class distinctions were clearly apparent in the battle lines on the ERA with more college educated, urban, upper middle-class women on the pro side and less educated, small-town, middle-class women against. This pattern often worked against the ERA supporters when, as in the case of North Carolina described in *Sex, Gender and the Politics of ERA*,[9] the militancy of NOW (National Organization of Women) campaigning in the state alienated many state legislators who had been planning to vote for the amendment. Legislators asked that NOW ads for the ERA not mention individual legislators. The reputation of NOW was that of an antimale, radical feminist group, and North Carolina lawmakers wanted no connection with it.

Beginning in the nineteenth century when women's groups first organized, women focused on single issues like slavery or suffrage. But buoyed by the success of the civil rights movement, by the early 1970s they had adopted broader agendas on equality. Their goals were to liberate women from all kinds of restrictions that operated in the marketplace, schools, and society. These broader goals mobilized large numbers of women, but the class distinctions noted in the ERA fight persisted.

More Divisions Among Women

Some women had a problem distinguishing women's issues from feminist issues; this confusion was apparent in the battle for the ERA. There was considerable criticism of NOW, the National Women's Political Caucus, the League of Women Voters, and the Women's Equity Action League as groups of educated, middle-class women working for their own benefit without consideration of their less educated, poorer sisters. Beyond class, questions of race were also raised as many black women remained alienated from the "movement," failing to see how the agendas of these groups would affect their lives. It has been very difficult for women leaders to bridge the wide racial and class divides and achieve a united movement for gender equity.

The leadership of the women's groups who were gaining increasing media attention was based in New York and often glamorous, including Gloria Steinem, for example. Many were writers and lawyers with whom average women could not identify. Although the civil rights movement was also largely middle class, it did attract a popular following, which the women's movement never did. Even some women who supported the ERA were frightened by the rhetoric and felt that their generation might indeed have much to lose if equality were mandated by law—for example, the loss of alimony and property. Women who had never worked and had no career training might wish for equality for their daughters, but they were apprehensive about what it might mean for their age group. Social change is always threatening, and the effective scare campaign run by the opposition heightened fears.

Given the high emotional content of the campaign for the ERA, it is surprising that the women's movement survived as well as it did. Many of the participants learned from their mistakes and attempted to broaden their constituencies. Furthermore, many had become expert at raising money, organizing, and media relations, so there were some gains as the result of the struggle.

The high-visibility issue of abortion dominated much of political discourse and a good number of election campaigns in the 1970s and 1980s, and continues to do so today. The demographics of support and opposition mirrored the battle lines of the ERA struggle. Perceptions of abortion as an upper middle-class issue created similar divisions. Just as in the battle for the ERA, fundamentalist religious beliefs fueled the "right-to-life" movement. The fervor of fundamentalism was at its peak in the 1980s. Again, the unresolved question of which policies would truly benefit women and which candidates would best represent women was in the forefront.

Not so surprisingly, the question of abortion energized politics, precipitating the entry of prospective candidates, many of them female, on both sides of the issue.[10] Party leaders agree that many candidates were attracted to politics by this issue. In Idaho, for example, after a tough anti-abortion law was passed (and vetoed by the governor,) a record number of candidates filed for office. Surveys of females running for office show that the majority take pro-choice positions. In an age of single-issue politics, the figure is of some importance.

Once again and inevitably, women in politics are entangled with the problem of children, wanted or unwanted. Can a man speak to this question as authoritatively as a woman? On whom does the responsibility for the decision to create life rest? What is the feminist position—the antifeminist position? These questions have become salient in American politics at a time when social reality and American mythology seem to be on a collision course. When a majority of women are working for pay outside the home, when their children are in daycare, when more and more children are being raised in single-parent-headed households, how can we continue the "mom and apple pie" pieties of decades past?

The Cost of Running for Office

One of the major factors that excludes many people from politics is the high cost of running for office. The "price tag" for some congressional seats has escalated to nearly a million dollars, while Senate seats can "cost" twice that much. This is especially onerous for women who are not part of the old-boy corporate network that contributes to men's campaigns.

As Connie Morella tells us, women are just now coming into their own in asking for money and giving money. Without this ability to raise funds, women will remain at a disadvantage in electoral politics. Recently, there have been encouraging signs that women are moving ahead in the financing of political campaigns.

Although Mary Boergers doesn't like fund-raising, she says it forces you out to the people and gives a touch of reality to your work. Yet it's a tragedy that you have to devote so much time to it rather than the issues. At the time of her interview, she was particularly interested in how to raise money because of a planned run for governor and felt she would need to raise $2 million. (She lost in the 1994 primary, the only woman gubernatorial candidate.)

Two fund-raising organizations have been in the forefront of the drive to support women running for office. One of them, the Women's Campaign Fund, founded in 1974, is a political action committee organized to help women whose positions are congruent with theirs. The litmus test for support is still the pro-choice one. Julie Tippens, political director of the Women's Campaign Fund, explains that the Fund has supported numerous

Republican women candidates if they are pro-choice (Personal Interview, March 13, 1992).

The second organization, EMILY's List, was established in 1985 by one woman, Ellen Malcolm, a key player in Washington, D.C. politics for over 15 years. In the late 1970s she served as press secretary for the National Women's Political Caucus, and during the Carter administration she was press secretary for Esther Peterson, the president's special assistant for Consumer Affairs. It is a Democratic women's fund-raising group, and EMILY is an acronym for "early money is like yeast." The former executive director of EMILY's List, Rosa DeLauro, followed her own advice exactly and was elected to Congress from Connecticut in 1990.

Both organizations were energized by the 1992 campaign with its focus on change and resentment of politics as usual. In addition, redistricting, as a result of the 1990 census, had reconfigured many constituencies, giving women a better chance to win election than they had ever had before.

Tippens, speaking for the Women's Campaign Fund, cited several possible victors in a wide range of states in the 1992 election as a result of redistricting, including Leslie Byrne, a Democrat in a new Northern Virginia district, and Elaine Baxter, a Democrat running in a new district in Iowa. Tippens emphasized these two because she said they had "broken the credibility gap." By this she meant they had so much political experience and reputation that men did not choose to run against them in primaries. They were perceived as politicians, not as women.

These two funding organizations have worked hard for women to run for national, state, and local office, and the inroads women have made in politics are largely due to the greater resources available to finance their campaigns. The representation of women in state legislatures has surged a remarkable 50 percent in the past decade. Since this is the traditional career path for national office, it is a very encouraging portent.

Another indicator that women have come of age in politics is the disparate positions that EMILY's List and the Women's Campaign Fund took in the New York 1992 Senate race in which two women faced off in the Democratic primary. The Women's Campaign Fund supported both Geraldine Ferraro and Elizabeth Holtzman, two women it had funded in the past, while EMILY's List supported only Ferraro. Its political director, Karin Johanson, says: "Supporting both Ferraro and Holtzman is the 'girl thing' to do," implying that women should be hard-headed and pragmatic and not be overly concerned about hurting feelings (Personal interview, March 10, 1992). They are learning to apportion their funds with discretion, aiding those candidates who have first shown they can help themselves and who have a fighting chance to win.

Even newer on the political horizon than these two groups is the WISH list, a GOP women's group organized to help Republican women. The financial help these groups can give is potentially great, and they are just in the embryonic stage. For example, EMILY's List in 1990 raised 1.5 million for 14 women candidates. This helped elect two women governors—Ann Richards of Texas and Barbara Roberts of Oregon. EMILY's List describes itself as "the nation's most powerful donor network and political resource for pro-choice Democratic women candidates." Many of the contributors to these groups are women in high-income jobs, and there are more and more of these. They are not necessarily political activists, but many have an interest in a particular campaign or generally in seeing more women in public life.

Although both groups are primarily fund-raisers, they also supply advice on how to utilize the media and offer help with other campaign strategies. They spend a lot of time as well as money giving candidates assistance in organizing and running a campaign. They give short courses on campaigning. It is particularly hard, even for good campaigners, to learn to ask for money. Tippens says they instruct prospective candidates in the obvious, but it seems to help.

The Crucial Election of 1992

The 103rd Congress has set a record for the numbers of women in office. Was it the media hype about the Year of the Woman, the coming of age of a generation of professional women? Was it the effect of redistricting and the number of open seats? Was it public disgust with old-style, old-boy politics? We can't be sure which of these factors dominated, but the end result was a clear breakthrough for women in the national legislature where their numbers had been stagnant for years.

In terms of percentage gains, the results are staggering, with the Senate up from 2 percent to 8 percent. In the House, the female delegation moved up from 29 to 47 (counting Eleanor Holmes Norton of the District of Columbia), bringing the percentage from its previous high of 6 percent to 10.8 percent.

The women in Congress are overwhelmingly Democrat. It may be that the Republicans are less hospitable to women, or the gender gap we have observed on social issues attracts women to the Democratic party. Thirty-five of the forty-seven women are Democrats. Four of the five newly elected senators are Democrats. Yet before partisan conclusions are drawn, we note that Republican women made great gains in the conservative revolution of 1994.

Writing in the *CAWP News and Notes,* Winter 1993, Susan Carroll suggests that the Democrats cannot always expect the gender gap to work in their favor because there is no single issue that divides women.[11] She says that Republican candidates can also attract women's support if they hit on the right issues; the 1994 election in which so many Republican women were elected may prove her point. Ms. Carroll goes on to predict that the gender gap will not disappear because "younger, better educated, and employed women were major contributors to that gap."[12]

According to an article in *The Wall Street Journal*, more women are getting elected to Congress, but they're still on the fringes of power.[13] They don't get a fair chance when it comes to party leadership. For example, no woman chairs a standing committee in the House or the Senate. Even Patricia Schroeder with twenty-one years in the House does not enjoy the power of men with much less seniority.

Most interestingly, the new congressional delegation is a veritable rainbow, a reflection of multiculturalism in contemporary society: eight African Americans (with Eleanor Holmes Norton of the District of Columbia, nine); three Latinas; and one Asian American.

Although she was elected in 1990, Barbara-Rose Collins, an African-American Democrat from Michigan, is typical of the women who won big in the 1992 elections (Personal Interview, March 10, 1993).

Collins became politically active in 1970. She is in her mid-fifties now. She ran for and won a seat on the Detroit School Board. She was angry when her daughter, a fourth grader, was not learning in public school after transferring from a private school. Collins had bought a house and could not afford the private school any longer. When Collins complained that her daughter was behind in math, the teacher said he couldn't teach multiplication to children who didn't know how to add or subtract. The teacher finally told her to come back in two weeks and her daughter would know multiplication. But Collins said that wasn't good enough; she wanted everyone to know multiplication. The black woman principal didn't back her up. Collins says black children never catch up because the teachers don't have confidence in them and don't teach them.

In fact the principal called her employer and asked what kind of job Collins had that allowed her to spend so much time at her child's school. Minority parents weren't welcomed in the schools if they criticized, only to make cookies and tea. Collins changed all that and got much more parental involvement. In 1980 the Chamber of Commerce initiated a referendum to vote on decentralization and this community control was ended. But while it lasted it was intense involvement and gave Collins the experience of how things get accomplished in politics.

Collins' childhood experience in Detroit schools was "racist, but good" because she was one of the "privileged few" who was chosen to go to the Detroit Symphony regularly and who received special attention as a "good middle-class girl," nicely dressed, with a mother and father at home.

"When I was married very young, both my husband and I were working and taking evening courses at Wayne State University." At 10 o'clock, she made the dinner, washed up, picked up after him while he watched TV, but she was not political and didn't know what to do. She did know she didn't want that kind of servitude again and she has never remarried.

Before she was elected to the Congress in 1990, Collins did a stint on the Detroit City Council and also served in the Michigan state legislature.

Collins' main interests are women's issues. She has sponsored a bill to include the work women do in the home in the GNP. Currently this measure of what is produced in the U.S. each year includes only paid work. There are 61 co-sponsors for her bill.

In the course of the interview, Barbara-Rose Collins talked about her attendance at the U.N. Conference on Women in Nairobi in 1985 when this issue of "homework" was on the agenda. The value of women's work has always been denigrated despite the fact that women do 80 percent of the work in Third World countries. "Women in China push huge loads of garbage and generally do very hard physical labor. Women in Africa build concrete houses, carrying bricks on their heads. Women's work must be counted for it is essential to the maintenance of society."

The recent congressional debate on funding for the National Institutes of Health is basically the same battle—asking that women (and minorities) be considered in medical research which has until now been done primarily on (white) men. Although the Director of NIH was at that time a woman, she didn't have the clout to push this.

Collins thinks the world is better now for black women in that "overt racism is over." Women have to be more assertive, they should stop having babies, should stop raising them, stop cooking, stop cleaning. But I'm trying to be reasonable about it, just asking the Bureau of Labor Statistics to put a value on this work."

She speaks of what would have happened if her mother, a housewife, had been divorced. She would have received nothing because it's the man's hard work that has value. The woman's lifetime work would not have been counted. Legislation is necessary to validate the contributions women make to men, the family and society.

All in all, Collins believes race has been a bigger barrier to her than gender or money.[14]

Are these women in office different from their male peers? It would seem so, looking at their backgrounds and career paths. More of them come from the "helping professions" such as teaching and social work. More of them have long years of community activism behind them. Most have worked their way up from local, county, and state government. Although there are a goodly number of lawyers, they are matched by the women who have come into politics via the school board or city council route.

As for patterns in state legislatures nationwide, most states have considerably higher representation of women than the Congress. Some states—Alabama, Arkansas, Kentucky, Louisiana, Oklahoma, and Pennsylvania—fall below the national average, but the total percentage of female representation in the states averages out to twice the national percentage at 20.4 percent. Some states have more than a third female representation—Arizona, Colorado, New Hampshire, Vermont, and Washington.[15]

Given the grassroots beginnings of the women currently in Congress and the rising percentages of women holding local and state office, we can probably say that the election of 1992 is not a blip on the screen, but that there are large numbers of women in politics at the local and state level who will be advancing into the national arena in future elections. There is now a critical mass moving upward, and it's unlikely that this trend will reverse. Progress that has been glacial may turn into an avalanche.

In ancient times, politics was the pastime, in fact, the responsibility and civic duty of the leisured class. It is ironic to think that in the nineteenth century when women of a certain class had more leisure, they were not accepted in politics. Now, when time is so limited for women who have what amounts to two jobs, one in the workplace and one in the home, they hesitate to enter politics.

Women often have good qualifications for politics because their lives have for the most part been centered on helping others. Furthermore, no special training is necessary so that they cannot be kept out by lack of credentials. What then has kept their representation in politics so low? To return to our definition of discrimination, if relevant factors such as education and backgrounds are held constant for men and women, and a huge gap in participation still remains, that gap can be explained as discrimination. It would seem that gender discrimination plays a role in keeping women from a field for which they seem uniquely qualified. If they are excluded from climbing the political success ladder, it can only be a result of social prejudice. Since the majority of political jobs are not full time, they would fit in with family life better than other more routine occupations for women.

The limits on progress for women in politics relate to an ingrained perception that even as we approach the twenty-first century, somehow public life is not the proper setting for a woman. Now that the barriers are down in education and the greater part of occupations and professions, it is difficult to find another logical explanation for the low visibility of women in politics. This is particularly unsettling when we realize that law, the traditional gateway to political careers, is rapidly filling with women as many law schools have edged toward female majorities. Perhaps it is just a matter of playing generational "catch-up," and we will have another generation or two before we see some indication that women are as well represented proportionately in legislative and executive branches as they are in the electorate.

What would reduce the costs for women entering politics and advancing in politics? We recommend public financing for election campaigns. This proposal would result in new blood coming into the political arena and would benefit not only women, but minorities and people with moderate resources as well. This would open politics to a greater range of candidates and ultimately provide more democratic leadership than we presently have.

Beyond that, public financing meets the criteria of democratic government in that it reduces the power of the few, gives more people a voice in a system where money talks, and levels the playing field for prospective candidates.

The central question for the observer attempting to evaluate the costs and benefits of politics for women is the exceedingly high cost of exclusion from decision making of a majority of the population. Too much of old-style politics lingers on with women ghettoized into those policy areas that seem "right" for women—education and welfare for the most part. While on the important budgetary issues of defense spending and foreign aid, women are generally out of the decision-making loop. Women are not perceived as qualified to formulate or advise on "hard" policy.

Whether this sort of ghettoization is connected to the small numbers of women actually serving in the Congress is problematic. Does this vast underrepresentation result in the absence of women from the inner circles at the highest levels of policy making? We can't say with certainty.

The Anita Hill hearings were a vivid reminder of the absence of women in key political venues like the United States Senate. When the petite African-American woman sat before the all-white male Senate committee who were her questioners, their discomfort was palpable. From the southern courtliness of the ancient Strom Thurmond (R-S.C.) and Howell Heflin (D-Ala.) to the prosecutorial rudeness of Arlen Specter (R-Pa.) to the tough-guy western style of Alan Simpson (R-Wyo.) to the tentative, almost wary, politeness of the committee Democrats, it was apparent the committee had no idea what approach to take with the ladylike, self-contained Ms. Hill as she responded calmly to charges and innuendoes.

Even before the Senate organized for the Clinton administration, newly elected women were actively recruited to sit on the Judiciary Committee. After some persuasion, Dianne Feinstein (D-Calif.) and Carol Mosely Braun (D-Ill.) agreed to do so, although the committee was not their first choice. Was it a coincidence or consciousness-raising on the part of the Senate leadership? In any case, when the committee acted on Ruth Bader Ginsburg's nomination, the comfort level was a lot higher.

POSTSCRIPT ON THE 1994 ELECTION

The Year of the Woman proclaimed in 1992 was overtaken by the results of the 1994 election. Many first-term women lost; all were Democrats. The number for women stayed the same at 47 seats, or 10.8 percent of the House, however the party ratio changed from 35 Democrats and 12 Republicans to 30 Democrats and 17 Republicans. Although the proportion of Congress that is female maintained its 1992 peak, these newly elected women largely support Speaker Gingrich's "Contract with America." These women are not likely to continue to support government programs that help women to balance work and family.

The cheering for women in politics after 1992 was perhaps excessive. After all, one election does not constitute a trend. Yet despite the loss of many Democratic seats, in numerical terms, women held on to their gains at all levels. What occurred in 1994 was a repudiation of "politics as usual." Democrats were the losers since they had been the majority in most state legislatures and in the House of Representatives for so many years. First-term Democrat women took a big hit, but CAWP Director Ruth Mandel points out that "election 1994 is but another year in the long push to parity."[16]

The connection between representation and women's interests is difficult to establish and goes back to the problem of women and their policy goals. Clearly, not all women think alike, and not all opt for the same policies. There is strong antigovernment sentiment among newly elected Republican women who espouse "family values." We have yet to see whether this position will have an impact on family policy or whether it is simply a dispute over means to the same end. For today there are still issues that women seem to regard differently than men, and these issues could certainly make significant differences in the direction of public policy if women united as a voting bloc.

Differences in partisan politics aside, it is simply not fair that women should operate at a disadvantage in contemporary politics. Republican or Democrat, women should have a fair chance at elective office. Attitudes are, of course, a long time in changing, but that is exactly why women need some assistance in catching up. This assistance has to be directed toward reducing the costs of running for office. Once that can be accomplished, women are on their own to compete with men. We recommend that women receive the equal treatment and recognition in public life that they are already guaranteed by law in education and employment.

A BRIEF CHRONOLOGY:
POSTWAR UNITED STATES—WOMEN AND POLITICAL EQUALITY

1950s	Minimal numbers of women are in legislatures. Policies do not benefit women.
1960s	More women run for office. Women are active in civil rights and antiwar movements.
	Women vote in greater numbers than men for the first time in the presidential election of 1964.
	Executive Order 11246 issued in 1965 guarantees equal opportunity for women at every level of federal service.

Women are given proportional representation in Democratic convention delegations under new rules voted in 1968.

1970s
Little change is made in congressional representation, but the number of women in state and local governments rises.

A gender gap appears in voting patterns, with women voting for less defense spending and more social programs.

The drive for passage of the Equal Rights Amendment stalls in state legislatures after a good start.

Abortion becomes the hot issue in election campaigns.

Affirmative action also has a high political profile as a result of conflicting Supreme Court opinions.

Women are admitted to most traditionally male schools, putting them closer to power networks.

1980s
Reagan appoints Sandra Day O'Connor to the Supreme Court.

The Supreme Court rules that the male-only draft is constitutional.

The ERA 1982 deadline passes without ratification.

Geraldine Ferraro runs for vice president on the Democratic ticket in 1984, the first woman to be nominated by a major party.

Elizabeth Dole, secretary of labor, raises the question of a "glass ceiling" for women in corporate America.

Congressional female representation seems stuck at less than 6 percent. Yet, as of 1988, women held nearly 16 percent of state legislative seats.

1990s
The Bush administration has one woman at cabinet level, Lynn M. Martin, serving as secretary of labor. She was defeated for the U.S. Senate seat in Illinois in 1990.

No women served as advisers during the Gulf War. The issue of women in combat is once again discussed, particularly women as pilots.

Mrs. Bush causes a stir as a commencement speaker at Wellesley in 1990 because she has no career of her own. Some students say they don't want to hear from someone who has subordinated her life goals to her husband's career.

The election of 1992 brings Bill Clinton to office, and he names his wife Hillary to head a task force on health care.

Women are appointed to prominent posts in the administration.

More women than ever before win in elections at all levels of government.

1994   Women in Congress win leadership positions. Republican women gain increased representation in Congress and in state legislatures.

NOTES

1. As of July 1993, they were Barbara Mikulski (D-Md.) and Nancy Kassebaum (R-Kans.). Elected in 1992: Barbara Boxer (D-Calif.), Dianne Feinstein (D-Calif.), Carol Mosely-Braun (D-Ill.), and Patty Murray (D-Wash.). Kay Bailey Hutchinson (R-Tex.) joined the group as a result of a special election to fill the vacancy left by Lloyd Bentsen.

2. William H. Chafe, *The Paradox of Change* (New York: Oxford University Press, 1991), p. 17.

3. Ellen Cantarow, *Moving the Mountain: Women Working for Social Change* (New York: The Feminist Press, 1980), p. xxvi.

4. Information obtained from literature published by the state of Wyoming for its centennial in 1990.

5. *Women and the Vote—1988* (Washington, D.C.: National Commission on Working Women).

6. Margery Elfin, "Learning from Failures Present and Past," *PS* 15, no. 4 (Fall 1982).

7. Jane J. Mansbridge, *Why We Lost the ERA* (Chicago: University of Chicago Press, 1986), p. 175.

8. Ibid., p. 179.

9. Donald G. Mathews and Jane Sherron De Hart, *Sex, Gender and the Politics of ERA* (New York and Oxford: Oxford University Press, 1990).

10. *Governing, Congressional Quarterly*, June 1990.

11. CAWP, the Center for the American Woman and Politics, is the most authoritative source for data on women in politics. It is part of the Eagleton Institute of Politics at Rutgers University.

12. *CAWP: News and Notes* (Winter 1993): 6.

13. John Harwood and Geraldine Brooks, "Other Nations Elect Women to Lead Them, So Why Doesn't U.S.?" *The Wall Street Journal*, December 14, 1993.

14. In 1995, Barbara-Rose Collins was the subject of an investigation into improper use of campaign funds. Ironically, a first-term Republican, Enid Waldholtz of Utah, a protégé of the Speaker, also found herself in trouble over correct reporting and misuse of campaign funds.

15. CAWP, *Fact Sheet: Women in State Legislatures*, 1995.

16. Ruth Mandel, "Stay Tuned for Women in Politics," *CAWP News and Notes*, 10, no. 1 (Winter 1994): 5–6.

3

THE COST OF BEING FEMALE IN SOCIAL LIFE

Caroline had never been career oriented and would have been perfectly happy to stay home as a wife and mother. But in the early 1980s, she divorced when her son was barely two years old. At first she worked part-time, but as he grew older, she moved into full-time work. Caroline has been bread-winner and childrearer for sixteen years now. Without a husband and a father in the family, Caroline worked double time.

Caroline resents being classified as divorced; she was married for five years. Yet, unless she remarries, for the rest of her life she will be classified as divorced. Although she thinks of herself as single, the Census Bureau insists that she is divorced. (Personal Interviews, 1992)

Tammy, a young white woman, had a baby when she was a teenager. She went on welfare, and Norplant was inserted in her arm to prevent future pregnancies. She finished high school and works full-time at a hardware store. She is the sole support of her child, although the welfare department pays for her child care expenses. (Personal Interview, 1992)

Discrimination against women in social life is harder to measure than that in economics and politics. The social cost of being female is a matter of status. We can measure economic status more easily by seeing whether men hold a disproportionate number of executive jobs and jobs in higher status fields. In politics we can easily see the vast gap in representation between men and women in higher elective office. Social life represents a grayer area, but we can nonetheless observe that women have lower status than men in the interrelationships that constitute society.

The basic unit of society is still the traditional family.[1] In the sexual division of labor within the family, women are responsible for childrearing and housework, and men are the breadwinners. This has been the pattern at least since the Industrial Revolution.

American social life has a history of separating men and women. Men have traditionally had their clubs and their social activities quite apart from women. For many, this voluntary separation is of no consequence, but since clubs have evolved as important professional networks, exclusion from them is decidedly harmful to women's careers. A woman attorney who cannot take a client to lunch at a downtown club is at a clear professional disadvantage. The old European custom of the ladies withdrawing after dinner is no longer common in any but the most formal diplomatic circles, but it was a clear signal that women did not talk business or politics.

Even in volunteer work, a woman who finds herself in the "auxiliary" group is bound to make less of an impact on the organization than a man who is a member of the parent organization. The very word "auxiliary" denotes second-place status, or as the Supreme Court decision stated in another context, a "badge of inferiority." Women carry the burden of charity work in the United States, despite the fact that most women are now employed outside the home. Charity organizers rarely solicit men to do the door-to-door canvassing or telephoning for good causes. However, it is usually men, rather than women, who turn up on the boards of the organizations.

The message is clear that in the drama of social life, women still get the supporting roles. What we need to know is why.

Table 2 presents an analysis of the social cost of being female. Our hypothesis is that women's relatively lower social status derives from society assigning them the role of childrearing. We measure women's social status by fertility rates; the higher the fertility rate, the lower the status of women in a society. Lowering fertility is a means of increasing women's status.[2] In the upper half of Table 2, we conceptualize the social COBF as it relates to childrearing.

Today, men and women share the benefits of children, but women pay all or most of the costs.[3] This is one reason why we chose the number of children per woman as our measure of the social COBF. Another reason is that childrearing, homemaking, and elder care are undervalued, low-status work. Having fewer children gives women a greater opportunity for social equality.

Once women's social status is based on their childbearing role, women not bearing or rearing children may have less status. In the lower half of Table 2 we consider the social COBF independent of childrearing.

Table 2
Social COBF—Related to Childrearing

Traditional Family	Dual-Income Family	Divorced Mothers	Teenage Childbearing
Women pay most, if not all, costs of childrearing	Second shift	Reduced standard of living	Poverty and/or welfare dependence

Social COBF—Independent of Childrearing

Single Women	Married, Childless Women	"Empty-Nest Women"	Widows
Once considered old maids, now independent women, more freedom	Once a stigma; now less pressure to have children; more freedom, more disposable income	Have more time but responsible for elder care	Live longer but alone, generally less well

THE "TRADITIONAL FAMILY"

As we have noted, men and women share the pleasures of having children, but women pay more of the costs.[4] Women have always been the primary parent responsible for childrearing.[5] In traditional society when women did not work outside the home, this was less of a burden. Women today who decide to stay home to rear their children often sacrifice important career time.

Mothers who have to work for pay or who choose to pursue their careers are faced with the childrearing responsibilities when they get home from work. This amounts to working a second shift, which raises the social cost of being female by depriving women of leisure time.

THE DUAL-INCOME FAMILY, OR WHO DOES THE HOUSEWORK?

As we discussed in the chapter on economics, most women work for pay. Society has not fully adjusted to the reality of working women, and thus when women come home from their paid jobs, they work a second shift at home. Women have moved into employment, but husbands have not moved into childrearing and housework. Consequently, women end up working more hours than men. Arlie Hochschild has called this *The Second Shift* in an eponymous book of interviews and narratives of many couples trying to cope with this problem.[6] Hochschild sees the problem as a stalled revolution: the division of labor in marriage has not changed to accommodate the working woman.

In *The Overworked American: The Unexpected Decline of Leisure,* Juliet Schor calculates that women work one month more per year than their husbands, when they both work and have a family.[7] Just as there is a wage gap, so there is a leisure gap for dual-income families. Schor also argues that we now have the most labor-intensive mothering process in human history.

Economist Heidi Hartmann calculated that "husband care" on average takes eight hours a week.[8] By husband care she means housework caused by the husband's presence. Hartmann suspects that husbands require more housework than they contribute. Data from Michigan suggest that single women spend considerably less time on housework than wives, for the same size family. Hartmann estimates that women who are full-time housewives work fifty-seven hours a week, while the husbands work eleven hours in the home.[9] It seems then that housework is more than a full-time job, which is usually defined as a forty-hour work week.

Wives who work for pay work more total hours, but they spend less time doing housework than stay-at-home wives. Husbands don't take up the slack when their wives go to work for pay. This is called the "dirty house" effect. To quantify this claim, Hartmann cites a study that found that women who work thirty hours or more outside the home work a total of seventy-six hours a week, counting housework.[10]

Hartmann argues that a full-time housewife with a child under the age of one works seventy hours a week, while there is no increase in the husband's housework. If the woman is employed for fifteen hours or more, then the husband works two more hours a week on child care and eight hours on housework.[11] She works thirteen more hours a week, and he works ten more hours a week.

The working mother does fifty hours of total work, of which twenty are spent in child care. As a family becomes a dual-income household with children, the effect is that women lose, on average, fourteen hours of leisure, and men gain 1.4 hours of leisure a week. Another study shows that for working couples with children, fathers have 1.3 hours more free time each weekday than mothers and 1.4 hours more on a Sunday.[12]

There is little agreement on exactly what housework is. For their part, economists ignore housework; it does not appear in the GNP. It is the daily drudge work that women do. Women cook every day and men handle the finances periodically. More research needs to be done on this ignored gender gap.

The social role of women as childrearers and homemakers has its economic costs as well. Economist Joni Hersch argues that women with heavy household responsibilities have less choice of jobs. Housework may have a direct effect on earnings by reducing the amount of energy and effort available for the workplace.[13] Statistical analysis of earnings and the number of hours of housework done by men and women shows that women's wages, but not men's, are reduced by each hour spent on housework. This means that, unlike men, women are doing so much housework that it affects their work.

Husbands and wives will just have to battle it out over the kitchen sink and the vacuum cleaner, but the problem of childrearing is more difficult and requires social intervention. Of course, couples do battle this one out also, but the cost is borne not just by them, but also by innocent children.

Often women choose a career that fits with family life. The Mommy Track has been a response to this problem as many women have chosen flexible hours, part-time work, or a job close to home over career advancement. Other women simply decide not to have children. Many women give up their careers for motherhood.

THE DIVORCE REVOLUTION

> *The doctor's wife was a pillar of the community. She was involved in a tremendous number of cultural activities. Married to a prominent surgeon and the mother of four children, she found her life very fulfilling. It was a shock when her husband told her the marriage was over and he was leaving her for a younger woman who "would be totally devoted to him."*

A divorce revolution has taken place in this country. Far more marriages end in divorce now than in the past. Divorce rates accelerated in the 1960s and 1970s and peaked in 1979. In the 1987 to 1991 period, according to the U.N. Human Development Report, 48 percent of marriages in the United States ended in divorce.[14] "No-fault divorce" may account for some of this increase, but there are other causes. Some people believe that women's increased independence and income have encouraged them to seek divorce. Other people argue that the relative ease of obtaining a divorce has pushed women into the workforce and into independence. Causality works both ways.

By the time the divorce rate leveled out after its peak in the 1970s, many middle-aged women in traditional marriages found themselves divorced. The much publicized male "midlife crisis" resulted in many men leaving their wives of twenty-five years for younger women. For these abandoned women, the situation was particularly painful and difficult because they were not trained to compete in the workplace and to be breadwinners.

The U.S. Foreign Service is a sad example of this phenomenon. A large number of Foreign Service wives were divorced by their husbands. These women had never had the opportunity to pursue careers or earn money because their duties as Foreign Service wives precluded that. This issue surfaced in the early 1980s when a group of first wives successfully sued to get their husbands' pensions, which were then going to their second wives.

Unlike these "displaced" middle-aged housewives of the 1970s, younger women are not so vulnerable to the costs of divorce. They are more likely to be able to support themselves if they are left by their husbands. They can even initiate a divorce themselves to get out of a bad marriage.

Divorce is not necessarily a negative social phenomenon. Now that women can get out of bad marriages, many feel liberated by divorce and say it is the best thing that ever happened to them. If there are no children and the woman is young and educated, she doesn't have any special disadvantage. In the past, many women stayed in marriages where they were physically and mentally abused. This is less likely to happen today.

In general, however, divorce is more costly for women than men. The most common impact of divorce on women is the financial insecurity it creates, increasing the possibility of poverty for them and their children. Data show that after divorce, women experience a 73 percent loss in their former standard of living and men experience a 42 percent rise. Alimony is rarely awarded any more; instead we have no-fault divorce. In her book, *The Divorce Revolution,* Lenore Weitzman says that divorce leads to changes in roles for women, a change in social status, a loss of family, friends, social networks, and social supports.[15] Often it also means a change in residence. It can lead to a change in jobs, or perhaps a return to the labor force, or an increase in hours worked. There may be mental health problems, distress, anxiety, and depression.

The Impact of Divorce on Mothers

Martha thought she would be married forever. As a young nurse working in a hospital she met a doctor and settled down to raise a family. When her youngest child was ten, she returned to school to get a liberal arts degree and decided she wanted to shift careers to sociology, even though she would have to start at the bottom of a profession in her mid-forties.

Her husband who had supported her in her desire for more education gave her a "graduation present"—he announced that he had met someone else at one of the many medical conferences he attended and he wanted a divorce.

Martha moved to an apartment, abandoned her career plans, and returned to nursing. Her husband moved to another part of the country, leaving her with increased responsibilities for the children and a severely reduced income. She had to raise two teenage boys alone.

In 1993, Barbara Dafoe Whitehead wrote in the *Atlantic Monthly* that divorce is the cause of the decline of the family and does great harm to children.[16] But what benefit is there for children when a man and woman stay together just for their sake and are battling all the time? Perhaps the harm done to women and children after divorce is not the fact of the divorce itself, but that men cannot be depended on for financial or emotional support. All too often the courts do not make men pay their financial share. Maybe the harm done to women and children is the recent phenomenon of the feminization of poverty. Maybe it is the unfair treatment of women in the workforce that adds to the problem. Maybe harm results from the lack of child care and paid maternity leave.

There was a time when no one was allowed to divorce. Ireland had no divorce until 1995, when legislation allowing divorce passed by a narrow margin. In the nineteenth century, in Great Britain, laws permitting divorce were finally passed, but often effectively worked only for those with the money to buy the divorce. At the same time that we truly lament the rise of divorce in recent decades, we should not forget the cost of being female in the days before divorce was possible. There were centuries of civilization when men could simply divorce their wives, while women did not have the right to divorce.

TEENAGE PREGNANCY AND CHILDBEARING

Teenage sexuality among females rose dramatically in the 1970s. In 1970, 29 percent of fifteen- to nineteen-year-old females were sexually active; by 1980, 42 percent were. This leveled off in the 1980s, but in 1988 it rose to 52 percent, according to the U.S. Public Health Service. A serious problem is that the pursuit of sexual enjoyment can lead to unintended outcomes: teenage pregnancy.[17]

Along with teenage sexuality, the teenage pregnancy rate rose in the 1970s. The rate stabilized in the 1980s. According to the U.S. Public Health Service, pregnancy among sexually active teens has declined owing to the increasing use of contraceptives and the legalization of abortion in 1973. Teenage childbearing fell from 1970 to 1986 but unfortunately is on the rise again. Two-thirds of births in the United States in 1989 were to adolescents (age fifteen to nineteen). This is an increase from 1970, when one-third (30 percent) of births in the United States were to adolescents according to the U.S. Public Health Service. These teenage mothers will pay a heavy lifelong price for their early childbearing. Study after study has shown that poverty is practically guaranteed for them and their children.

It is not easy to sort out public health problems from social problems and moral issues. One change in the problem of teenagers bearing children is that in the past, the teenage mother and infant would remain with the extended family. Today, teenagers and their infants generally leave home. This is an important cause of their poverty. Social conservatives denounce teenage childbearing but oppose school-based health clinics.[18] Another associated problem is the confusion and anger in the United States over abortion. At the same time as teenage pregnancy is decried, teens are denied abortions. The issue has become highly politicized. In the current welfare debate, some social conservatives want a family cap on welfare mothers: no more money if they have children while on the dole. They are opposed by people who fear the cap will lead to abortions. There is also hesitancy about using contraception. Public provision of contraceptives could reduce dramatically the teenage childbearing, if we could only accept human sexuality. But this is not likely inasmuch as religious fundamentalism is very strong in the United States in the 1990s.

FEMALE HEADS OF FAMILY

Polly was married for many years to an abusive man. She wanted to have children but was unable to conceive. She divorced the man and decided that she would have a child on her own. At the age of forty she became pregnant by her long-term boyfriend. She is happy to struggle to support her child.

Shantel is a female head of family. Like her parents, she is employed by the Post Office. Her mother always worked, even as she raised her family. There was little violent crime in those days. There is considerable violent crime in Shantel's neighborhood now. She wishes she could send her two daughters to a private school, but she can't afford it. She wishes she could buy a house. She works a second job toward that goal. (Personal Interviews, 1992–1995).

Sarah, a clinical psychologist, is not married and has adopted a child from overseas. Without a husband's income to supplement her own, she will face a heavy economic burden as her child grows older. But many women have followed this pattern in spite of the difficulties.

Like divorce, the rise in female heads of family is perceived as a major social problem of our era. It is women and children who pay the cost. More and more women are solely responsible for the financial and emotional support of their children. More and more single mothers are poor.

Birth out of marriage is sometimes called the social evil of our day. Welfare reformers want to deny benefits to women who bear children out of wedlock. In connection with the new Crime Control Act of 1994, the secretary of Health and Human Services prepared a study of out-of-wedlock births.[19] But if you look at the statistics for Sweden and France compared to the United States, an interesting idea emerges. In the period 1985 to 1992, according to the United Nations Development Program, 52 percent of births were outside of marriage in Sweden, 32 percent in France, and only 27 percent in the United States.[20] Illegitimate children in Sweden and France are not impoverished the way they are in America. This difference needs to be explained. In Sweden and in France, men generally live with their partners and their children, and thus there is less of a threat of poverty. In the United States, men do not live with their partners and children, although we do not know exactly why. Thus the likelihood of poverty is very high. The problem is not childbearing outside of marriage, but the poverty that it brings in countries like the United States with its puritanical culture and stingy social welfare system.

Over 7 million women are heads of households in the United States today, accounting for 8 percent of families.[21] Although the rise of female heads of households has been a trend for over forty years, the pace increased in the 1960s. We can see the impact of this change on children by looking at the following statistics: in 1959, 92 percent of children lived in a family headed by a married couple. By 1979, only 81 percent did, and in 1992, the figure had dropped to only 74 percent.[22]

The cause of the increase in female heads of household is twofold: (1) the increase in divorce of mothers with children, and (2) the increase in unmarried motherhood, especially among teenagers. Katha Pollitt writes that marriage and motherhood are separate commitments now.[23] Some women want children but not husbands. Some men want sex but not a family commitment, and society lets them get away with it.

Incidence of Poverty Among Female Heads of Family

Being a female head of household puts a great deal of strain on the mother. If the woman is young and has no skills to support herself and her children, this can lead to crushing poverty. The market does not pay women as well as men. Evidence for this is that a single male head of household is less likely to be economically insecure or to be in poverty than a single female head of household. The government allows this problem to be worse than it need be by its failure to help significantly with child care and with employment training.

There is a strong correlation between poverty, race, and ethnicity. Eighteen percent of white families are headed by women, and 39 percent of them are in poverty. Fifty-five percent of black families are headed by women and 57 percent of them are in poverty. Twenty-six percent of Hispanic families are female headed, and 57 percent of them are in poverty.[24] Women may be forced to go on welfare owing to a lean labor market and discrimination against women in the workplace.

Middle-class single mothers may suffer less economic pressure, but the psychological costs for the children who have only one parent may be great. Murphy Brown, the heroine of a television series, and her single parenthood sets an unrealistic example to less affluent women who cannot afford to have a child without a husband.

Middle- and upper-class women who want to have children without husbands do not create a pressing social problem. Since they can support their children, we are tempted to regard it as a matter of choice. Their children will not be poor and undernourished. They will not be uneducated, and they will not be a burden on society. Currently there is also a growing number of unmarried women adopting children, often from overseas. Rather than adding to the population by having babies themselves, they are in effect saving children from impoverished futures.

At the same time, can this individual choice of lifestyle be beneficial for children? Despite the economic security they will enjoy, their futures as fatherless children do not seem particularly bright. The message to the child that fathering is only a biological function—the sperm bank or a willing male—is a peculiar message to send. Finally, raising children is the hardest job in the world, and to do it intentionally with only one parent is foolhardy.

The social COBF in relation to childrearing could be reduced with the introduction of subsidies for child care, more vigorous enforcement of child support, daycare centers, and private-sector cooperation.

BEING SINGLE

Let's take a look at the marital status of women in the United States today. In 1992, there were almost 100 million women over the age of eighteen, of whom 59 percent were married, 12 percent were widowed, 10 percent were divorced, and 19 percent had never been married.[25] Summing up the last three, we see that 41 percent of women are alone.

Today women stay single longer and marry later. Many women reason that they can have an interesting life without a man by having an interesting job. Why marry unless he is a wonderful man? Women no longer have to marry to have their own home or to have a sexual relationship. It's easier for couples to live together now and not make the marriage commitment. Women may feel more independent outside of marriage. More and more women are keeping their names after marriage, especially those who marry later and have already established themselves professionally.

Unfortunately, the single life poses serious drawbacks for women. Many women who live alone are in poverty and face the risk of loneliness and isolation. The decline of "marriages-for-life" causes unhappiness for women who want to marry. For single women, the decline of marriage means that they must support themselves.

Are unmarried women scorned in our society? Once, society labeled women who did not marry as "old maids." Being unmarried is less of a stigma today, but it still can be painful for single women. Often women are made to feel that since no man "chose" them, they have less value. Social life in America still revolves around couples. Are unmarried women devalued because they are not fulfilling their role of childbearer and -rearer? Or is it because women must always take the status of the adult male in their life? The wife takes the status of the husband. The unmarried woman takes the status of the father; so in this case she has not grown up—she is not an adult female, she is still her father's daughter. We feel that to be an adult we need to be the source of our own status.

From Traditional Marriage to Partnership in Marriage

Amy is a budget analyst for the city's nutrition program for woman and infants. She is the only economist in her department and feels appreciated. It is an all-female office. She is thirty-three and has a Ph.D. in economics. She is more educated than her husband. "I make my own decisions. I cook. My husband does all the washing and cleaning. He was raised by his mother." (Personal Interview, 1994)

Although a high proportion of marriages fail, marriage is still the norm. In recent decades, changes in the institution of marriage have seriously affected family life. Paradoxically, these changes have benefited women in some ways and harmed them in others.

Traditional marriage is more beneficial to men than to women. Studies have shown that married men experience less stress and are in better health than single men. Men put less effort into maintaining and developing their marriages than do women. Perhaps that is why men feel less stress. For men, traditional marriages have provided security and many social support services. If men's lives run smoothly at home, because of their wives' care, time, and effort, they function better at work.

The reverse situation is true for women. Single women are under less stress and are healthier than married women, whether or not they work. Wives expend more effort in building the marital relationship and the couples' social life. Women tend to be the caregivers in a marriage, devoting a good deal of their time to what we call "husband care."

Women still perform all the roles of a traditional marriage; that is, they are primarily responsible for the child care and the housework. Later in life, wives are expected to provide elder care for their own elderly parents and for their in-laws.

In the past women were subordinate to men. They were dependent on men for social status and economic support. Women were defined by their husbands' positions. The choice of one's husband determined practically everything in a woman's life. This is still the case, though to a lesser degree.

Attitudes toward marriage have changed. In dual-income families, women have more autonomy (46 percent of families had a wife in the paid labor force in 1991). This usually results in a more egalitarian relationship. More couples work on sharing household chores and childrearing. Although the husband usually makes decisions about job location, it is becoming less unusual for a husband to follow his wife to her new job.

With regard to egalitarian marriages, we can look to some Victorians who experimented. Josephine Kamm in her book *John Stuart Mill in Love* describes the partnership and collaboration of Harriet Taylor and John Stuart Mill.[26] Phyllis Rose also describes this Victorian marriage, as well as the partnership of George Eliot and her companion.[27] Intellectual women have traditionally striven to find men who can accept their intellectuality.

Empty Nest or Elder Care

Alice was an only child. When her mother was widowed, she took on many financial responsibilities for her. When her mother became ill, she arranged for nursing care and finally took her into her home, although Alice worked full-time. For five years, until her mother's death, Alice's life was circumscribed by her mother's illness, psychologically and financially.

Margaret found herself in an unwanted role of caregiver to both her mother and mother-in-law just when she thought she could retire and enjoy her own hobbies and some travel. One of these elderly women was in a nursing home several states away, and the other one would soon need to be. It fell to her to make the arrangements since her husband and brothers were too busy.

Three women in their sixties who had returned to their college for a fortieth reunion all discussed their lives as primary caregivers for their husbands, all of whom had suffered incapacitating strokes.

The woman's caregiver role is not just for her children but extends to the elderly. Over their life cycles, women first care for children and then for their parents and the parents of their husbands. Directors of nursing homes will tell you that most of the visitors are women. It is the daughters and daughters-in-law who come the most often, not the sons and sons-in-law. This is the woman's sphere, even though the woman is now middle-aged and not in the best of health herself in many cases.[28]

Women live longer than men. They live to be caregivers to their husbands. They outlive their husbands by an average of six years.[29]

Age discrimination has an impact on both men and women. We are not a society that is sympathetic to old age. Age discrimination hits women harder than men. First, women often take longer to get to their career goals than men. They may have entered the workforce when there was still a good deal of discrimination against women in their fields. They may have taken time out to rear children. Therefore, they are older when they first get into positions of responsibility. Ageism is bound to harm them in their prime.

Second, physical appearance seems to count more for women than for men. Women cannot afford to show that they are growing old if they are in any kind of public position. They are given less slack than men. Men are distinguished-looking; women are wrinkled and old-looking.

In America we have no long-term elder care policy, so the burden falls disproportionately on older women.

THE CONTRACEPTION REVOLUTION

Barbara, a 1950s woman, had two children in the 1960s. She stayed home with the children for ten years. Her mother was a full-time housewife and raised five children during the Depression. Her grandmother, an immigrant, had thirteen children and worked in the family business.

"Through most of history the survival of the species has been dependent upon the willingness of women to bear (on the average) six to eight children so that two or three might survive to adulthood. Until the decline of mortality rates in the nineteenth century, the rebellion of even a minority of women from this taxing maternity regime could threaten a group with slow or rapid extinction."[30]

In 1960, the Food and Drug Administration approved the contraceptive pill for women. In 1965, in *Griswold v. Connecticut,* the Supreme Court established the right of married couples to use contraception. In 1973, in the case of *Roe* v. *Wade,* the Supreme Court legalized abortion.

The trend toward reduced fertility began before the contraception revolution. The first country to reduce fertility rates was France. Next came the United States where rates began to fall when land became scarce. This is called the demographic revolution, and it occurs in all countries that have experienced industrial revolutions.

In the past hundred years in the United States, there has been a decline in the fertility rate. Women now spend less of their life cycle in childrearing and more in employment, leisure, or playing other social and political roles.

In 1991, the fertility rate in the United States was 2.0 pregnancies per woman.[31] This is below the rate needed for reproduction of the population, which is 2.1 children per woman. European countries have even lower rates: the rate in France, for example, is only 1.8.

Women are also having their children later in life. Many women now have their first (and last) child in their 30s, not their 20s.[32] In addition, more women are remaining childless. In a survey of women aged twenty-five to thirty-nine years, researchers found that in 1960, 18 percent of these women were childless; in 1986, 28 percent were.[33] In 1988, 30 percent of households in the United States were married couples without children. This compares with 27 percent in France and 33 percent in Sweden.[34]

This reduction of fertility means that women can contribute to the economic, political, and social life of the community. Women can reduce their COBF economically and socially by not having children or by having fewer children. Having no children or having fewer children increases the woman's bargaining power vis-à-vis her husband.[35]

There is also a downside to fertility reduction. Democracies need citizens. Businesses need workers. Not reproducing the population can lead to increased immigration, which is controversial. Moreover, if women don't have children, they miss out on the benefits of motherhood, which include the pleasure of rearing children, a sense of achieving adulthood, and a hedge against loneliness in old age.[36]

Technology has intervened in the biological evolution. One key gift of science has been the great reduction of mortality rates achieved in the nineteenth century, so that women no longer have to have six to eight children to ensure that at least two survive. This change radically reduced the cost of being female. Technology has given us the contraception revolution, although the diffusion of birth control and family planning is very far from complete.

The woman's role in marriage has traditionally been a complementary one. Economically, once women entered the workforce in appreciable numbers, they were expected to contribute to the household income, but they were not the primary breadwinners. In fact, women were often turned down for jobs if they were married, the logic being that they didn't need the job and were taking a man's income away. Politically, women's role has been in the background of men's political careers. The smiling, supportive political wife was the sine qua non for every candidate, but she was not to have personal political ambitions.

Perhaps because women were in the backseat for so long, when they were finally in a position to take control, they did in a big way. Dominating the household, deciding on the direction the family would take in every area from church affiliation to vacations, and setting priorities on expenditures, women often ruled their private domains. This led to the stereotype of the hen-pecked husband handing over his paycheck and his virility simultaneously. The social mouse, meekly deferring to her husband in public, was a lion in the home.

In this new era of shared responsibilities, women remain the primary organizers of family life and hence, social life. Many women choose not to exercise this authority and would prefer men to help out with the tasks of arranging get-togethers with family and friends, remembering family birthdays and gifts. But these mundane details that make life work smoothly are not among the most appealing, and so women will undoubtedly continue to handle them without much help from men.

We have traced the social cost of being female to women's childbearing and childrearing. Childbearing is not a cost of being female; it is a biological fact. Marriage, family structure, and gender are social constructs and are determined more by culture than by biology.

Caroline believes that men and women are equally capable of raising children, but that men and women are not equally capable of waging war. She says that natural sex differences may underlie traditional gender roles "only in some cases possibly, but not necessarily in situations that require physical strength." (Personal Interviews, 1992)

Mary Lou says that men and women are equally capable of raising children and waging war. She does not believe that there is a natural sex difference underlying traditional gender roles. Her husband cared for their son while she went off on many trips to Europe in the 1960s. Her husband did the cooking all of their married lives. Her husband had a stroke recently and is currently teaching her to cook. (Personal Interviews, 1992)

Dorothy says "some men are equally capable of raising children as women. Otherwise, men are influenced by the hidebound way of thinking that changing diapers is not for them." As to men and women being equally capable of waging war, she says "here, again, individual differences. . . . Physical differences may not figure as much as psychological ones; the accretion of centuries of attitudes still hold strongly. I was happy to see that the new Air Force Secretary is a woman." She says that there are fewer sex differences underlying traditional gender roles as time goes by. (Personal Interview, 1992)

It is a biological fact that women bear children and a cultural fact that women rear children. In much of human evolution, we were organized in hunting and gathering societies. Survival of human groups was precarious. Women had to have many children in the hope that a few would survive. Human behavior patterns reflected this important role of reproduction in prehistoric society. Scientist Sarah Hrdy argues that female anatomy was destiny then, but it was not oppressive for it benefited everyone.[37] It is oppressive to organize society where one gender benefits to the disadvantage of the other gender. It is oppressive for men not to respect what women do in the sexual division of labor, when that division of labor is necessary for the survival of the human race.

Men and women in hunting and gathering societies had relatively equal status. It could be said that the biological or sexual division of labor was based on females' ability to nurse infants.[38] The female gatherer would nurse a child for two to three years, and most of her adult life (only thirty to forty years in prehistory) was spent pregnant, childbearing, and nursing. Thus women chose economic tasks compatible with mothering duties. This is not gender discrimination, but merely a fact of being female in the hunting and gathering days of prehistory.[39]

The authors, an economics professor and a political science professor, have concluded that the essence of the cost of being female is based on our capacity to bear children. It is a biological fact that we can bear children. It is a social cost that we are assigned the role of childbearer when the human race no longer needs this for survival. In fact, we have a problem with too much population, not too little.

The "major shift" took place around 5,000 years ago after the discovery of agriculture, when more intensive methods of farming began to be implemented. Once plows came into being and animals were domesticated by agricultural use, men's work was no longer compatible with child-rearing.[40]

One clue we would pursue is from women evolutionary biologists. For example, science writer Mary Batten argues that in our highly developed, industrial society, sex differences have been manipulated for social and political ends. This is the creation of gender, as opposed to the biologically based sex differences of the past. Female choice has been subverted. It is this manipulation and subversion of women that is the cause of the COBF, not biological necessity.[41]

The fact that women are expected to rear children is the root of the COBF. Society must share in the costs of rearing children. Our major policy recommendation is universal, high-quality, affordable child care.

NOTES

1. In fact, the unit of society is the family. Morally, however, the unit of society is the individual. This is the basic tension in our society. Respect for the individual is an Enlightenment value. See *The Portable Enlightenment Reader* edited by Isaac Kramnick (New York: Penguin, 1995).

2. To prove our hypothesis that women's relatively lower social status derives from society assigning them the role of childrearing, we would first have to measure social status independently of fertility. The hypothesis treats social status as separate from (an effect of) fertility. To measure social status, we use the number of children born per woman on average, as a proxy. It is beyond the scope of this book to *prove* our hypothesis. Further research is needed on the social and economic roles of women and on the causes of women's lower status than men.

3. Some would go so far as to claim that the subordination of women persists because it produces a group that can be exploited as childbearers. See Alan Wolfe, "The Gender Question," *The New Republic*, June 6, 1994.

4. For the argument on why women pay the costs of childrearing, see Nancy Folbre, *Who Pays for the Kids?* (London: Routledge, 1994).

5. Margaret Polatnick, "Why Men Don't Rear Children," *Berkeley Journal of Sociology* 18 (1973–1974).

6. Arlie Hochschild, *The Second Shift* (New York: Avon Books, 1989).

7. Juliet B. Schor, *The Overworked American: The Unexpected Decline of Leisure* (New York: Basic Books, 1991).

8. Heidi Hartmann, "The Family as the Locus of Gender, Class, and Political Struggle: The Example of Housework," *Signs: Journal of Women in Culture and Society* 6, no. 3 (1981): 5.

9. Ibid., p. 378.

10. Ibid., p. 379.

11. Ibid., p. 382.

12. Ibid., p. 383.

13. Joni Hersch, "The Impact of Non-market Work on Market Wages," *American Economic Review* (May 1991).

14. United Nations Development Program, *Human Development Report 1994* (New York: Oxford University Press, 1994), p. 48. Note that Sweden has the same divorce rate as the United States: 48 percent of marriages end in divorce. Norway's divorce rate is 45 percent and France's is 39 percent.

15. Lenore Weitzman, *The Divorce Revolution: The Unexpected Social and Economic Consequences for Women and Children in America* (New York: Free Press, Macmillan, 1985).

16. Barbara Dafoe Whitehead, "Dan Quayle Was Right," *Atlantic Monthly* (April 1993): 47–84.

17. Newsletter of the Committee on the Status of Women in the Economics Profession, Fall Issue, October 1995, "Women's Contribution to Economic Demography," by Rachel Connelly.

18. Zero Population Growth Backgrounder, "Teens and Taboos: Fact and Fiction: Adolescent Pregnancy and School-Based Clinics" (Washington, D.C.: 1990).

19. Department of Health and Human Services, *Report to Congress on Out-of-Wedlock Childbearing* (Washington, D.C.: Government Printing Office, 1995).

20. UNDP, *Human Development Report 1994*, p. 186.

21. Ibid. Again, to gain perspective on single-female parent homes in America, which account for 8 percent of families, in Sweden the number is 6 percent and in France it is 7 percent.

22. Ibid.

23. Katha Pollitt, "Bothered and Bewildered: Why So Many Single, Middle-Class Mothers," *The Nation*, July 22, 1993.

24. U.S. Public Health Service, Family Planning Program.

25. Women's Research and Education Institute (WREI), *The American Woman 1994–95*, edited by Cynthia Costello and Anne J. Stone (New York: W. W. Norton, 1994), p. 257.

26. Josephine Kamm, *John Stuart Mill in Love* (London: Gordon and Cremonesi, 1977).

27. Phyllis Rose, *Parallel Lives: Five Victorian Marriages* (New York: Vintage Press, 1984). See also Gertrude Himmelfarb, *Marriages and Morals Among Victorians* (New York: Vintage Press, 1987).

28. Some analysts go so far as to claim that the subordination of women persists because it produces a group that can be exploited as emotional nurturers in the household. See Alan Wolfe, "The Gender Question," *New Republic*, June 6, 1994.

29. The life expectancy of Americans at birth as of 1992 is 75.6 years, according to the UNDP, *Human Development Report 1994*, pp. 129 and 189. The life expectancy of American women is 79.1 years. As a gender index of life expectancy, 109 means that women live 9 percent longer than men. Interestingly, French, Swedish, and Norwegian women have longer life expectancies than American women: French and Swedish women can expect to live to be 80.7 years old on average, and Norwegian women 80.3 years. Is the difference explained by culture? By public policies? We pursue this issue in later chapters.

30. Sheila Ryan Johnson quoted in Mary Batten, *Sexual Strategies: How Females Choose Their Mates* (New York: G. P. Putnam's Sons, 1992), p. 201.

31. UNDP, *Human Development Report 1994,* p. 207.

32. William Chafe, *The Paradox of Change: American Women in the 20th Century* (New York: Oxford University Press, 1991), p. 221.

33. Victor Fuchs, "Sex Differences in Economic Well-being," *Science* (1986): 15.

34. WREI, p. 428.

35. Nancy Folbre, "Of Patriarchy Born: The Political Economy of Fertility Decision," *Feminist Studies* 9, no. 2 (Summer 1983).

36. Irwin Garfinkel and Sarah S. McLanahan, *Single Mothers and Their Children: A New American Dilemma* (Washington, D.C.: Urban Institute, 1986), p. 84.

37. Sarah Blaffer Hrdy, *The Woman That Never Evolved* (Cambridge, Mass.: Harvard University Press, 1981).

38. With the invention of the rubber nipple and the development of infant milk formulas, women are no longer needed to nurse their offspring. Women may want to nurse, and society may want mother-nursed children. Nursing is no longer necessary, however; it can be the woman's choice.

39. Margaret Ehrenberg, *Women in Prehistory* (Norman: University of Oklahoma Press, 1989).

40. Alan Wolfe, "The Gender Question: Women and Men in the Mirror of Feminist Theory," *The New Republic,* June 6, 1994, p. 29.

41. Batten, *Sexual Strategies.*

4

THE EDUCATIONAL COST OF BEING FEMALE

The year is 1956: Ruth Bader Ginsburg enters Harvard Law School, one of ten women in a class of 514.

The year is 1957: The graduating class of a women's college is exhorted by a male commencement speaker to go forth and be the mainstays and support for their successful husbands.

The year is 1993: An eight-year-old girl doesn't understand why she isn't called on much in her summer science class for gifted children.

The year is 1993: A junior at a women's college, a math major, says she would never have majored in math if she were at a coed institution. She would not have felt that she could succeed.

This is our good news chapter. Of all the aspects of women's lives we have investigated, education is the one area where women have come closest to equality with men. We are well aware that the battle is ongoing despite great gains, but we are optimistic and want to explore the struggle for this equality and the differences it has made in their lives.

What is education worth today? What impact does it make on one's life chances and on the quality of life? No one would disagree that education is a powerful influence on the lives of Americans and has an almost mythical hold on our imaginations. Therefore, it's heartening to see that most barriers are now down in education. Girls and boys, women and men, attend schools of their choice and obtain the educations they seek without prejudice. Admissions offices of colleges and universities, of law schools and medical schools no longer consider women as a special category nor exclude them altogether. The doors of higher education are wide open for women now. The fact that women have largely caught up with men in this area is encouraging. We can see just how encouraging by looking back to another generation and the effects of discrimination against women.

THE COSTS OF DIVORCE—THE 1950s GENERATION

A story out of the 1950s. An Ivy League setting. Marriage after graduation for a typically achieving male and female. The male goes on to law school courtesy of his partner who takes a low-paying job teaching at a private school. For her, as for many women, a job was only a means to an end . . . seeing her husband complete law school and go on to an economically rewarding career. Women had jobs; men had careers.

Ten years later, the couple have two children. The husband is launched on his career. The wife is immersed in volunteer work and caring for the children. She has not furthered her career preparation, although she has learned a lot about management and human relations. She is always too busy to be bored, although there are times when she questions the importance of her major activities, which are centered on her children's school and related interests.

Twenty years later, the husband informs his wife he plans to divorce her and remarry. They have grown apart; they no longer share interests. The children are teenagers. He will pay for their education but has no intention of paying alimony, nor does she really want it because she thinks she should be able to support herself. After all, she has a bachelor's degree and a solid liberal arts education.

A woman of forty plus, with virtually no job history, is pushed into the labor market with her Phi Beta Kappa key and not much else. She is competing with better trained women twenty years her junior. Her resume is blank.

This was the pattern for Miriam, an economics major who had never worked in the field. She had lots of company among educated, untrained women of her generation. She was able to find an editorial job in an economic research institution, and after ten years worked her way up to a policy analyst position. By now she was 50 and had perhaps another decade of working years ahead. Her salary was far below that of her former husband, and her lifestyle had changed from the comfortable suburban home to a small in-town condominium in a not very safe neighborhood.

The story is ironic in that it portrays an educated woman at a transition point in American higher education. She is educated but not trained. She is educated but is not expected to use her education in the working world.

No one would dispute the value of education in and of itself. In the 1950s there were many liberally educated women caught in a bind similar to Miriam's, but these days we expect some vocational reward for our investment in education. This was not true for Miriam's generation in which society expected women only to be wives and mothers, albeit educated and civically responsible ones. Then when nuclear families began breaking up in record numbers, these women were forced out to work and, like Miriam, found themselves at a tremendous disadvantage. It proved costly to be female even with the same education as a male.

The story is not simply that of a failed marriage and an educated, unskilled woman; the costs exceed the psychological scars of a woman "scorned." Married or not in the 1950s, women's chances for professional training or employment were meager. The tale is often told of two English majors applying for an entry job in publishing in New York. One has an average academic record; the other has received academic honors and has won writing prizes. The average graduate gets the job reading manuscripts; the brighter one is asked whether she can type because there is a secretarial position open. One guess as to gender.

EDUCATION: DISPARATE EFFECTS OF GENDER

Yet, as we have said, the cost of being female in education has been reduced more than the cost in any other part of their lives. Education is undoubtedly the area in which women have achieved the most equality. Why haven't these achievements translated into economic gains? This is a question that must be addressed. Are women being educated in the same way as men?

The 1980s version of the story would have Miriam proceed directly to graduate school (now open to her) and then enter her chosen profession. (Antidiscrimination laws, in fact, encourage hiring women.) She probably would marry later, so at this early stage there would be no question of career or marriage. The hard choice would come later. It would be on her way up the ladder that barriers would be raised, particularly if she had children. We have considered those barriers—the glass ceiling and the steel door—in Chapter 1 on the economic cost of being female.

Why has discrimination been reduced more sharply in education than in occupations and professions? Women fought for the right to education. It was the first thing they wanted. Indeed, it is the first thing any group that has experienced discrimination should seek. Eventually, women won the right to higher education. However, in the 1950s, the feminine mystique told women not to take their education seriously, that they would never "use" it.

When women became discontented with being housewives in the 1950s, some people argued that the problem was that these women should not have been educated. Their education was the problem. As Betty Friedan pointed out in *The Feminine Mystique,* perhaps it was the role of women in the 1950s society, the occupation "housewife," that was to blame, not education.

THE EDUCATION OF WOMEN IN HISTORICAL PERSPECTIVE

Since colonial times, girls and boys have attended public schools in this country, although they were usually segregated by gender until well into the nineteenth century. It was always accepted that girls would receive less education and worse teachers than boys. Girls were treated more or less equally depending on the predominant religious denomination of the community. But it was always thought less necessary for girls to be educated, a reflection of the conventional wisdom on appropriate roles for women as well as a response to mainly agricultural societies where feminine skills and labor were not dependent on literacy. Educating girls was a luxury many families felt they could not afford.

Many female seminaries were founded in the first part of the nineteenth century, producing more and more women teachers. Again, preconceptions about the feminine nature led to the belief that teaching was a natural profession for women. The sister of Harriet Beecher Stowe, Catherine Beecher, who established many seminaries, wrote to Governor Slade of Vermont saying:

Our creator designed woman to be the chief educator of our race and the prime minister of our family state, and our aim is to train her to this holy calling and give her every possible advantage for the performance of its many and difficult duties.[1]

By 1888, the United States had the highest ratio of women to men teachers of any country except for England (63 percent women, 37 percent men). When the statistics were broken down for cities alone, then women accounted for 90.4 percent of teachers. This imbalance has continued into the twentieth century. Why did teaching remain a female domain in the United States? Why did men not enter the profession in significant numbers? Does it have to do with status or remuneration—or both?

> *Mary Mae grew up on a farm in the late nineteenth century. Her uncle was the principal of the high school in a nearby town. He said to Mary Mae and to her cousin Frances, why don't you do something with your lives? Become teachers. And they did.*

Teaching used to be one of the few occupations that was proper for middle-class women. But as other occupations opened up, women chose it less. In 1960, 50 percent of female college graduates majored in education. By 1985, only 13 percent did.[2]

Nancy graduated from college with a degree in English literature. She wanted to be an educated woman and she liked to read novels, so she chose to major in English. She married a graduate student who pressured her to get a job and earn money for them. Nancy was shocked that she was not prepared to be employed by anyone. When in trouble or in doubt, women can become teachers. So she did.

Today a higher percentage (41.3 percent) of women complete high school than men (35.4 percent), and the percentage of women enrolled at the college level is 43.7 percent compared to 36.5 percent of men.[3] By the late 1980s, women's postsecondary educational achievement had begun to surpass men's. By 1988, more than half of college students were female, and one out of every five was a person of color. Thus the diversification of the student population in higher education was evident for both women and minorities.

What Do Women Study?

There is still disagreement about the object of women's education, although it usually remains beneath the surface of debate, mostly a topic of discussion when the concentration of women in the humanities and men in math and science is observed. The concern is that women are still not entering the fields with the most job opportunities. But there has been some movement. By 1988 one out of every five female college graduates had majored in business/management, and one-third of the degrees in biological science were earned by women. In 1993, three-fifths of all doctorates awarded to African Americans were awarded to black women, but half of the women earned those degrees in education.[4]

Barriers to graduate schools have long since been removed, enabling more women to enter previously male-dominated fields than ever before. In law schools the percentages of women are approaching majorities, and the percentages of women in medical schools rose geometrically in the period from 1989 to 1995 when women constituted 42.3 percent of all applicants.[5] In fact, in 1995, women made up 46 percent of the total enrollment at Harvard Medical School and were in the majority at fourteen medical schools, including two historically black institutions, Howard and Meharry. Women are beginning to outnumber men at many schools of veterinary medicine.

Jennifer went to law school in the 1980s. She is now a practicing lawyer, but she does not like the man's world of corporate law. She hopes to find a position outside that world where she can use her legal education for some-thing she believes in.

EDUCATION THROUGH THE LIFE CYCLE

Starting Out in School

Why is equality still a problem? We have to start with the early school years to attempt an explanation. The origins of the puzzle go back to the first experience children have in school. Are the children off to an equal start? Do teachers have the same expectations for girls and boys? Do girls and boys develop skills equally? Evidence in study after study reveals wide gaps, especially in math and science. Why would girls who are generally higher achievers than boys in school not excel in math and science? The biological explanation would be that the right brain/left brain balance dif-fers according to sex, but no study has ever established this difference.

Next we turn to social conditioning, and here a more plausible expla-nation arises, though still unproven: namely, expectations for girls in the family, the classroom, and society generally are different from those for boys. When girls do break away from traditional paths of achievement, they have very often had the benefit of fathers who took a great deal of time encouraging their interests.

A study conducted for the American Association of University Women[6] by the Center for Women's Research at Wellesley brings a volume of evi-dence to bear on this question of early learning conditions. The classroom atmosphere is not one in which girls will be successful in subjects thought by teachers to be "male." And it doesn't seem to matter whether the teach-ers are male or female. It is really disturbing that girls would be short-changed in school situations where the overwhelming majority of their teachers are women!

The Wellesley researchers summarized and evaluated 35 studies on learn-ing between 1983 and 1991 to come up with their findings and recom-mendations. As part of this research, they conducted a study of 3,000 boys and girls between grades four and ten to look at the differences in self-image according to gender.

The report was released in February 1992. In the foreword to the report, the president of the AAUW Educational Foundation goes back through history to review other AAUW studies—one as far back as 1885 that was intended to dispute the theory that education was bad for women's health. She says that this report dispels a more modern myth—that girls are treated equally with boys in American schools.

We live in a new era. Girls are not circumscribed and boxed in from following their natural predilections in school. After all, it would be against the law to keep girls from doing so. Yet an anecdote from the summer of

1993 in a Maryland town makes the opposite case. When an enrichment science program was made available to elementary school children, the class of nearly 20 included only two girls. The little girls who had obviously been enthusiastic about science were made to feel like oddities by the male teacher in a joking, rather than a mean, sort of way. They were called on less than the boys and soon began to retreat from participating in the class. At the age of eight, they had been subtly discouraged from pursuing scientific interests.

According to the AAUW's comprehensive study, girls are not getting the same education as boys. The researchers entered hundreds of classrooms to explore these inequalities. They found an educational system biased against girls, one where girls do not receive the attention and encouragement from teachers that boys do, especially in math and science, nor in speaking out and asking questions in class. Minority girls fare even worse because they are ignored to a greater degree.

What is interesting about these findings is that the overwhelming majority of teachers are women. As we have noted, this is a longstanding American tradition. Why would they be ignoring and underestimating girls? The researchers do not consider that question, although they do emphasize the importance of the effect that teachers' attitudes have on the self-images of girls.

When teachers have lower expectations of girls than boys, something happens to deter girls from pursuing math and science courses and future math and science-based careers. The report argues that lack of teacher support is a vital factor, contributing to a lack of confidence in girls far greater than boys experience. This lack of confidence steers girls away from courses they are told are "hard." Thus a segregated curriculum develops whereby girls follow one set of courses and boys another, as soon as they can choose their courses—generally at the high school level. Girls don't choose math and science, despite the fact that math and science backgrounds are key to well-paying jobs.

The report also looks at the sexual harassment of girls and at sex education and concludes that girls are "marginalized" in the curriculum and the classroom. The researchers call those courses that are not taught the "evaded" curriculum, and they say it works against girls and society. For example, the United States has the highest rate of teenage pregnancy in the world, along with a high rate of sexual disease, yet schools don't deal with these problems adequately. In the September 1993 confirmation hearings on Joycelyn Elders, Clinton's nominee for surgeon general, it was clear that there was disagreement as to whether the schools are the proper venue for such education. Nevertheless, many schools have tried and failed.

Therefore, for a variety of reasons, the report finds that girls remain second-class citizens in American classrooms, out of the mainstream of education that will prepare them for good jobs and advanced training and education. The AAUW has issued forty policy recommendations to meet the challenge this presents. The recommendations range from a different approach to teacher training to modifying current curricula to dealing with gender questions.

For many the Wellesley research is unconvincing. For our part, we do not pretend to judge the quality of the research. What is of major concern to us are the low numbers of girls studying advanced science and math, which will sharply reduce their value in the job market in later life. We can see no justification for differential treatment.

Adolescents in School

Generally, the researchers found it to be true that, although both boys and girls suffered a loss of self-esteem as they approached adolescence, girls were harder hit. Moreover, it appeared that girls consistently felt less confident about "doing things." They had far less confidence in their abilities in sports and in technical areas. Most boys came to school knowing something about how things work; they were more comfortable with science than girls. This is clearly a result of role conditioning within the family, but the schools tend to reinforce it. The survey concludes that teachers are particularly important in directing and reinforcing career aspirations.

As recently as 1993, some schools were trying to come to grips with the problem of educating girls in science and math. In California and Michigan, independent schools were experimenting with separating girls from boys for math and science instruction.[7] Most students felt that this separation was beneficial, giving them more confidence to ask questions in the classroom and to focus on their work. The idea of separatism is discouraging to those who feel that boys and girls need to study and work together in the classroom if they are to compete in the same marketplace after school.

It is important to use the term *self-esteem* with care, for it has become a catch-all term in pop psychology, a "feel good" word that is used to rationalize the sense of failure most of us feel from time to time. In a critique of the AAUW study published in *The Wall Street Journal,* Christina Hoff Sommers argues that young black males who are clearly the most deprived group educationally in the country consistently rate high in self-esteem.[8] The group that rates the lowest are upper middle-class girls and, of course, that fact was the basis of the AAUW recommendations. Sommers says that the AAUW researchers did not publicize the very "awkward" finding on young black males, but we need to think through that seeming contradiction and deal with the problem of how to define self-esteem when evaluating academic performance.

By high school, where students have a choice of a range of courses, we have seen that fewer females elect math and science. Although we have already noted the lack of encouragement in the lower schools, there is something clearly wrong with the counseling system at the high school level when girls are not directed into courses of study that will help them in careers. This lack of guidance has a negative impact on their career choices. This is true despite the fact that more women are entering and graduating from college than males—and most significantly—more black women are entering and graduating from college than their male peers. By 1988 more women were enrolled in college than men, and over half of all undergraduates were female.

Higher Education, Law and Social Attitudes

The Promise of Title IX

Title IX of the 1972 Education Amendments was designed in response to discrimination against girls and women in education. Institutions receiving federal funds were barred from discriminating against females:

No person in the United States shall, on the basis of sex, be excluded from participation in, be denied the benefits of, or be subjected to discrimination under any educational program or activity receiving federal financial assistance.

Despite this guarantee, several exceptions to Title IX weakened its force. The four exceptions are: public or private preschools, elementary schools, secondary schools, and private colleges. Historically, single-sex institutions lobbied for this exemption. Therefore, it is not unlawful to discriminate by sex in the aforementioned areas, leaving only four prohibited areas: vocational schools, public undergraduate institutions, professional schools, and graduate schools. Enforcement of this provision has resulted in the rise of women in law and medical schools and in Ph.D. programs.

An irony in interpreting one of the strongest administrative protections, Title IX of the 1972 Education Amendments to the Civil Rights Act of 1964, is the continuing battle waged by women in college athletics for equal treatment. The argument that football is a revenue-producing sport and thus deserves special attention for that reason, and not for reasons of gender, seems a specious one. Football is also an expensive sport; its transportation, promotion, equipment, and medical care costs do not come cheaply. Women's sports have always received minimal support from educational institutions. The crucial question is whether these sports fulfil some educational function or whether they are merely entertainment.

As some have suggested, if these highly publicized sports are entertainment and profit-making for educational institutions, then colleges and universities should simply buy the best teams and end the charade that they are in fact providing players with a college education. But if athletics are meant to foster good health, team spirit, and a friendly rivalry between institutions, then women's sports should receive the same treatment as men's.

This radical idea was put to the test at the University of Southern California in 1993 when a female basketball coach, Marianne Stanley, disturbed that she was earning less than her male counterpart, refused to sign a contract and was dismissed. She promptly brought suit under federal sex discrimination law. Counsel to the university contended (in defense of differing pay scales) that the men's and women's basketball programs are not the same. An attorney arguing against the female coach's request for reinstatement before a federal judge compared the male coach job to being head of a large corporation and the female coach job to running a "mom and pop" business.[9] For him there was no equality issue at stake. As of April 1996 the case is still on appeal from the decision that went against Ms. Stanley. After being effectively blacklisted for a few years, she has just been hired by the University of California where her pay will be equal to the coach of the male team.

Social Expectations for Girls

Perhaps it's peculiar to Texas where cheerleading is an important component of the high school culture—to the point where one mother attempted to hire someone to kill her daughter's chief rival on the squad—but a flap over pregnant cheerleaders in a Texas town tells us something more universal about the perceptions and images of teenage girls. Four of the fifteen members of the cheerleading squad were pregnant, and the community was up in arms. The issue seemed to be whether the one girl who had an abortion should be allowed to continue when the others who were having their babies were not. The question of male responsibility for the pregnancies, and whether they should undergo any punishment or be prevented from playing, was hardly considered in the initial coverage of the story.

> *A woman who is very successful in a traditionally male specialty, sculpture restoration, spoke of her career path this way: "I always thought of myself as a boy, I guess. I liked mechanics, enjoyed getting my hands dirty, but I got some pressure from my parents to be more like a girl. When I got to college, I thought I would major in physics, but then I discovered art and became terribly interested. I was lucky because my college had a joint program with an engineering school so I was able to combine my interests and major. But I was really unusual then (in the early 70s) and still am."*

Proof that American women place a great premium on education was the greatest phenomenon of the 1970s and 1980s—the number of women returning to college and graduate schools. These returning women are the chief financial support of many educational institutions struggling to survive. What do these women expect to gain from their degrees? Do they share the expectations of their daughters? What are the costs and benefits of education to women of different generations?

Institutions have changed. Doors are open that were previously closed. Affirmative action seems to have achieved its goals of creating a larger recruitment pool that results in greater numbers of women in educational institutions. Society has also changed in accepting women as professionals and in occupations that were previously reserved for males. What problems remain for women in education despite legislative and administrative protections?

Do other cultures have different gender perceptions of career training? Why would the former Soviet Union, for example, think medicine a field particularly suited to women while reserving hard science for males? We have seen that teaching, a feminine profession, has been traditionally low-paying in the United States. An article in the *Christian Science Monitor* on academic opportunities for women reports that gender differences in education persist in all countries, that "the destiny assigned to each sex seems to have a fixed form that repeats itself the world over."[10]

It has become particularly crucial to explain the persistent gender gap in technical areas of learning. We must understand how girls are conditioned differently from boys in the home and in the school setting. It's important to know because these differences in education and training have lifelong implications in the job market. Is there a hidden agenda in our culture that continues to operate—one that says educate women, but only for those fields where they won't compete with men?

Women in Graduate School: The Big Chill

By the early 1970s, many individuals and organizations were asking these questions and studying the problem. The research produced several answers. Among them were that girls were subject to a "chilly" climate in the classroom, one that lasted through graduate school; that teachers gave boys greater attention and respect than girls; that girls were conditioned not to do well in the hard sciences and math and that they had few role models to emulate in these fields.

Nancy experienced the chilly climate her freshman year of college. She loved her first semester of the History of World Civilizations; she participated in class and earned an A. Somehow by the second semester, she got the message that women were not supposed to speak out; she deferred to convention and earned a C.

Barbara attended a women's college and thus did not experience the chilly climate until she was in a Ph.D. program in the 1960s; no one stepped for-

ward to be her mentor. There were no women professors. By the 1980s, a
woman professor was a mentor for Nancy during her Ph.D. work. Twenty
years makes a big difference.

Legislation to protect women from discrimination has been on the books
since the 1970s and has resulted in the opening of all institutions of higher
learning and all fields of study to women. Bernice Sandler, a pioneer in
equality for women in higher education, sees vast changes in the academic
landscape since that time. For example, at the hearings on sex discrimination in higher education in 1970, not one educator testified. The people
who controlled hiring and firing at the university level did not see it as a
problem. Yet women have not been made welcome in many of their new
locales. A 1982 report issued by the Project on the Status of Women details
the environment in which women find themselves in higher education and
notes that many women actually experience a *decline* in their career aspirations as a result of what the report terms "a chilly climate."[11]

This report describes the subtle ways in which women are disadvantaged
in higher education. Most of the behaviors stem from attitudes that women
are often married, mothers, older, part-time, and, therefore, not serious
students. Most damaging for future careers is the lack of mentoring of
female doctoral candidates because this affects their job search profoundly.
Prejudice by professors against older women returning to school makes it
difficult to find mentors. If women are outnumbered by males in the pro-
fessoriate in general, they are only now beginning to be visible at the graduate level. As recently as twenty years ago, it was possible to obtain a
doctorate at many leading institutions without ever encountering a female
professor. Numerous interviews with female graduate students highlight the
problems: "[the] instructor spoke in snide and derogatory terms of the role
of housewives and women [as not being economically useful to men] without examining reasons why this may have been so." "In classes, I experienced myself as a person to be taken lightly. In one seminar, I was never
allowed to finish a sentence. There seemed to be a tacit understanding that
I never had anything to say." This woman, like many of her peers, was
invisible in the classroom.

More than invisible, women are too often unheard at the graduate level.
At a doctoral seminar at Columbia University in 1960, eight people and a
professor sat around a table for a weekly seminar. Five were male, three
were female. The male professor engaged in dialogue primarily with the
men; the women had to assert themselves to get into the conversation. They
were rarely asked to contribute. They were unseen and unheard. The professor found it easy to ignore them. At that time, there were no women
professors in the program so that there was no possibility of mentoring.
The professor was not intentionally discriminatory; he merely felt uncom-

fortable with women. But his lack of support and interest would follow the women in a negative way as they tried to establish academic careers.

Anyone in academe will confirm that mentors are the means to the end—a tenured position. Women are far less likely to have the opportunity of a mentor and, consequently, are out of the loop to success. The access to professional publications and professional associations which result in visibility and employment is less available to women for the same reason. Their response in terms of starting their own publications and groups does not begin to address the problem. They remain out of the mainstream.

Thirty years after the seminar experience recorded at Columbia, in a lecture hall at the University of Texas law school, a conservative constitutional law professor routinely ignored women, failing to call on them. After students registered a protest with the dean, he summoned the professor to convey the complaint. The professor admitted he did not call on women and announced that he would accordingly change his policy in response to the complaint by not calling on anyone!

Written a decade after the passage of legislation establishing the Equal Employment Opportunity Commission and authorizing it to sue employers who discriminated on the basis of sex, "The Classroom Climate" reveals patterns of discrimination.[12] These were not apparent in the data collection that was used to assess the effectiveness of the legislation. A happier story was told. For example, enrollments of women were significantly higher in the ten years, and so were the numbers of women on faculties of colleges and universities and the female recipients of advanced degrees. It appeared that the law was working as intended.

What has happened is a peculiar kind of squeeze play in that girls are still shortchanged at the lower levels and are therefore often not qualified to enter the courses of study now open to them. If they do qualify and complete their education as professionals or as workers in previously all-male occupations, they then hit a glass ceiling or a closed steel door when they try for promotion and advancement. It is as though all the red lights have turned to green except for the one at the end of the road to success; that one is still registering red.

In July 1994 an article appeared in *Forbes Magazine* tracing the careers of the first eight women who had been accepted in the M.B.A. program at Harvard Business School.[13] They were in the class of 1965, so it is immediately apparent that the business school lagged behind Harvard's other professional schools in accepting women. Only one of these women had a business career more than 25 years later! What had happened was in many ways typical. Few of these women were even interviewed by the leading recruiters who invade Harvard every year to look over the graduating class. Those who planned to marry classmates were ignored by recruiters until their future spouses knew what their plans were. Professionally, it was a disaster, although the academic track record of these pioneers was good; all had made it through, unlike many of their male counterparts.

Years later, most of these women speak of placing their families first. (All but one are married.) They say the satisfactions of raising children surpass success in the world of business. They all talk about incorporating their business backgrounds into their daily lives as community volunteers and organizers. They seem to prove the old-fashioned cliché that education is wasted on women. None seem to have envisioned that it would be possible to have both family and career. One woman says that her daughter, a recent Princeton graduate, will find out soon enough that she can't have both. For these women, more than 25 years later, the choices between family and career remain the same, and it is the woman who must choose.

The good news is that women are now allowed in—to schools, occupations, and professions previously denied them. The sad news is that they continue to confront barriers in those schools, occupations, and professions because so many are still dominated by outworn traditions. They are frequently invisible in the classroom, underutilized and underrated in occupations and professions.

Out in the World

As for professional training, the same law and medical schools that women had worked to put their men through for the most part discriminated against women in admissions. In a survey done for *U.S. News and World Report* in 1994 of the Classes of 1939, 1949, 1959, 1969, and 1979 at Wellesley College, the class of 1979 was the first one to produce more lawyers than lawyers' wives. This represents a monumental change since the percentage of women in law schools in the 1950s hovered around 5 percent. For women who did become lawyers in the 1940s and 1950s, employment opportunities were scarce. Justice Sandra Day O'Connor, for example, upon graduation from Stanford received no job offers. Untold others were rejected by major firms simply on the basis of gender or marital status and never actually practiced law.

Ruth Bader Ginsburg who was later to ascend to the Supreme Court was one of ten women in the entering class at Harvard Law School in 1956. The class totaled 514! It was not surprising in view of the fact that Harvard did not open its doors to women until 1950. Women graduating from Harvard in the 1950s recounted some of their experiences at a recent reunion reported in the press. Justice Ginsburg, speaking to the group, recalled that as a Jew, a woman, and a mother, no major New York law firm would hire her. (Justice Ginsburg actually graduated from Columbia Law School because she followed her husband to New York.)

A survey of women lawyers in 1991 showed that women accounted for 37 percent of the associates in law firms but only 11 percent of the partners.

The current environment lets women in but places subtle obstacles along the route to partnership. Women have fewer mentors, are considered less able as "rainmakers" (bringing in business to their firms), and if they have children, less dependable. The social costs of being female intersected with the professional costs when an associate in an Atlanta law firm was denied partnership. She contended that she had been unable to compete as a "rain-maker" because she was denied membership in a downtown eating club where deals were made.

A 1985 graduate, practicing at a major New York law firm, asked the firm to consider the possibility of part-time partnerships and was told that if fathers didn't spend that much time with their children, why should mothers expect to?

Career preparation, even at the women's colleges, was nonexistent as recently as thirty years ago. The assumption was that upon graduation, women's work was to provide support, emotional and economic, if need be, for men. Work was an activity to fill the time before marriage. It was not career oriented. After marriage, the role of wife, that is, helpmate, was the one the woman filled. This role was a supporting one in every sense of the word.

Even in the traditionally female professions, such as teaching, there was tremendous prejudice against married women, and in many cases there were absolute bans against married women teaching. In later years, this ban was largely overcome, only to be replaced by a ban against pregnant women in the classroom.

Some true pioneers in women's education founded the much maligned field of home economics, which by the 1940s and 1950s, was regarded as preparation for the MRS. Yet the women who promoted home economics as a field of study in higher education were scientists concerned with health and nutrition. Ellen H. Richards, the first president of the American Home Economics Association, was the first woman to receive a B.S. degree from the Massachusetts Institute of Technology. For Richards and women like her, home economics was a scientific means of improving the sanitation and diet of the American family. Like the social workers in the early settlement houses, they had a mission far removed from the courses in retailing that appear in a home economics curriculum today.

REASONS FOR UNEQUAL TREATMENT

In elementary school classrooms, treatment by teachers, the style of teaching, and even the textbooks used have all helped reinforce sex roles that are no longer operative in contemporary society.

By the high school level, many behavior patterns have become institutionalized—girls are less aggressive intellectually, and they are steered away from "heavy duty" courses like physics and advanced math. If they are not going on to college, they are directed into "feminine" occupations. The high school advising system has been notoriously sexist. Why would girls ever expect to enter occupations like car sales or fire fighting when all the cues they've received have been to become hairdressers or secretaries?

In an article in the *Washington Post,* Malcolm Gladwell concludes that men have no inherent superiority to women in math.[14] His article, based on an interview with Janet Hyde, a psychologist at the University of Wisconsin, who analyzed more than 4 million math scores of American high school students, reports that there is effectively no difference in *average* scores. The differences show up at the top and at the bottom where more boys tend to score at the highest end of the scale, but also at the lowest, whereas more girls score in the middle range. In other words, although there are more boy math geniuses, there are also more boys who are low math performers than girls. No one ever publicizes this fact.

Girls get better grades in math courses than do boys, but this is not reflected in aptitude tests. Meredith Kimball, a psychologist at Simon Fraser University in British Columbia, offers an interesting explanation for the disparity: girls work harder in school; boys tend to think of themselves as naturally talented. Girls are far less confident about test-taking than boys and far more apt to opt out of advanced math courses. Is the elusive self-esteem factor at work again?

Believing that girls get less attention from teachers in math and science and are accordingly more intimidated in the classroom, a coed private school in California decided to experiment by segregating girls in math and science classes. Other schools have followed suit as more evidence has been produced to show that girls are more successful in single-sex classrooms. One San Francisco principal was quoted as saying, "In a co-ed computer learning class which is dominated by boys, girls feel like foreigners."[15] Most girls reported they felt more confident and were better able to learn in this environment, although one girl asked to go back to the coed classroom, saying she saw no difference and thus, no reason to be separated.

It's not clear whether it's a case of competitiveness or distraction by the opposite sex that gives girls some trouble in high school classrooms. Most of the data are anecdotal, but many schools are willing to give single-sex learning a try in order to build confidence among girls. In the same way, single-sex academies for young males have been founded to help them "catch up" with girls, says Kevin Mercer of Morgan State University.[16] Separate schools have been around for centuries in order to teach girls and boys different subjects. What exactly is this "new" experiment with single-sex learning?

Single-Sex Education

There have always been concerns that educating women makes them less satisfied wives and mothers. This argument was made as late as 1920 in

England when women were finally admitted to Oxford (albeit in single-sex colleges.) Women who wanted to go to Cambridge would have to wait until after World War II. Even today it is true that women returning to school in the 1980s and 1990s have often sought education as a way to independence and out of unhappy marriages.

Women's colleges were founded in the last decades of the nineteenth century because higher education was for the most part available only to men. Traditionally, male institutions of higher learning have been accepting women since the 1970s, often over the emotional protests of male alumni. In 1972 there were nearly 150 women's colleges in the United States; in 1993 there were only 84. The president of Wellesley College, Diana Chapman Walsh, a Ph.D. in health policy from Boston University, responded to a journalist's question on Wellesley remaining a women's college in this way: "If women are taken very seriously across all aspects of life from sports to the classroom to governance of the community; if half of the tenured faculty are women and play very important roles in running the institution at the highest levels of management; if the rest of academia were to look like that—then I'd say maybe Wellesley's job is done. But we are so far from that point that I don't see a day in the foreseeable future when Wellesley College won't be needed."[17]

An interesting twist to the single-sex controversy is the case of VMI. The Virginia Military Institute is a state-supported institution that was sued by a woman seeking admission on the grounds that its all-male admission policy is in violation of federal law. The case had been dragging its way through the court system for several years. Although the Appeals Court ruled that VMI was in violation of equal protection of the law for women, it gave VMI the option of creating a plan for training women. Douglas Wilder, the first black governor of Virginia, provided unlikely support for VMI by coming up with a plan that would offer similar training for women at Mary Baldwin College, a school some thirty miles away from VMI. He proposed giving Mary Baldwin a $6.9 million grant to establish a "leadership" program for women on its campus. (Its total endowment is $20 million.) That's a very juicy carrot and one the administration at Mary Baldwin accepted. A federal judge approved the plan, but the Justice Department is appealing. (This program was implemented in the fall of 1995.)

In 1954, in the landmark *Brown v. Board of Education* of Topeka, the Supreme Court unanimously declared separate but equal to be an unconstitutional remedy. Nearly forty years later, Virginia was exhuming this theory in an attempt to keep an all-male institution going. The irony of a black governor at the forefront of this attempt was patent. It takes us back to the time when one class or race or gender was categorized as inferior; it places a "badge of inferiority" on a group. Why should women be unqualified to participate in a male leadership program? The answer is obscure.

The argument replicates the discredited thinking of the 1950s by placing one group of people in a superior position to another simply on the basis of gender. Military training, and by extension, leadership training, is assumed to be a male preserve. If women want this training, they can receive it in a different form. Constitutionally, of course, the argument is flawed in that separate cannot be equal unless the Court overturns Brown after forty years. Legally, denying women admission to a state institution is a violation of federal law as well as state laws. Socially, the double standard established is counter to all the advances women have made in their progress in education.

A separate program at a women's college validates the belief that women are incapable of completing the same training as men. What kind of leadership program is deemed suitable for women? That a women's college could even consider being used for this sort of program sets women back in their efforts to attain equality in higher education.

It is true that permitting women to enter VMI (and it is unlikely that the gates will be stormed by hundreds of women seeking admission) may necessitate changing some of the old-boy practices like hazing, but no one has ever proved that some of the childish, and even sadistic, rituals of military academies were beneficial and produced good officers. Admitting women may force the all-male institution to reconsider some of its traditions and modify its training accordingly.

A similar case originated at The Citadel, an all-male military college in South Carolina, sued by a young woman who was finally admitted but was denied full participation in the community. The arguments against her participation in the military drills and exercises are standard—her presence would destroy the unity of the men, her sex would make it impossible for her to meet the standards of physical endurance, the school's long tradition of male bonding would be disrupted by the presence of women. Since the nation's tax-supported military academies have been open to women, the arguments presented by VMI and The Citadel have an anachronistic ring to them. They present clear difficulties to those lawyers representing the all-male point of view. (On July 22, 1994, a federal judge ruled that The Citadel must place the plaintiff in the corps of cadets in the fall. This made Shannon Faulkner the first woman granted full admission in 152 years. She began the training but soon dropped out. Other women are now seeking admission.) Judge C. Weston Houck gave The Citadel 60 days to come up with a plan for dealing with future female applicants.

The Classic Study on Education and Achievement

If education is the card of entry for better paying, more satisfying jobs and careers, why haven't women who are becoming better educated than men, at least in Western countries, experienced more success? The answer, as we have seen, lies first in the learning environment, but the work environment provides another explanation.

A comprehensive study of how women's education relates to occupational achievement was conducted by the Department of Education, written by Clifford Adelman and published during the Bush administration.[18] Data were drawn from a sample of 22,652 people who were high school seniors in 1972. These people were tracked through the time they were 32 years old. The word "paradoxes" is used in the title of the study because the findings revealed a paradox that, although women had consistently stronger academic performances, they were not correspondingly rewarded in the labor market.

The report attempts to probe the puzzling question of why education has not been linked to occupational success for women. American women are the best educated and trained in the world, says the report; they will constitute 64 percent of the growth of the workforce in the last decade of the century. What is the problem? According to Kerstin Keen of Volvo, commenting at an Organization for Economic Cooperation and Development (OECD) meeting in Washington in June 1989, "you're not utilizing women as well as you have prepared them," whereas in Europe the problem is mostly the opposite."[19]

A quick view of the problem would seem to show that educational equity does not lead to occupational equity, but reading Adelman's research in more detail reveals that behind the screen of comforting statistics on equality rests an entirely different body of evidence. His data reveal areas of segregation within education that help us to understand the effects we witness later on in the workplace. For example, from an early age girls self-segregate by not taking as much math and science as boys do. They prepare themselves to enter traditionally low-paid professions like teaching, while men enter engineering in greater numbers. These patterns are well-established and slow to change.

Thus the curriculum itself is segregated by preference, not by design. Accordingly, women prove to be better educated than men, but they have chosen different areas of study. The effects are clear; Adelman found that the only women who achieved pay equity with men were those who took more than eight credits of college math. The question is not whether women are better educated, but that they are differently educated, and hence, differently rewarded.

LOOKING AHEAD

Given the barriers women face in education despite legislation requiring equal treatment, remedies seem to reside in the culture more than in the courts and the legislatures. The remedies most frequently suggested are to change the kinds of attitudes projected by elementary classroom teachers, to base classroom activities more on cooperation and less on competition because girls seem to learn better collaboratively, to foster an atmosphere of gender equity in the classroom, and to bring more women into educational administration, which is still largely a male preserve.

Minority women are leading the way as their education levels regularly exceed those of minority males. They demonstrate the importance of credentials to careers. Black women graduate from both high school and college at greater rates than black males and are making gains in occupations and professions. Unhappily, black men, for a variety of reasons, have not remained in school. They need to see the importance of educational attainment in gaining entry to better jobs and careers. As we enter a century when the economy will be increasingly based on knowledge, they will continue to lose out on opportunities.

Not that long ago, only the rare woman was a high school principal or a superintendent of schools or a president of a coeducational institution. Attitudes that kept women out of executive positions in education are changing, and perhaps there will be a trickle-down effect so that girls, seeing these role models, realize that they can succeed at the highest levels.

Only recently has the number of women in administrative positions in higher education begun to climb. Until Hannah Gray was named president of the University of Chicago in 1978, no woman had been president of a major coeducational institution. Today, although the numbers are still small, women are much more visible than they were, accounting for 16 percent of college and university presidents.[20] Of that small percentage, 16 percent are minority women. When Ruth Simmons, an African-American woman, was named the ninth president of Smith College in 1995, her inauguration was treated, quite correctly, as a momentous event.

The number of women presidents of public four-year institutions increased considerably in the 1980s, finally enough to provide useful data on their career paths and their perceptions of their roles. A study conducted by the American Association of State Colleges and Universities reveals that almost every woman president (93 percent) assumed that it was part of her job to assure equality for women on her campus.[21] Many of these women, however, were concerned that this sort of advocacy would have costs.

Patricia O'Donnell Ewers, president of Pace University, is quoted in *Liberal Education* as saying that it takes so long to get the credentials to become a college president that the biological clock is ticking away with the credentials clock and the biological clock often takes precedence. In other words, women dead-end themselves.[22] Bitter proof of the conflict between career and family that creates this dilemma is a federal appeals court's dismissal of a suit against Vassar College in 1995 brought by a biology professor who sued because she said she was denied tenure for having taken time off to raise a family.[23] The professor intends to appeal to the Supreme Court.

The connection between education and success has been so important in this country that equalizing opportunities for women is certainly a major achievement. Yet, as we have seen, the opportunities must go beyond admission to programs and schools. If women are not encouraged to take math and science, to be trained for the high-technology society of the twenty-first century, patterns of occupational segregation will persist, and those patterns will continue to keep women from better paying jobs and careers.

Our research reveals support for several hypotheses about women and education. Although we announced this to be our good news chapter, the residue of many entrenched attitudes lingers on. There is still some debate on the object of women's education. For example, some latent fears remain about educating women to compete with men. In economic hard times, these fears tend to surface in the form of worries over women taking jobs from men. A seemingly intelligent Englishman offered the opinion that the way to cut the unemployment rate in Britain was to make women return to their homes! And he was a man with professionally trained working daughters!

Thus, although we have good news to report in education, it is superimposed on layers of myth and fear that tend to peel away when a period of recession sets in. Women should be educated and trained in a postindustrial society, but some men would like to have more control over what women are educated and trained for because they see it as a zero-sum game: When times get rough women win, men lose. Nevertheless, we remain optimistic, believing that the resistance and the social lag will erode and that equality in education will prevail in our time.

NOTES

1. Thomas Woody, *A History of Women's Education in the United States* (New York: Octagon House, 1929), Vol. I, p. 323.

2. Claudia Goldin, *Understanding the Gender Gap: An Economic History of American Women* (New York: Oxford University Press, 1990), p. 215.

3. *The American Woman 1992–93, a Status Report,* ed. Paula Ries et al. (New York and London: W. W. Norton, 1992).

4. "Black Women Achieving More Ph.D.s But Not Advancing in Academia," *The Monthly Forum on Women in Higher Education,* December 1995, p. 13.

5. Source: Association of American Medical Colleges.

6. "How Schools Shortchange Girls," Wellesley College Center for Research on Women for the American Association of University Women, a report released in February 1992.

7. Sharon Massey, "Co-Ed Schools Are Studying All-Girl Classes," *The Wall Street Journal,* September 10, 1993.

8. Christina Hoff Sommers, "The Myth of Schoolgirls' Low Self Esteem," *The Wall Street Journal,* October 3, 1994.

9. Malcolm Moran, "Dispute over Equality Leaves a Coach Jobless." *New York Times,* September 13, 1993.

10. Christian Baudelet and Roger Establet, "Academic Opportunities, for Women Are Opening," *Christian Science Monitor,* September 8, 1993.

11. *Project on the Status of Women: The Classroom Climate: A Chilly One for Women?,* (Washington, D.C.: Association of American Colleges, 1992).

12. The Civil Rights Act of 1964 banned sex discrimination in employment in the professions. Title IX of the Education Act of 1972 banned sex discrimination in education.

13. Dana Wechsler Linden, "The Class of '65," *Forbes Magazine,* July 4, 1994, pp. 92–98.

14. Malcolm Gladwell, "Pythagorean Sexism," *Washington Post,* March 14, 1993.

15. Sharon Massey, "Co-Ed Schools Are Studying All-Girl Classes," *The Wall Street Journal,* September 10, 1993.

16. Angela E. Couloumbis, "A New-Old Experiment in Separating Girls, Boys In Schools," *Christian Science Monitor,* April 18, 1994.

17. Laurel Shaper Waters, "New President for a Top Women's College," *Christian Science Monitor,* August 12, 1993.

18. Clifford Adelman, *Women at Thirtysomething: Paradoxes of Attainment,* 2nd ed. (Washington, D.C.: 1992).

19. Ibid., p. 1.

20. *American Council on Education Survey, 1995,* reported in *The Monthly Forum on Women in Higher Education* (December 1995): 9.

21. Judith A. Sturnick, Jane E. Milley, and Catherine Tisinger, eds., *Women at the Helm* (Washington, D.C.: American Association of State Colleges and Universities, 1991).

22. "On Campus with Women." *Liberal Education,* Association of American Colleges, May–June 1991.

23. "Court Upholds Tenure Denial to Woman Who Took Extended Leave to Raise Children," *The Monthly Forum on Women in Higher Education* (December 1995): 9.

5

THE HEALTH COST OF
BEING FEMALE

Our theme, the cost of being female, is clearly seen in the area of women's health. Of course, there are specifically male health problems, and we in no way wish to diminish their importance. Our point is that female-related problems have not received the research funding that other health problems have. This disparity is not fair, and it has proven costly to women.

Restating the obvious, we recognize that there are physical differences between men and women, and these differences are most apparent when health problems are involved. But why must these differences result in inequalities of treatment? Why have health issues relating to women been unrecognized for so long? We return to our theme of fairness and conclude that discrimination in so many areas of our lives over centuries has resulted in neglect of what is most crucial to any human being—health. We do not question that men also have health concerns that are gender specific. Prostate cancer would be an example. But in this chapter we will detail how little awareness there has been of female health. Fortunately, this disregard for women's health is diminishing, but we have already lost ground, and it will take a lot of time to catch up. Entire generations have been deprived of the benefits of research.

At a seminar in June 1993 sponsored by the Advancement of Women's Health Research, Kenneth Olden, the director of the National Institute of Environmental Health Sciences of the National Institutes of Health (NIH), said that women were particularly susceptible to environmental toxins. He explained that estrogen and changes brought on by menstrual cycles and menopause were sensitive to chemicals like PCBs and DDT. This interaction can produce dire results. For example, the toxins can lodge in fatty breast tissue over decades. A study conducted by New York University of stored blood from 14,000 participants found significantly higher levels of DDT in women with breast cancer. Exposure to lead in pregnancy can also be transferred to the fetus. There are other concerns over bone density loss and reactions to chemicals that put women at risk, as shown by Dr. Ellen Silbergeld, a toxicologist. Her research has demonstrated how lead levels in the women's blood through the life cycle mobilize and remobilize, with harmful effects.

What has been the cost to women of so many years of indifference to their health? Could deaths from breast cancer have been reduced if money had been poured into research? Would more women be serving in elective office and in the boardrooms if menopause had not been regarded as a psychological mystery? Would generations of children have been healthier? The Population Crisis Committee, in an addendum to a 1988 briefing paper, states that better data on women, including new statistical indicators, are prerequisites for sound strategies to improve the status of women.[1] The committee says that gender-specific data are essential to make recommendations that will improve women's well-being worldwide.

Politics has had a direct and beneficial effect on women's health as the rise in representation in the Congress has resulted in a higher priority given to the subject. Legislators such as Constance Morella (R-Md.) and Patricia Schroeder (D-Colo.) have held hearings and raised consciousness about women's health among male members as well. One important outcome has been the Women's Health Equity Act.

The first Women's Health Equity Act was introduced in the House of Representatives on July 27, 1990. It contained 20 separate bills in crucial areas of women's health: research, services, and prevention. It was introduced in the Senate four days later by Barbara Mikulski (D-Md.), who inserted key provisions that women be included in clinical trials and that a women's health office be created at NIH.[2]

NIH began following most of the policies set forward in the WHEA even though final approval did not come until the reauthorization bill for NIH was approved in June 1993. Meanwhile other provisions of WHEA were also passed as "free standing" bills. The goal of this legislation is to require the NIH to conduct research without gender bias. An immediate effect has been the creation of a center for women's health research, which we discuss later in the chapter.

A FRIGHTENING HEALTH COBF: THE POSSIBILITY
OF BREAST CANCER

In Texas in 1983, a group of women organized the Komen Foundation in memory of a woman who had died of the disease to raise money to fight breast cancer. It began typically out of loss, and it expanded as the experience of loss was repeated hundreds of thousands of times throughout the country as women continued to die of breast cancer in frighteningly high numbers. The centerpiece of this campaign was an annual run or walk, to be held in several locations across the country. It was called "The Race for the Cure." By 1993 the race had been scheduled to take place at thirty-five sites. This number increases yearly.

At one of these sites, Washington, DC, people began lining up to enter the race early on a muggy Saturday morning in June. As they were handed placards to put on their backs, they were asked to write the names of the persons they knew who had died from breast cancer and in whose memory they were running. It was an appalling sight. Many people had more than five names written on their backs!

Money raised from registration for the various races is, of course, targeted for breast cancer research, but another goal is to ensure that mammograms are available to women who may lack the information or funds to obtain them. Years from now, women will look back at the days when they had to fight for insurance coverage of mammograms in wonder. The failure of many insurance plans to cover mammograms surely reflects insensitivity more than considered medical judgment. But more and more companies are becoming aware of the seriousness of breast cancer, and that problem is sure to disappear. More problematic is the effectiveness of mammograms as a screening device.

A blue ribbon group of corporate sponsors including Hallmark, MCI, Gannett, Time Warner, and Johnson and Johnson have supported the Race for the Cure. In only two years, the Washington Race for the Cure grew to be the largest 5K race in the world. This was due to the ability, energy, and tenacity of Gretchen Poston, a successful Washington events planner, who organized the Race by raising most of the corporate money. She died of breast cancer in January of 1992 and left this race as her contribution to women's health.

In some ways, Gretchen Poston's battle with cancer reflects the culture of the 1980s when success in business was paramount for many men and women who were first entries into a competitive market and were beginning to make it very big. Ms. Poston was a partner in a very successful convention and conference planning business. When she was first diagnosed, she was unwilling to speak of the disease. She felt that her business would suffer if clients thought she was not healthy. Since she worked about a year ahead on events, Ms. Poston thought that some clients would feel they were taking a risk using her, so she kept up her usual pressured routine without letup, only occasionally collapsing at home on her free evenings and weekends. When she went in for chemotherapy, she would say, even to people in her office, that she was out of town on business. She maintained this deception for two years, until she decided that "coming out" about her cancer might help other professional women. She chose a journalist friend to write an article for a mass-circulation women's magazine, detailing all she had learned about how to cope with the disease, from when to get a wig to the best type of clothing to wear after a mastectomy. Then she became seriously involved in raising money for a cure. It was a tremendous relief not to have to hide her illness, although to the end, she never admitted it had debilitated her.

A major study produced by the newly created Office of Research on Women's Health of the NIH in September 1992 gives a comprehensive picture of the state of women's health and the current research. It is projected that one in nine women will develop breast cancer in the 1990s, whereas the rate in the 1960s was one in twenty. Although the mortality rate for breast cancer has remained constant for the past fifty years (27 deaths per 100,000 women), the incidence of breast cancer has increased. (The first documented decline in the death rate from breast cancer was announced by the federal government in January 1995: from 27.5 breast cancer deaths per 100,000 in 1989 to 26.2 in 1992.) This, of course, is good news and perhaps shows that increased awareness has helped promote early detection. This is a reduction in deaths, not in incidence, and reflects earlier and more aggressive therapies. But a sobering aspect of these statistics is that breast cancer mortality has actually increased among black women, who may not be benefiting from increased awareness and earlier treatment. These women are less likely to get treatment. Perhaps most disturbing is the finding that most women (no one can agree on the exact percentage, but well over 50 percent) have had no known risk factor—that is, there has not been a history of cancer in their families, nor did they give birth late in life.

While cancer is second to heart disease as a cause of death among women, it is the leading cause of *premature* death. There are still circles of medical opinion where these data are considered questionable. A quarter of the cases diagnosed in 1993 were in women from forty to sixty years old. Some scientists downplay the notion that breast cancer is becoming epidemic and suggest that groups avoid using statistics that may be unreliable. But there are many women who want to explore every possibility, and they are convinced that more research needs to be done on environmental causes. Activists on Long Island, for example, reacting to a study of breast cancer there (it's a very high cancer area), which had concluded that environmental factors were unimportant in causing cancer, decided to design their own study and have begun collecting data in a grassroots manner. After years of pressuring the New York State Legislature to fund such a study, the findings were inconclusive as to cause, but supported the fact that the breast cancer rate was abnormally high. This is enough of a lead to compel more research on environmental factors. As we have seen, the massive study done by New York University suggests that women may process toxic chemicals differently from men.

Perhaps more alarming than the incidence of breast cancer is the incidence of lung cancer as a cause of death for women. In 1991, according to the NIH report, 51,000 women died of lung cancer compared to 45,000 who died of breast cancer.[3] Yet these deaths are easier to explain, for they correlate directly to the increase in smoking among women. Today more young women are likely to begin smoking than young men. Minority women are particularly liable to smoke. The concerted effort of advertisers to appeal to very young women needs no comment, but presents a difficult challenge to those who care about the health of these women.

Diseases that have taken their toll on women have been traditionally neglected in medical research. This has not been due to any conspiracy against women, but simply because there has been little public awareness of the omission of female health problems from scientific consideration. Thanks to the increasing activism of women in Congress and other women in public life, along with "survivors" groups, breast cancer and other forms of cancer that strike women have recently been receiving attention and, consequently, funding. Yet these efforts have provoked a controversy typical of American politics.

As Susan Ferraro puts it in a hard-hitting article, "The activists may be a health movement first, but theirs is a feminist cause as well: Many believe that breast cancer has been ignored for decades because it is a woman's disease. It may be wishful thinking on their part, but some activists suggest that breast cancer is *the* feminist issue of the 1990s."[4] The extraordinary mobilization of public opinion and awareness to the cause supports this idea.

Fighting over Funds

It is characteristic of American pluralist politics to pit group against group in lobbying Congress for funds, but when it comes to funding for health, the sight is particularly appalling. The Chronicle of Higher Education[5] reports that President Clinton's budget request for increased funding for breast cancer has sparked a battle between researchers and breast cancer activists.[4] In the fiscal year beginning October 1, 1993, funding for breast cancer was $262.9 million, up from $197 million the previous year.

Many researchers disagree about earmarking for a particular disease and think that too much money is being directed toward research of this form of cancer. The dispute has gone public in a most unpleasant way, polarizing the groups and making it especially uncomfortable for women researchers. An example of this dilemma is a female professor of genetics at Berkeley who testified before the Congressional Biomedical Research Caucus on the projected funding. First, she said that researchers should not be constrained by specific guidelines for what they researched, and next, under pressure from women's groups, she stated that not enough attention had been paid to women's diseases and that every effort should be made to eradicate breast cancer.

Reporting in the *New York Times,* Gina Kolata writes about the problems of allocating funds for research.[6] This is a dilemma for scientists who want to pursue research in a particular disease. Many believe that earmarking funds can be carried to the extreme and other promising avenues of research are overlooked. Another concern is that money does not always prove to be the answer and that funds poured into studies don't make a difference as in breast cancer. The chief of medical oncology at the University of California, Dr. I. Craig Henderson, suggests that scientific leaps forward often come from unexpected directions. This is especially true in cancer research where there is so much overlap in the disease.

In the past decades, despite this increased funding, the incidence of breast cancer has jumped 25 percent. What can possibly account for this rise? Everything from diet to medications to environmental hazards has been suggested, but nothing substantive has been identified as causal. Ironically, because women are living longer, they stand a better chance of contracting breast cancer in the postmenopausal years. Many elderly women do not examine themselves, nor are they encouraged to do so. Thus, the cancer is not always caught in its early stages.

Recently, there has even been a backlash against the surgical procedure of mastectomy: some maintain that there is no better chance of survival with mastectomy as opposed to lumpectomy. Since the cure seems so far from realization, discussion now focuses on the best type of treatment; the medical community remains divided on the subject. Dr. Susan M. Love, director of the UCLA Breast Center, describes the standard treatment for breast cancer as "slash, burn and poison."[7]

Today the Office of Research on Women's Health and the Office for AIDS Research share a small suite at the NIH. Whether this is more than coincidental is a matter of perception, but the health concerns will surely become more closely linked as the number of women infected with the AIDS virus increases. The figures are not reassuring, for AIDS increased alarmingly in several urban areas in 1990 to make it the largest killer of women ages 15 to 49.[8] The unhappy outcome of this situation may well be a generation of infected children. Again, as with breast cancer, the data for minority women are particularly upsetting. For example, Hispanic women are disproportionately affected by AIDS; they constitute 15.8 percent of all women with AIDS, and Hispanic children, 20.5 of all children under 13, although their percentage in the U.S. population is 9 percent.[9]

ANOTHER HEALTH COBF: WOMEN AND CARDIOVASCULAR DISEASE

The NIH Report on Opportunities for Research on Women's Health summarizes several interesting facts about the disproportionate impact of cardiovascular disease on women. Heart disease is the leading cause of death among women, although, until recently, all the research has focused on the male population. Women have poorer outcomes after heart attacks than men do. Indeed, women are *twice* as likely to die after a heart attack. They are also less likely to survive procedures such as angioplasty and bypass surgery. Survival rates are better for breast cancer because fewer female heart patients receive hospitalization and sustained treatment. Fewer of them undergo standard testing procedures, and fewer participate in cardiac rehabilitation programs.

Researchers are now looking at different responses, both male and female, to stress, to behavioral risk modification, and to poorer compliance with postcoronary rehabilitation programs. They are also studying the effects of hormone replacement therapy on female heart patients. This therapy is in its early stages so the long-term benefits are uncertain, but most doctors think it provides protection to women from heart disease and osteoporosis.

The data on cardiovascular problems are still so limited that it is impossible to recommend specific treatments with total confidence. But more and more researchers are concluding that women do respond differently than men and that treatment that may work for men may be ineffective or even harmful for women. Menopause also makes a difference in what sort of therapy should be prescribed. Since most women experiencing heart attack, stroke, or high blood pressure are menopausal or postmenopausal, responding to these differences requires far more knowledge than we yet have. Nearly half of the 500,000 Americans who died of heart attacks in 1993 were women, most past menopause. The American Heart Association calls heart disease the "silent epidemic" for women.

ABORTION AND REPRODUCTIVE RIGHTS

For most of history, women were regarded as reproductive machines; their purpose was to have children. Despite the horrifying mortality statistics of women dying in childbirth, little attention was paid to these deaths. They were accepted as natural, for there were always more women to have children. An excellent account of the difficulties of childbirth in postcolonial America is given in Laurel Thatcher Ulrich's, *A Midwife's Tale*.[10] Along with these dangers were a series of other problems that were related to pregnancy: fetal and perinatal deaths and difficult pregnancies, which resulted in disabling physical conditions.

Women's life expectancy was for centuries lower than men's because of the hazards of pregnancy and childbirth. There was a very high COBF for women until well into the twentieth century as the most natural function turned out to be one of the most dangerous. This shorter life span for women persisted until this century. Even now, childbirth remains a hazardous business throughout the Third World. Today a major research priority at the NIH is to treat reproductive biology as a critical health concern.

The strong focus of the women's movement has been on abortion. Until abortion became legal in this country with *Roe v. Wade* in 1973, women's health was endangered by their attempts to end unwanted pregnancies. A woman's right to choose was a unifying principle for many women of all classes and politicized women who heretofore had had no interest in politics. Unfortunately, the issue of abortion has become so politicized that it is virtually impossible to engage in rational discussion and to consider the health implications of the procedure and the social and psychological effects of having unplanned children.

The development of the contraceptive pill was another major force in reshaping the responsibilities of men and women in reproduction. The reported risks of the pill have since lessened its popularity, but the newly approved French abortifacient pill, RU-486, may modify the fear of medication to cope with unwanted pregnancies. Yet RU-486 is no panacea either, for it must be taken very early in pregnancy and has some physically painful effects unlike a standard abortion procedure.

THE WOMEN'S HEALTH INITIATIVE

Even reflective people in the medical community have given very little thought to the uniqueness of women's health. Since it is generally known that women live longer than men, it has been easy to dismiss women's health problems. But living longer does not necessarily mean living healthier. Many of the illnesses women experience are a direct result of the aging process. Another fact that until recently has been overlooked in medical research is that similar forms of illness such as heart disease can affect men and women differently and may require different therapies. More and more scientists are discovering that drugs may be metabolized differently by sex. Since drugs are not usually tested on women, it is not possible to judge the effectiveness of drugs for both sexes. Although heart disease ranks ahead of breast cancer as the number one killer of women, no major study of the disease had ever included women!

By 1991, the U.S. government, under pressure from women in Congress and the public, announced that it would ask the NIH to undertake the largest study of women's health ever with hundreds of thousands of women as subjects. The new head of the NIH was Dr. Bernadine Healy who, in response, created a new office of research on women's health. She was quoted in the *New York Times* on April 20, 1991, as saying that "The good news is that women live longer; the bad news is that their quality of life, from a medical and behavioral perspective, is not what it could be."

Dr. Healy, who left office when the Clinton administration was sworn in, was instrumental in placing women's health concerns high on the list of NIH research projects. Believing that social attitudes have too long influenced research priorities, she has set out to change that. The Women's Health Initiative developed under her leadership is a broad-based initiative to include women in the biomedical research sponsored by the NIH and to provide information to women on how to maintain health as well as to focus on health problems specific to women.

Directing this research division is Dr. Vivian W. Pinn, a physician whose specialty is pathology. Dr. Pinn is a dynamic African-American woman with a bachelor's degree from Wellesley and an M.D. from the University of Virginia, earned in the 1960s when it was quite unusual for a black woman to be enrolled at medical school, particularly a southern school. But Vivian Pinn is used to being a trailblazer. She has had long years of teaching experience at Tufts and Howard Universities where she mentored many women, encouraging them to go on in the profession and telling them just what obstacles they might expect to encounter.

Dr. Pinn, whose mother died of breast cancer at an early age, is totally committed to women's health. She has long been sensitive to gender issues, noting that as the only woman in her medical school class, she observed how little attention was paid to women patients' complaints when doctors made hospital rounds. From the very beginning of her career in the 1960s, she has been an advocate for women and has helped sensitize male doctors to their problems. Growing up, Dr. Pinn had never met a woman doctor; the only female medical personnel she knew were nurses. To this day Dr. Pinn is known as a mentor for younger women in medicine. In fact, she first encountered Bernardine Healy when she, Dr. Pinn, was a pathology resident and Dr. Healy, a medical student. She helped Dr. Healy interpret a series of kidney slides with such patience and thoroughness that Dr. Healy never forgot the experience. Years later when she became head of the NIH, she chose Dr. Pinn to lead the new Women's Health Initiative. Now that the context has changed and public consciousness has been raised, Dr. Pinn continues her job as educator with considerably more support (Personal Interview, August 8, 1993.)

Can we hypothesize that the growing numbers of female physicians are proving to be a moving force in this type of research? And, conversely, that the small number of women in medicine over the years has been counterproductive to the consideration of women's health? Judging by the change in the professional climate today, it seems fair to conclude that this is the case. As the director of the Office of Research on Women's Health, Dr. Pinn has been able to use her position to bolster ongoing programs and to set priorities for new programs to advance the cause of women's health and of women's advancement in the sciences. As she says, "By the year 2000, women's health should be an integral part of the mainstream, with gender disparities in research programs relegated to historic interest."[11]

One such program is designed particularly for women who have "left" science in order to cope with family responsibilities. Dr. Pinn does not believe, as many scientists do, that one can't leave science and get back in. She thinks there can be flexibility in career paths and wants to encourage women to reenter scientific research. Thus she has become an advocate for women returning to work in medically related areas. Ironically, as Dr. Pinn has made this a clear priority, the NIH is under siege and has lawsuits pending for failure to promote women, for giving them less grant money than men, and for a generally hostile environment for women.

According to Shirley M. Tilghman, Ph.D., professor of molecular biology at Princeton University, the underrepresentation of women in scientific professions makes recruitment of women important. Women have a very strong attrition rate in the sciences as they move up through their years of schooling (see Chapter 4). Dr. Tilghman believes that women's low participation in science is a result of what she calls "the male-dominated culture of science." Roselyn Payne Epps, national president of the American Women's Medical Association, Inc., states:

More women researchers will be needed. Programs should be designed to identify and nurture the female researchers among high school and college students, mentors should be found for women medical students, residents, and researchers, and technical assistance should be provided to overcome past inequalities.

The COBF for women in science has traditionally been high because of the long years it takes to attain professional status. Women in science today, looking ahead at demographic and economic patterns, are seeking to encourage more flexibility and open-mindedness among those who still control entry and promotion in biomedical research. Dr. Tilghman concludes that gender disparities in the medical treatment of women would quite probably be reduced by increasing the number of women in positions of leadership in the field.

THE SHAME OF MENOPAUSE AND THE PROMISE OF HORMONAL THERAPY

For too long, hormonal changes accompanying menopause have been the subject of humor rather than serious clinical investigation. But recently there has been a shift in opinion, reaching as far as Capitol Hill. Testifying before a Senate subcommittee on aging, Senator Brock Adams (D-Wash.) told Dr. Healy that more research was needed on the health of older women and menopause. Menopause is thought to be an important factor in osteoporosis, a bone-weakening disease. The committee made clear that menopause was to be taken seriously. Not so long ago Dr. Edgar Berman, a physician active in Democratic politics and close friend of Hubert Humphrey who traveled with him in the 1968 campaign, suggested that menopausal women were not competent to serve in leadership positions because their judgment was impaired. Despite the questionable medical history of many of our presidents, no such assertions have ever been made of men. Only recently has the mythology of menopause been eroding as the women of the baby boom generation have come of age and begun writing about their experiences. If it happens to them, it must be important.

In an article published in *American Demographics,* Patricia Braus suggests that this baby boomer population is responsible for the new scientific interest in menopause.[12] For the increase in this age group has made menopause and its attendant problems a fruitful market for drug manufacturers and other businesses. One-quarter of the female population between the ages of 45 and 64 was on hormone replacement therapy in 1994.[13] It is projected that between 1990 and the year 2010, the number of women aged 45 to 54 will grow 73 percent, while the number of women 25 to 34 will decline 12 percent. Braus also notes that the medical profession has already begun to respond to this phenomenon, with many ob/gyn specialists dropping their obstetric practices to concentrate on gynecological disorders. (This, of course, may also be connected to the desire to avoid the mounting malpractice suits in obstetrics.) Thus, menopause has become "trendy," and the media have been covering it, whereas decades ago it was not worth researching or writing about.

The Women's Health Initiative, the fourteen-year $625 million effort Dr. Healy sponsored when she took over at NIH in 1991, will ultimately include 150,000 women at 45 clinical centers across the country. The women studied are postmenopausal women between 50 and 79. The study takes aim at the most prevalent killer diseases for women: cardiovascular disease, cancer, and osteoporosis. It explores the connection between behavior and health, evaluating the effect of diet, calcium and hormone replacement therapy. To quote from the NIH statement, "The broad geographic distribution of the . . . centers allows for recruitment efforts in medically underserved areas and targets minority populations—African-Americans, Hispanics and Native Americans." The goal is to encourage behaviors that have proven to be of value to women's health—low-fat, high-fiber diets, for example.

ANXIETY AND DEPRESSION

At a meeting in May of 1993, the American Psychiatric Association voted to classify PMS (premenstrual syndrome) as a "depressive disorder," an action that provoked the wrath of NOW. Characterizing PMS in psychiatric terms can perpetuate the cultural myth that women's behavior is linked to their hormones and cannot be trusted. Women's groups express concern that a diagnosis of "depressive disorder" could work against women in court and in the workplace.

The incidence of depression is much higher among women than men. The reason is unknown and most explanations tend to be stereotypical, such as women are more emotional, women spend more time alone after their children are grown than do men, or, the slightly more rational—it's hormonal.

Mary Batten, a science writer, comments on the statistic in the report of the American Psychiatric Association's 1990 Task Force on Women that women are twice as likely as men to have mental problems.[14] The APA cites these reasons: (1) women are more likely to be unhappy in marriage, (2) they suffer from physical and sexual abuse, (3) they earn unequal salaries in employment, (4) they are more likely to be poor and be single heads of families, and (5) they encounter the problem of hormones with the menstruation cycle and after childbirth. Batten argues that women are vulnerable because they make greater parental investment in their offspring than men do and, accordingly, experience high guilt levels when they go off to work. She says that natural selection favored the evolution of a mother's strong devotion to her children and that a natural anxiety about their ability to nurture their young is compounded by their need to work, especially when they become single heads of households through divorce or desertion. Depression is a problem for women in each age group; much of it is likely due to the isolation of younger women at home with small children or, in their later years, to women living alone without much contact with the outside world.

In the nineteenth century, upper middle-class women often took to their beds for months at a time suffering from "nerves." (In fact the origins of Coca-Cola lay in the patent medicine women took for those "nervous times.") These women, frustrated by the social constraints placed on them, resorted to illness as a way out.[15] For some Victorian women, illness could save them from a sexual relationship and years of childbearing. The darkened bedroom became the safe haven from the masculine world of sexual demands. Harriet Taylor, an Englishwoman and strong feminist who was later to become Mrs. John Stuart Mill, sought refuge in a platonic relationship with the philosopher. She found the "demands of marriage" too distasteful to bear and spoke out against the treatment of women as simply vessels for their husbands.

Middle-class women had "nerves" and female "complaints," but received very little serious medical attention. Working-class women died young and suffered chronic illnesses, many of which originated in the lack of pre- and postnatal care. Nobody paid much attention to them either except for marketers of patent medicines who had found themselves a large pool of customers. There seems to be a correlation between middle-class female illness and the separation of home and work as we moved from an agrarian society to an urban one. This separation left many women with nothing to do but organize their households. They did not have the freedom of public life that their husbands did, nor did they have productive work to do. Illness soon became associated with leisure and refinement.

In the nineteenth century, men were also edging women out of the health profession. Women who had long been in charge of "birthing" found themselves pushed to the sidelines as modern medicine and the use of forceps became standard (though brutal) procedure. In the book, *A Midwife's Tale,* we get a graphic picture of revolutionary America and women's roles in helping each other as midwives and herbalists.[16] Childbirth, though difficult and painful, was regarded as natural. When nineteenth-century modesty took over, the perspective changed radically, and the midwife was scorned by the middle classes. Their healing activity was mostly over by the middle of the nineteenth century.

COBF FOR THE HEALTH OF OLDER WOMEN

Osteoporosis is a serious health issue for women. Think of the numbers of elderly women with frail bones who fall down and break their hips and can no longer leave the house. Because women have less bone density than men, they are much more likely to suffer fractures in the course of their daily lives. Some steps can be taken to prevent osteoporosis. For example, estrogen replacement therapy decreases a woman's chance of getting osteoporosis. But most women do not even know about it. According to a Louis Harris Poll, 62 percent of women 65 and older are not familiar with osteoporosis, although it can be chronically disabling.

Since women live longer than men, they are more likely to need long-term care. Women constitute the overwhelming number of nursing home patients, and because they outlive men, they are less likely to have a spouse as caregiver. For example, 37 percent of men over the age of 65 receiving care were cared for by their wives; it is estimated that only one-tenth of the women were cared for by their husbands. Home care is not usually covered by insurance. If women are poor or become poor as a result of medical expenses, they can qualify for nursing home care under Medicaid, but middle-income women will not be able to use Medicare to meet these custodial needs. According to data published in *The American Woman 1994–95,* Medicare pays less than 5 percent of the country's total costs for nursing home care.[17] Moreover, this institutional care is not always high quality.

Women in Medicine

Well into the twentieth century, only the rare woman entered medical school; the profession, together with many of its more lucrative specialties, was closed to women. Talking with female doctors today, we are told about their experiences in their medical education of twenty or thirty years ago as if it were a century removed from our lives. During an oral interview for medical school, one woman, now a practicing psychiatrist, was asked whether she planned to have a family and, if so, how she would be able to practice medicine. All her interviewers were male. In medical school all her professors were male.

An important objective of the Women's Health Initiative is retraining women to reenter scientific research. Ironically, as Dr. Vivian Pinn advocates for women whose careers have been interrupted by family responsibilities, instances of discrimination abound at her home base of the National Institutes of Health. Dr. Pinn, aware of this, finds it all the more reason to start reducing some of the barriers.

In 1994, a medical school in New York and a hospital settled the case brought by a woman who is a research specialist in nuclear medicine and associate professor of radiology for $900,000. She charged that she had been denied promotion based on sex. The case took seven years to decision, but should set a precedent for the medical research community which is dominated by men.

Although women are entering medical school today in record numbers, most are still practicing within specialties considered to be appropriate for women such as obstetrics and gynecology, pediatrics, and psychiatry. Few women enter surgery, traditionally the most prestigious of the medical specialties. The sex prejudice in medicine may boomerang as more and more women seem to be choosing women for their physicians.

Another advantage for women in the rapidly changing approach to health services is the emphasis on the primary or family physician where women often choose to practice. Although traditionally considered the least prestigious areas of medicine, women appreciate the flexibility of family practice, and under the new systems of managed care, they may find themselves better employed than some of their male specialist peers.

Many women in medicine today entered the profession after they married and raised children, something that was unheard of until the past few decades. Medical schools traditionally excluded older candidates, claiming that the expensive training would be wasted on people who became doctors later in life. That resistance has apparently ended as mature women graduate from medical school and begin the practice of medicine. And since women live longer, they can practice longer!

EATING DISORDERS

What is there about culture in developed societies that places pressure on women to be thin? It used to be that the plumper the wife, the prouder the husband, for her weight was proof of his ability to feed her well. Those days are long gone, and a different standard has been set in affluent societies. This standard takes the cliché, "You can't be too rich or too thin," quite seriously, with dire results. A pattern of starving and bingeing can affect the menstrual cycle and the ability to have children.

Fashion magazines, in particular, with their underweight models who admit to starving themselves, the heavy advertising of diet products, an inordinate concern with body image, all contribute to an epidemic of fasting, bingeing, and purging that is physically harmful and can even lead to death. Young women seem to lose all sense of reality as they try to look like the models they see advertising clothes.

Female athletes are particularly at risk. An article in *Harvard Magazine* reports that women athletes, especially runners and swimmers, feel they must be very thin to do their best, and so they engage in harmful eating behaviors that can result in loss of bone mass (osteoporosis) at a young age.[18] They are so blinded to the reality of their physical condition that they can sustain unnecessary fractures because their bones have become brittle through diet. Although male athletes are prone to the same behaviors, they don't run the risk of osteoporosis.

Women athletes also suffer possible long-range difficulties in childbearing because of amenorrhea (the disruption of the menstrual cycle). Whereas the general population's rate of amenorrhea is 2 to 5 percent, the figure for women athletes is 3.5 to 66 percent. Since eating disorders are just now coming out of the closet, data are not reliable, but *Harvard* estimates that one out of five female students has some kind of eating problem. Almost half the women at Harvard University are chronic dieters, and 70 percent state they would like to lose 10 pounds or more.

Obsessive behavior about food intake is commonplace for young women who are usually intelligent about other areas of their lives. A recent movie, a quasidocumentary entitled *Eating,* chronicles a fortieth birthday party. The guest are all women; they all are obsessed by food, and they tell their stories while scrupulously avoiding eating the birthday cake. How much this sort of behavior is culturally induced has been questioned very recently when the results of a study by the Pittsburgh School of Medicine were reported at the annual meeting of the American Psychiatric Association by Dr. Theodore Weltzin. He found a physical explanation for bulimia in the low level of serotonin (a substance used by brain cells to communicate) in bulimics. Somehow their brains were not getting the message that they were not hungry. It is estimated that 4 percent of women get bulimia at some point in their lives, whereas men are hardly ever afflicted.

PREGNANCY AND CHILDBIRTH

Nothing is more unique to women than their ability to reproduce. For many this is a very natural, even a spiritual, function and not one to be considered in health terms. Yet the global statistics on deaths in childbirth and infant mortality are evidence that, even in these modern times, childbirth is not risk free.

Health problems connected to the reproductive functions are not confined to Third World societies or low-income women. Socioeconomic changes in the United States in the past two decades have resulted in women having their first children later, which often means a high-risk pregnancy. More and more obstetricians, concerned about malpractice suits if they deliver less than perfect babies, perform caesarean deliveries. Caesarean deliveries are major surgery and result in far longer recovery time than vaginal deliveries. Women's advocacy groups, upset at the high rate of caesarean births in the United States, have gone to the media to draw attention to this medical practice, which many doctors agree has more to do with protecting themselves than with the condition of the mother.

On the other hand, the hospital stays for women giving birth have been drastically reduced to a typical 24 hours or less. Women sent home before they have mastered feeding their babies have a very difficult adjustment period, as pediatricians report. Moreover, infants do not generally manifest the dangerous symptoms of some illnesses until the third day after birth— jaundice, for example. By that time they are out of the hospital and not yet scheduled to see the pediatrician for their first checkup after the hospital check. Enough infants have died to make this a serious problem and one that can be avoided by a longer hospital stay.

A health system such as ours, driven by costs, does not readily respond to human concerns. Recently, however, several hospitals have announced publicly, that whatever insurance practices are, they will insist that postpartum women remain in the hospital for more than one day.

PREVENTION AND ACCESS: POOR INNER-CITY WOMEN

The United States has a high incidence of teenage pregnancy and high infant mortality rates. In Washington, D.C., in June 1993, a 20-year-old young man indicted for a shooting spree turned out to be the father of three children, all sired in one year with three different teenage girls. Imagine the lives of those three babies and the cost to society! The policy implications of unplanned pregnancies are enormous, ranging from infant mortality rates to low birth weights and malnutrition to the later social problems caused by children raising children.

Despite the anecdotal evidence that these young teenagers want to get pregnant because they need someone to love or for reasons of self-esteem, most studies show that half the pregnancies in this country are unintended. The rate of teenage childbearing would undoubtedly be even higher, especially in the middle-class population, without legal abortion. More specific research would have to be done, of course, to demonstrate the validity of these data. In the heat of the current welfare debate, hard data on teenage pregnancy and correlations with the availability of contraceptives, abortion, and access to medical care will prove valuable in determining public policy response.

Prenatal care would solve some of the problem of low-birthweight babies born to teenage mothers. Good nutrition alone could produce healthier babies. The huge investment we make to sustain low-birthweight, mostly premature babies could be better used to prevent these types of births by teaching teenagers how to eat, to see a physician regularly, and to avoid drugs during pregnancy. Adolescent pregnancy is substantially higher among blacks (23%) than among any other social group. The birthrate for blacks under fifteen is seven times higher than that for whites. As in low-income countries where higher birthrates are linked to poverty, so do we in the inner cities have higher birthrates and more babies born to younger women. Writing about health and socioeconomic status, the authors of a *World Bank Report* say that low-cost health interventions are highly effective in developing countries.[19] These interventions, such as access to information on nutrition, sexually transmitted disease, and prenatal care, would be equally effective in our inner cities. According to the report, "more than half the years lost to poor health by women up to age forty-five could be partially or substantially saved through low-cost health interventions."

In addition, the problem of drug addiction has an impact on reproduction in that many babies are being born to mothers on crack. The babies, in turn, are born addicted and experience withdrawal that makes them very difficult to care for. Many of these babies are hospitalized as boarder babies. As these babies mature and enter school, their performance has been tracked and the results are not encouraging. They seem to exhibit the aftereffects in the form of ADS (attention-deficit syndrome) and other behavioral problems. Findings are still tentative, but reports from elementary schools indicate that there are noticeable differences between children born to mothers who have used crack and those who have not.

American girls are sexually active at younger ages than in many other cultures, leading to increases in teenage pregnancy and sexually transmitted diseases, including AIDS. The declining age of puberty is reason for concern. The main factors that determine the age of menarche, which is when a girl begins to menstruate, are health and nutrition. Dr. John Tanner, a pediatrician at the University of London, estimates that in 1840 in England, the age of menarche was at about 17 years. By 1900 it had dropped to 15 as health and nutrition improved. In countries like the United States, today the average age is between 12 and 13.[20] Early pregnancies resulting from earlier menarche have a particularly disastrous effect on inner-city populations. The correlation between the declining age of menarche and increases in early adolescent fertility is the quintessential case of "more research is needed"[21] because so many sociological factors are present as well to complicate the picture.

The NIH report notes that among girls fifteen years old, 25 percent are sexually active. Sexually transmitted diseases are so commonplace that NIH uses the acronym, STD, to refer to them. The working group on immune function and infectious diseases concluded that research needs to be done on STDs because they have an enormous impact on women's health. They may be linked to the immune system and most particularly to reproductive capacity. They can cause pelvic inflammatory disease, infertility, ectopic pregnancies, spontaneous abortions, prematurity and low birth weight—the entire spectrum of reproductive mishaps.

Thus the sexual revolution which has hit the American culture hard in many ways has taken a special toll on the health of younger, poorer women. This is harmful to society at large because it extends beyond a particular generation. Despite attempts to counter the problem with birth control information and the promotion of condoms, we are going to be dealing with its consequences for many years to come.

The Outlook for the 1990s

Unlike the European countries, the United States does not emphasize preventive health care. A large proportion of adult women do not have basic preventive health services, such as Pap tests. According to a Louis Harris poll for the Commonwealth Fund, 35 percent of adult women in the United States had not had a Pap smear in the past year.[22] In addition, roughly a third of all women in the United States do not have a yearly breast exam, a pelvic exam, or, for those over fifty years of age, a mammogram. The Commonwealth Fund poll also found that 13 percent of women and 9 percent of men had not gotten the care they needed in the past year. It is even worse for uninsured people: of this group, 35 percent of women and 23 percent of men were not getting the care they needed.

Again the inevitable link between poverty and health is harmful to women in particular. Since women account for most of the poor in this country, their limited access to health care doubly disadvantages them and their children. And because a higher proportion of minority women are poor, they are doubly disadvantaged. The future is not bright. Mary Batten writes, "The first casualties of budget cuts usually include maternal and infant health care."[23]

As Bernadine Healy states in her foreword to the NIH report on women's health research, "In recent years, Americans have experienced an awakening about the importance of women's health: not only to women themselves but to our society as a whole. . . . This awakening has been spearheaded by advocacy groups and members of Congress. . . . The National Institutes of Health, . . . has heard this call and has responded with an awakening of its own."[24] Society cannot afford to ignore the health concerns of those who will raise the next generation. Attention to women's health could not be more critical.

NOTES

1. Population Crisis Committee, *Country Rankings of the Status of Women: Poor, Powerless, and Pregnant,* Population Briefing Paper, No. 20, June 1988.

2. Source: The American Woman 1994–95, ed. Cynthia Costello and Anne J. Stone (New York: Norton, 1994), pp. 97–102.

3. U.S. Department of Health and Human Services. *Report of the National Institutes of Health: Opportunities for Research on Women's Health,* Washington, D.C., 1992, p. 11.

4. Susan Ferraro, "The Anguished Politics of Breast Cancer," *New York Times Magazine,* August 18, 1993.

5. Stephen Burd, "Clinton's Budget Increase for Breast-Cancer Research Divides Scientists and Activists and Satisfies No One," *The Chronicle of Higher Education,* June 9, 1993, p. A22.

6. Gina Kolata, "Weighing Spending on Breast Cancer," *New York Times,* October 20, 1993.

7. Ferraro, *New York Times Magazine,* p. 27.

8. *Report of the National Institutes of Health,* p. x.

9. Ibid., p. 14.

10. Laurel Thatcher Ulrich, *A Midwife's Tale* (New York: Vintage, 1991).

11. Editorial, *Journal of the American Medical Association,* October 14, 1992.

12. Patricia Braus, "Facing Menopause," *American Demographics,* March 1993.

13. Robin Herman, "The Dilemma of Menopause," *Washington Post,* March 8, 1994, p. 11.

14. Mary Batten, *Sexual Strategies: How Females Choose Their Mates* (New York: Putnam, 1993), p. 93.

15. Diane Price Herndl, *Invalid Women* (Chapel Hill: University of North Carolina Press, 1993).

16. Ulrich.

17. *The American Woman 1994–95* (New York and London: W. W. Norton, 1994).

18. Sandy Kendall, "Not Eating to Win," *Harvard Magazine* (July–August 1993).

19. *Women's Health and Nutrition: Making a Difference* (Washington, D.C.: World Bank, 1994), p. 4.

20. Daniel Goleman, "Theory Links Early Puberty to Childhood Stress," *New York Times,* July 30, 1991.

21. Harriet B. Presser, "Age at Menarche, Socio-sexual Behavior, and Fertility," *Social Biology* 25 (Summer 1978): 94–101.

22. *The Health of American Women,* a Louis Harris poll for the Commonwealth Fund released in July 1993.

23. Batten, p. 189.

24. *Report of the National Institutes of Health,* p. ix.

6

THE COST OF BEING FEMALE IN SWEDEN AND NORWAY

Birgitta is in her sixties and has been living with Hans for twenty years. It's for the children's sake that they don't marry, as both of them are divorced and have grown children. She says that when a marriage is willed and is not just a piece of paper, it is better. Not getting married is not a shame in Sweden; it's normal. People who live together get the same benefits that married people get from the welfare state. (Personal Interviews, Summer and Fall 1993)

Back in 1947 when Birgitta married and had her first son, she received some allowance from the new welfare state. Hospitals were free then. In 1950, she had her second child. Birgitta stayed home for sixteen years raising her two sons. After twenty years of marriage, her husband "ran off with a girl twenty years younger than himself." At the time, Birgitta's sons were teenagers. The father wanted to take the flat they lived in, to keep the two sons, and have Birgitta move to a one-bedroom apartment. But the youngest son said no; he did not want to leave his mother. It was decided that Birgitta would keep her sons and her flat.

Birgitta cried for one day. Then she went to the Labor Office. They paid for her to attend the Royal Library School in Stockholm. In the late 1960s she graduated with a library degree at the same time that her sons earned their baccalaureates. She got her first job, which was part-time, and was able to combine family and work for the five years that her sons lived at home. She worked part-time for twenty-two years in a Social Science Statistics Library and draws benefits as if she had worked full-time for eleven years. Everyone in Sweden gets a social pension when they reach the age of sixty-five.

THE WELFARE STATE IN SWEDEN AND THE
RIGHTS OF WOMEN

After World War II and into the 1950s, Sweden built its welfare state and began its policy of promoting gender egalitarianism. In a study of ninety-nine countries by the Population Crisis Committee, Sweden is ranked number one on the status of women.[1] The status ranking covers five areas of women's well-being: employment, social equality, marriage and children, health, and education. The study includes more than 2 billion women or more than 90 percent of the world's female population.

What does it cost to be female in Sweden? Women with whom I spoke during a trip in the late spring of 1993 had many complaints, ranging from the glass ceiling that keeps women out of higher executive positions to the stress of working the "second shift." Nonetheless, their status compared to that of American women is remarkably good.

With the exception of one election in 1976 and the election of 1990, Sweden has had socialist governments, which tend to enact pro-family legislation. The so-called welfare state has been a fact of life in Sweden since the end of World War II. Although conservative regimes may back-pedal a bit on the extent of policies, the concept of paternalistic government has been fairly well set in the Swedish psyche for more than two generations. The income distribution in Sweden is quite equal with only a handful of wealthy people. Taxes are about 40 percent, compared to the average 30 percent paid in the United States. Critics of the Swedish lifestyle engendered by these policies would like to reverse the pattern because they think it is damaging Sweden's ability to compete in the global market. Although a majority of the Swedish economy is private sector, the safety net provided by government protects citizens from the uncertainties of a free market economy. Swedish citizens live in a comfortable environment that many say makes life in Sweden boring, but if it were a contest between boring and secure, most people would choose boring.

The Swedish constitution guarantees equal rights for women. In a country relatively untouched by race and class problems, the chief possibility for discrimination resides with gender and both the constitution and Swedish law guard against it. Sweden is an anomaly—an ostensible monarchy that has had decades of socialist rule. Although a conservative government was elected in 1990, conservative in Swedish terms would be liberal for Americans. The liberals returned to power in 1994, but there is concern that many of the social policies will suffer nevertheless since the government is faced with an economic situation that requires taking a hard look at their social spending. The budget deficit in the United States is considered bad at 4 percent of GDP, but in Sweden the budget deficit is 12 percent.[2]

In a factsheet published by the Swedish government in 1992, a statement on equal opportunities policy prefaces a brochure on the status of women.

"Swedish equal opportunities policy is fundamentally concerned with the ability of each individual to achieve economic independence through gainful employment. . . . The introduction of separate taxation for husbands and wives, and amendments to matrimonial legislation that clearly uphold the economic independence of all adults, have done much to transform attitudes concerning the traditional role of men and women."[3]

Sweden has a homogeneous population of only 8 million, whereas the United States has a heterogeneous population of 250 million. Nonetheless, we can learn from the experiences of other societies no matter how different. These population facts are important to keep in mind, but should not get in the way of learning what societies can do with social and economic policies.

THE ECONOMIC COBF IN SWEDEN

In a 1968 report to the United Nations, the Swedish government stated that the achievement of the rights of women would require changes in men's roles and priorities. They made the following three recommendations:[4]

- Every individual shall have the same practical opportunities for education and employment.
- Every individual shall have the same responsibility for his or her own financial support.
- Every individual shall have shared responsibility for child upbringing and housework.

It is official policy in Sweden to promote equality of the sexes. Sweden has progressive social and family policy because it had a population and labor shortage after World War II.

Swedish Women Join the Paid Workforce

Sweden has the highest ratio of women to men in the paid workforce of all the developed countries of the world, followed by Norway, the United States, and France.[5] Forty-five percent of the labor force in Sweden was female in 1993, as compared to the United States where only 41 percent is female.[6] According to a publication of the Swedish Institute, women's employment intensity is roughly twice as great in Sweden as in the European Community. The overwhelming majority of Sweden's women are in the labor force; in 1990 the figure was nearly 85 per cent of the female population between twenty and sixty-four.[7]

Although Swedish women work in great numbers, many of them are employed part-time—in 1989, 41 percent of employed Swedish women worked part-time, compared to 6 percent of men.[8] Swedish women have paid maternity leave and subsidized child care, so they do not drop out of the labor market because of childbearing; instead they shift to part-time work. In this way, Swedish women keep their skills, and Swedish children get personal care from their mothers. On the other hand, by working part-time, Swedish women often give up good jobs that rarely exist at the part-time level.

The Pay Gap for Swedish Women

The pay gap in Sweden is much smaller than that in any other country, followed by France and the United States. Moreover, Sweden is number one in closing the pay gap rapidly. The unions in Sweden have worked hard to narrow wage differences between men and women. Here is the evidence from various sources:

- The ratio of women's to men's hourly earnings in manufacturing in 1988 in Sweden was 90 percent; in the United States it was 70.[9]
- In the United Nations' *Human Development Report 1994*, Sweden was ranked number one in lack of gender discrimination in pay: Swedish women made the equivalent of 90 cents for each dollar made by Swedish men. The number for the United States was 59 cents.[10]

But Swedish women still earn less than men. In 1988, the average income of a Swedish woman was 78,000 kroners, and the average income of a Swedish man was 111,000 kroners.[11] This gap is probably due to the fact that so many Swedish women work part-time in occupations that are female dominated and thus low paid.

Studies in the United States have shown that the more housework women do, the greater the pay gap between women and men. Swedish men do more housework than American men, which may explain why the pay gap is less in Sweden than in the United States.[12]

Occupational Segregation for Swedish Women

Sweden has a higher rate of occupational segregation than France and the United States.[13] The occupational segregation index which measures the percentage of women that would have to change occupations in order to achieve equal distribution of men and women among the occupations is 42 for Sweden. This compares with 37 percent in the United States and 38 percent in France. It may be that Sweden, by focusing on social policy more than employment policy, and by solving the second shift problem by having women work part-time, has paid the price of more occupational segregation than the United States or France.

The dual labor market—one for men and one for women—is a recognized fact in Sweden. Fifty-eight percent of women work in the most common thirty occupations, such as child minders, home-helpers, nurses, and kitchen assistants. Forty-two percent of working women are working in occupations that are 90 percent female.[14] Only five occupational fields of fifty-two surveyed in the Swedish labor force had an equal balance of the sexes in 1990. There was a more than 90 percent rate of segregation in thirteen of these fields.[15]

Despite a forward-looking family policy, traditional attitudes are slow to change in Sweden. Studies show that the percentages of women choosing typically male areas of employment are very low and that occupational choice, as in most other cultures, is usually an extension of the female roles of caring and service. Aware of this occupational segregation, the Swedes are making a special effort to attract more young women into technical subjects at the secondary level. Since women comprise almost half the labor force, this would have a strong impact.

Swedish Public Policies That Help Women in the Workplace

Progressive Family Leave Policy. In Sweden, women and men are entitled to fifteen months of parental leave after the birth of a child. When women in Sweden have a baby, they get paid leave and they are guaranteed their jobs back without loss of seniority. Fathers have the right to ten days of leave at childbirth. Women get fifty days of leave before delivery and childbirth at 90 percent of their pay.[16]

After World War I, the International Labor Organization in Geneva, then part of the League of Nations, now part of the United Nations, adopted a convention urging countries to establish maternity leave policies. As early as 1937, maternity insurance benefits were introduced in Sweden.[17] In 1979, it was legislated that people have the right to a six-hour workday to care for small children.

Sweden was the first country to establish parental leave in 1974. They actually have five kinds of parental leave:

- Twelve weeks of maternity leave, six weeks before and six weeks after birth.
- Longer maternity leave if medically necessary.
- Paternity leave for fathers of ten days after the birth.
- Nine months of parental leave, for either the father or the mother.
- Extended parental leave for another nine months, again for either the father or the mother.

Employees receive 90 percent of their usual salary when on leave. This is financed through a national social insurance system—85 percent from payroll taxes and 15 percent from general revenues. This is job-protected leave for new parents with pay.

Swedish policy encourages men to take parental leave, but it is women who take advantage of the policy. Linda Haas, who has studied this problem in Sweden, writes that Sweden has tried to "liberate men from gender stereotypes," but that men are so "pressured to advance and compete and raise the family's standard of living" that women are still primarily responsible for childrearing.[18]

Haas found several barriers to equal parenthood in Sweden. Of course, there is biology: women give birth and breast-feed, but a more important barrier is sociopsychological, or people's attitudes toward gender roles. Women may feel that they want to monopolize childrearing, that this is their calling. Friends and family may not support a couple's desire to share parenting. The husband's father plays a role here. And finally, there is an economic barrier. Men earn more than women, and so if a man takes family leave, the family loses more money, as it gains only 90 percent of the earnings. Part of the Swedish solution is to have women work part-time; this way Swedish women can rear the children.

Personal Income Tax of Individuals. Sweden taxes everyone separately as individuals; there are no joint returns inasmuch as they discriminate against women in dual-income families. This has been the case since 1971 when separate income tax assessments for wife and husband were introduced.[19]

Each individual has her own pension. In Sweden, one has to work for thirty years for a full pension. In 1990 the legislature passed a new law that ended the granting of widow's pensions. A woman is to have a pension in her own name. This policy began as early as 1935 when equal pensions were adopted for women and men.[20]

Equal Employment Opportunity Policy. In 1980, Sweden enacted an antidiscrimination law and set up a commission similar to the Equal Employment Opportunity Commission in the United States. However, as early as 1947, Sweden legislated the principle of equal pay for equal work for state employees.[21] The United States adopted this as a federal principle only in 1963. As early as 1939, it became law in Sweden that gainfully employed women may not be dismissed from employment due to pregnancy, childbirth, or marriage.[22] The United States did not legislate this protection until 1979.

THE POLITICAL COBF IN SWEDEN

As for the COBF in politics, representation in Sweden is more reflective of the population than in the United States. Women have been voting since 1921. Yet although women comprise about one-third of all elected bodies in Sweden, their roles in policy-making are minimal. Their presence on boards and commissions is low, and their assignments throughout government still tend to be those connected with social policy. The situation in corporate life is worse, with very few women in top management jobs. Women speak of the glass ceiling in Sweden much as we do in the United States.

In 1921, Swedish women got the vote, and now more women than men vote in Sweden. In the 1988 parliamentary elections, 87 percent of women and 84 percent of men voted.[23] Women hold 113 of 349 seats in Parliament. In 1989, 38 percent of members of Parliament were women.[24] Perhaps this explains why Sweden has so many family-friendly social policies.

Speaking with a government official who was formerly in corporate public relations, I heard a lot of criticism of the conservative perspective and much concern about setbacks in progress for women. (Personal Interview, 1993)

Lillemor Sillen, spokesperson for the Swedish equivalent of the EEOC, thought that antidiscrimination laws were not being strictly enforced, mainly because women were afraid to bring complaints, that sexual harassment and unequal treatment were prevalent, and not much was being done about it. As a strong feminist, she had contempt for those women who chose not to work. She feared a backlash against women now that Sweden was experiencing recession; she is evidently not alone in this belief, as Susan Faludi, the author of Backlash, *spoke to packed houses during a Scandinavian tour in early 1993.*

THE SOCIAL COBF IN SWEDEN

When I talked with a young woman, a Swedish citizen, but one educated, living, and working in the United States, I was interested to learn that she felt her Swedish contemporaries were far less success-oriented than comparable Americans. She found it depressing that they seemed to have so little interest in pursuing career opportunities and felt minimal pressure to do so. If they lost their jobs, they went on unemployment and stayed out of work as long as possible by signing up for "retraining" programs. The tensions and anxieties of the American job market for educated young people were absent. (Personal interview, 1993)

Who is to say whether the comfort of such a safety net is entirely bad, but my Swedish friend, looking to the future productivity of her native land, was concerned about the relaxed and even passive attitudes she observed during her annual visits. On the other hand, her Swedish cousins thought her to be a typical American "yuppie" and found nothing to admire in her competitive orientation. There is a clear tendency for recent Swedish generations to look to government to help. For some, this represents the success of the welfare state; for others, it represents its ultimate failure.

An older Swedish man had a negative view of Sweden's social policies:

> *In talking with Swedish citizens about their country, I learned that there are generational differences in the way social policy is perceived. (Personal interviews, 1993)*
>
> *For example, when I interviewed a retired shipping executive, Bo Johanson, whose wife is still working as a university administrator, I had the sense that he was discouraged at the direction of his country. Naturally, part of this was due to the fact that the shipping industry, once Sweden's pride, was virtually defunct, but more than that, he expressed disappointment in the younger generation and the way children were raised under several decades of socialist governments.*
>
> *Most critical, he said, was a lack of respect for authority and a corresponding decline in civility which he attributed to long years spent with peers in daycare rather than in family settings. His wife took ten years off to raise their children which he felt was important. He sees much less creativity among the young today and feels it's dangerous to have all "kids the same." For the first time in his life, he has experienced uneasiness when he sees groups of teenagers together on the subway. He sees them out of control and contemptuous of senior citizens. He thinks too many are used to receiving benefits without working and that there is a general decline in morality and a lack of initiative.*

A younger Swedish man of twenty-six who had chosen to stay home with his baby, a little boy of sixteen months, had an entirely different perspective on the welfare state:

> *From Pieter's point of view, government policy gave him the chance to know his son in a way he never could if he were working outside the home. He was enjoying the experience enormously and regretting his return to work, particularly because he did not want to put his son in daycare. If it were up to him, children would remain at home until they were four. I wondered if this reflected his own childhood experience.*
>
> *Rather than saying that the welfare state had dulled his initiative, he said that it had taught him the value of family, which was more important to him than climbing a success ladder at work. He had changed his mind about what was important. He liked the idea that subsidies offered by the government provided an economic cushion so that it was possible to live decently on one income. (Personal Interview, 1993)*

Changes in Social Life for Women in Sweden

The Decline in Fertility Rates. In 1890, Swedish women had four children on average; this rate fell to two children in 1930; and in 1980, the total fertility rate was only 1.7 children per woman. (Total means the estimated number of children a woman will have over her entire reproductive period.)[25] After the war, Sweden had a baby boom as we did in the United

States, but then the rate continued its decline as it did in most other industrialized countries.[26]

Most Swedish families with children have either one or two.[27] Very few households have three children, and it is rare to find four or more. One in seven women in Sweden do not have children.[28]

The Rise of Out-of-Wedlock Births. According to Swedish statistics on Sweden and the European Community, in Sweden about one in two children are born to unmarried parents.[29] For comparative purposes, the rate is 52 percent in Sweden; 27 percent in the United States; 32 percent in France; and 34 percent in Norway.[30]

The Rise of Divorce. The number of divorces in Sweden has only doubled since 1960, whereas in the European Community countries, divorce has quadrupled.[31] However, the level of divorce in Sweden is high: 48 percent of marriages contracted between 1987 and 1991 ended in divorce. The rate in the United States is the same; in Norway, it's 45 percent and in France, it's 39.[32]

The Rise of Cohabitation in Sweden. In the early 1980s, the number of cohabiting households increased by nearly 20,000 per year.[33] Today, 95 percent of Swedish women cohabit for some period of their lives. Since Sweden has a high percentage of couples cohabiting without being married, a new marriage code was drawn up in 1987 to clarify the ambiguities of these relationships in terms of property. Two strong themes underlie this act: first, that the weaker economic partner must be protected upon divorce or death of the other, and second, that divorce must be based on the best interests of the child.

Accepting the reality of cohabitation, these partnerships count as family units. As a result of this type of calculation, 81 percent of minors in Sweden live with both parents—a very telling figure compared to the American picture where the percentages of children growing up without both parents are rising geometrically. By 1992, 24 percent of unmarried American women were mothers. For black unmarried American women the figure was 56 percent.[34] The number of children who will grow up without fathers is dishearteningly high, especially because of the likelihood they will grow up in poverty. Two-thirds of black children born today are out-of-wedlock without the comforting cohabitation situation that prevails in Sweden where fathers are present. In Sweden parents who do not live with their children are required to help support them in proportion to their financial status.

The Rise of Female Heads of Household. In Sweden, 6 percent of households with children are headed by women alone. The percent in France is also low, 7 percent.

Is There a Second Shift in Sweden?

As early as 1884, August Strindberg, a Norwegian playwright, spoke of housework as real work and not just something "to be tacked gratis onto a full-time job."[35] Sweden is the first country to place a strong emphasis on the achievement of equality of men and women in the household as well as in the market.

After the war, Sweden had no more servants; women wanted real jobs and no longer cared to work in someone else's home. As a result, all Swedish women and men would have to clean up after themselves. Even the wealthy are discouraged from hiring housekeepers.[36]

In 1984, Swedish men did 18.1 hours of housework and Swedish women 31.8 hours a week; this compares with 13.8 hours for American men in 1981 and 30.5 hours for American women.[37] In Japan, men only do 3.5 hours of housework per week.

Feminization of Poverty in Sweden

Swedish men live with the Swedish women with whom they have children. This makes a big difference in poverty rates. If the man does not stay, then the Swedish government provides child support (in addition to the child allowance that every child gets), parental leave, child care, and pensions. So even if a woman is alone with her children, she is not disproportionately poor compared to men, as such women are in the United States. The behavior of Swedish men and the generous welfare state have prevented the feminization of poverty.

Swedish Social Policy

Reproductive Rights. Swedish women have full reproductive rights. Over three-quarters of Swedish women use contraception.[38] In 1938, contraceptives were legalized; in 1964, the birth control pill was approved in Sweden; and in 1975, a new abortion law was passed, giving women the right to decide through the eighteenth week of pregnancy.[39] In 1989, the number of abortions in Sweden as a percentage of live births was 33, and the policy is abortion on demand. In France, which also has the policy of abortion on demand, the percentage is only 22.[40]

Child Care. Swedish social attitudes favor women working for pay and collective daycare. There has been a tripling of infants to two year olds in full-time daycare centers in about fifteen years. Three to four times more children age three to six are now in full-time daycare centers. Swedish women make less use of child care than French women because the supply of child care in Sweden is smaller, and the price is relatively high. In addition, since more Swedish women than French women work part-time, they need less child care.

Child Support. Child support is required if a parent is not living with the child. If a man is required to pay for the children he produces, then he may be less likely to leave. Perhaps if we in the United States had a child support system like Sweden's then we would have fewer female heads of household, or at least fewer poor ones. Sweden provides eighteen years of child support, if the father cannot or does not pay. The children in Sweden are taken care of; thus women can have children and they get help. These are universal programs, not just for the poor.

THE EDUCATIONAL COBF IN SWEDEN AND NORWAY

Boys and girls ages seven to fourteen attend Swedish elementary schools in equal numbers. Home economics and technology are compulsory for all children.[41]

At the secondary level, boys and girls aged fifteen to nineteen attend school in equal numbers, but they are still channeled into male and female subjects, such as woodworking for boys or typing for girls. Thus in 1991, Parliament passed legislation requiring more balance between the sexes at the secondary level and in municipal adult education.

At the university level, slightly more women than men attend: 14 percent of women compared to 13 percent of men.[42] Technical subjects are male dominated.

Norway parallels Sweden in equal opportunity in education. Roughly the same proportion of females and males attend school when they are seven to fourteen (near universal), when they are fifteen to nineteen (72–73 percent, slight edge to females), and when they are twenty to twenty-four (23 or 25 percent, again slight edge to females).[43] Yet educational segregation persists as it does in Sweden; women simply do not acquire the technical skills that men do. The result is occupational segregation; the labor market still divides along sex lines.[44]

THE HEALTH COBF IN SWEDEN AND NORWAY

Health care in Sweden is universal as it is in Norway. The two countries have very similar health profiles. Norway has a better ranking in maternal mortality rate and is rated above Sweden (third compared to fifth for Sweden) in the U.N. Human Development Index. All women receive free prenatal and obstetric care. All children get free care, so mothers don't have to worry. But the world economic recession and problems with immigrants are putting a strain on the Swedish system, and some charges for care are being made now.

In a country known for its pro-family policies, one would expect quality health care. Although many Swedes complain about the system, it is undoubtedly superior to that of the United States overall, if only because everyone is covered.

Swedish and Norwegian women have a life expectancy of eighty-one years, which is seven years longer than that of the men. Sweden has an excellent record in infant mortality. Elderly people are taken care of in decent institutions. No one is impoverished by sickness.

Swedish authorities are particularly conscious of women's special health problems. They have commissioned studies on the work environment and its effect on women's health, both physical and mental, and have also investigated the burden of housework for women who work outside the home.[45] In addition, they have looked at the burden of caring for the elderly in this regard. Since the future of the Swedish welfare state stands or falls by women's economic activity, women must improve their position in the labor market, and working life must change so that people have more control over their environment. This reform would be in the interests of women and men alike.

NORWAY, THE ETERNAL UNDERSTUDY

In most people's minds, Scandinavia is a unit and Sweden is the key component. Norway has always been an afterthought and, for a considerable amount of time, an appendage of Sweden, until it won its independence in 1905. In that year, Norway began its slow progress from an agricultural to an industrial economy.

Although Sweden, as a larger economy, receives much more attention, Norway ranks high in all the quality of life and human development indices that the United Nations and the World Bank use and in some cases, is slightly ahead of Sweden.

An accident of nature has helped bolster Norway's economy and elevate its status vis-à-vis its neighbor Sweden. The discovery of the North Sea oil has given Norway a solid resource that Sweden lacks. This has helped Norway survive a recession better than Sweden and permits the Norwegians to maintain their strong social welfare policies. (The Norwegian economy is 70 percent public sector.) The old image of Norway in Sweden's shadow is surely changing.

The current portrait of solidly middle-class Norway is encouraging for women. In computing the gender gap in the paid labor force, the Population Crisis Committee ranked Sweden second and Norway fourth, followed by the United States.[46] On the more general question of social equality, Norway is ranked in the top group, though lower than Sweden.

Norway has a history of progressive policy toward women, paralleling Sweden and the United States. Women acquired inheritance rights in 1854, were given access to higher education in 1882, and with industrialization, began to join the workforce by the early twentieth century, though mostly as secretaries, teachers, and industrial workers.[47] The working woman, at that time, had a life similar to that of women in nineteenth-century American industry—long hours, low pay, and low status. Many Norwegian women were in domestic service.

Eventually, a labor union movement developed and women became more militant in seeking improvements in working conditions. The fight for better working conditions took place at the same time that the woman suffrage movement was growing among middle-class women. Women obtained the franchise in 1913, fifteen years after Norwegian males did.

It is difficult to explain the relatively strong position of women in Norway that we know of from Henrik Ibsen's *The Doll's House* and *Hedda Gabler*. Some hypotheses suggest themselves: Norway is a homogeneous society, with a consensus on values. It is a small country, geographically and demographically. Communication is good; there are no language problems. During the Nazi occupation in World War II, German became the second language. Now it is English. Norway is unified racially and religiously. There are no significant ethnic divisions, nor has there been significant immigration, except for guest workers.

Given the climate and the topography, it is easy to see why Norwegians are nature lovers. With low population density, even in the cities, people enjoy space and freedom. Perhaps the weather keeps families close, for it may isolate them from other contacts. In any event, the country is family and recreation oriented. Despite a high divorce rate, family ties are solid, and spouses tend to share responsibilities more than in other countries.

THE ECONOMIC COBF IN NORWAY

Norwegian women do not work for pay as much as Swedish women do, but the majority of them do work. The rate of labor force participation in 1989 was 62 percent and had risen from 55 percent in 1980.[48] This compares with Norwegian men whose rates were 77 percent in 1989 and 79 percent in 1980. Norwegian men now have lower rates than Swedish men.[49] The gap between the average income of Norwegian women and men is larger than the gap between the average income of Swedish women and men. In 1988, a woman made 82,881 kroner in Norway and a man 137,595.[50]

Occupational segregation, as in Sweden, is also prevalent, with women concentrated in "caring" work: hospitals, daycare centers, and schools. Many people believe that women are missing from the most responsible and lucrative jobs because they don't want them. This echoes a familiar argument in the United States—that women are unwilling to put in the hours necessary to hold the key positions. The subtext is, of course, that women, unlike men, put their families before their careers.

THE POLITICAL COBF IN NORWAY

The Norwegian national legislature is more than one-third female, comparable to that of Sweden and much greater than the 10 percent in the

United States. Interviews with two women members of Parliament illustrate the differences between the major parties in Norway, Conservative and Liberal, as well as the underlying consensus on social policy.

The Conservative Point of View: Member of Parliament

Annelise Hoeth is a very attractive woman in her fifties, blonde and well-groomed; she speaks fluent English. She is a conservative and is married to the president of the Norwegian Parliament (the Storting). Since 1991, she has been the chair of the Committee on Family and Public Administration. The subject matter of this committee is pensions, child abuse, and daycare. She was elected to Parliament in 1981 and has served on pensions and social affairs as well as foreign affairs.

Her background is that of a third-generation Oslo resident with a university degree in History, English, and the History of Ideas. As noted earlier, about one-third of the 165 members of Parliament are women; in the 1996 session, a very liberal maternity leave act was passed. Annelise says that she never describes herself as a conservative when she visits the United States. By American standards, she would be a liberal, and calling herself a conservative would give the wrong impression. Her explanation of how she differs from a Norwegian liberal is that the conservatives made a campaign promise to give women money for the purpose of child care, which they can choose to use for preschool or which they can keep and stay at home.

Mrs. Hoeth would not turn back social programs. She shares the same goals as the liberals but seeks other ways of arriving at them. Thus, despite a difference in means, there is an important consensus in the politics of Norway.

The Socialist Point of View: Member of Parliament

Mrs. Hoeth's opposite number and co-chair of the Family Committee is Kjellborg Lunde, a left-wing socialist who represents a district south of Bergen. Unlike Mrs. Hoeth, Lunde is very open and eager to talk about herself and her ideas. She is an avowed feminist who mobilized a group of like-minded women and overturned the incumbent old-style politician in her district in 1975; she has held the seat ever since.

Lunde is energetic and outspoken, a determined advocate for children. She began her career in special education and has strong views on child development. She says there is less of a tradition in Norway than in France for preschool learning and says you have to fight local politicians who have only daycare in mind. She would be a formidable opponent in any such fight. At the moment, a movement is under way to lower the entering school age from seven to six.

As a feminist and a realist, Lunde says that most women need to work, that the dual-income family is a fact. Yet most women want to work part-time because role differentiation is still strong in Norway, with women needing to perform the majority of household chores. As in other developed countries, men earn more and have more important jobs than women, still playing the breadwinner role. It is estimated that 15 percent of the pay gap in Norway can be attributed to discrimination. There is now a comparable worth movement in Norway to help value women's work. Lunde admits that further progress has been made in Sweden and Finland. Since the 1980s, the public sector has been prohibited from discriminating against women in employment. The legislative intent to balance the labor market has been implemented by a quota system.

With the advent of socialist governments (although Norway is technically a monarchy) came much progressive social legislation which characterizes contemporary Norway. These laws have provided many benefits for families ranging from child subsidies to daycare. Norwegian women have attained a great measure of social equality, and their lives have been made a great deal easier as a result of government policies on employment, maternity leave, and daycare arrangements. Although daycare is less universal in Norway than in France, compared to the American situation, Norwegians have a good deal.

In the national election of September 1993, women headed the tickets of three major parties. Most party platforms emphasized women's issues, and women were prominent on party slates. The present prime minister is a woman, Gro Harlem Brundtland, and she has eight other women in her cabinet. More than one-third of the Parliament is female, so women have a fairly high profile in national politics. Unlike American politics where women serve in greater numbers in local and state legislatures, there are few women in these capacities in Norway. Women have tried to counter this by crossing out male names on local party lists of voters.

Supporting this movement toward numerical equality is a rule promulgated by the Equal Status Ombud, which requires equal representation for both sexes on public committees and boards. If this proves impossible, there should never be less than 40 percent female representation. Norwegians refer to this type of ruling as part of the "feminine political revolution." Despite their strong representation in Parliament, women do not fare well in the civil service where few women hold high administrative posts. Most are frozen in the lower echelons and lower pay brackets.

THE SOCIAL COBF IN NORWAY

The social status of women in Norway is reflected in the following interviews with Arni Hole of the National Science Board and Fride Ege-Hendricksen of the Institute for Women's Research.

No question about it, both women agreed, there is discrimination against women in Norway, and certainly in academe. Both women are academics, though neither pursued a strictly academic career. There is indeed a "chilly climate" in Norwegian universities in the classroom and in the faculties.

Both Arni and Fride said that, despite liberal maternity leave and cooperative husbands, they were nonetheless exhausted returning to work. The Parliament had just extended maternity leave from six months to one year. When I asked how realistic that was for the private sector, they acknowledged that the company could lose on the arrangement. Yet both felt that the "second shift" placed a burden on women that they experienced both physically and in terms of career advancement.

Arni is chair of the Board of Technology and Human Values and is also the only woman delegate to the European Community science advisory. She feels the EC is very discriminatory, employing women mostly in low level positions.

Fride, who heads the Institute for Women's Research in Oslo, recalls unpleasant experiences as a graduate student in the male-dominated university. She is fighting for recognition of women's studies as a major field. She is hopeful that there is now a resurgence of feminism after a decade of quiescence. When Susan Faludi, the author of the best-seller, Backlash, *came through Oslo, her talk was a sellout, even though it had hardly been publicized.*

Both spoke about their daughters with hope that their lives would be easier. They know that women have made great strides in Norway occupationally, but the attendant pressures are of great concern to them. They see differences in the way boys and girls are conditioned in the school system. Arni, as a specialist in technological progress, believes that technology should be more accessible and that women could redesign ordinary household equipment that would be more efficient, something male engineers who don't use the appliances very much don't seem to give a very high priority.

Both women talked about stress. They mentioned the growing problem of eating disorders for young women. They expressed concern about backlash with growing unemployment, saying there were some who blamed social problems on the absence of women in the households. There has been an increasing incidence of wife-battering and general violence toward women which has been making the news.

A Very Modern Marriage: Marit and Sverre Mauritzen

Marit and Sverre Mauritzen have been married for twenty-five years; they have raised three children and have been active parents, sharing the job of child care. Marit helps operate a resort hotel for half the year. Sverre managed the family business until he decided to run for Parliament as a conservative.

They have had a commuting marriage between three locations. Both are absorbed in their work. Marit began her career as a college administrator and is now a businesswoman managing the old hotel that has been a family enterprise for decades. She is away from home for months at a time, although the family gets together at the hotel for the summer months.

Sverre has a small apartment in Oslo during the parliamentary session. He goes back to the district on weekends; by now, the children are in their twenties and on their own, but for a long time, life was very complicated in arranging schedules so that the children would be supervised and the household kept running. Thanks to Sverre's competence around the house and involvement with the children, this was not a gender-based concern.

Oddly enough, Marit, the daughter of two teachers and a businesswoman herself, does not think of herself as a feminist. She is very matter of fact about the bifurcated life she has led for the past ten years. Now Sverre has resigned from Parliament and has taken a job with the European Community in Brussels; two of their children will accompany him in order to improve their French. Both partners are comfortable with his decision, and both remain staunch conservatives, which in Norway means that they believe more emphasis should be on the private sector and on individual initiative. It does not mean that they believe in ending social programs.

Norway has a better record on equality between the sexes than most countries. The position of women in Norwegian society is strong. They don't, however, have a comparably strong position in the economy. Like Sweden, occupational segregation and part-time work for women persist and keep women from the most well-paying and prestigious jobs. Thus, one's view of the status of women in Norway depends on the standard for comparison. For most women in other developed countries, the Norwegian women have reached a standard worth emulating.

Can it be that women do more work outside working hours than do men? Are women in Norway, like their sisters in the United States, subject to the "second shift?"

All the women I met in Norway told me this was indeed the case—that they carried most of the burden of the home whether it was arranging for child care, general housework, cooking and shopping. As in Sweden, many women work part-time in order to be able to keep up with their household responsibilities. Unlike the United States, where part-time workers lose benefits, Scandinavian women do not; it is possible for them to exercise the part-time option. This choice, however, keeps them from the best jobs.

So much of what I heard in Norway was a familiar tune. The arguments of employers struck the chord we've often heard. Women are seen as employees who will always be applying for leave to have babies or take care of babies, whereas men can commit themselves to careers (thanks to their wives). If women can afford to, they take advantage of Norway's liberal maternity leave policy (increased in 1993 to one-year paid leave) and the opportunity to come back to work with reduced hours for a time thereafter.

The necessity for two incomes and economic security undoubtedly puts more women in the labor force than want to be there. The government has tried to encourage men to take paternity leave and reduce the burden on their wives, but few men take advantage of the opportunity. Therefore, one sees two-income families where the primary earner is male and the primary caregiver and, accordingly, leave-taker is female. This has been the pattern throughout affluent countries for the past twenty years.

The need for better child care arrangements is clear in Norway, particularly in the less populated areas. There is no universal system as in France; rather, it is a municipal responsibility. All preschools in Norway are publicly financed this way: one-third national, one-third local, and one-third parents. But the municipalities can decide whether they'll finance private as well as public schools. The conservatives would permit the parents to decide the question of whether the federal share could go for private schools. For school-age children, the school calendars have not been adjusted to match either work hours or days, and there is much concern about children being left alone and unsupervised.

Statistically speaking, there has been a decline in marriage in Norway. Whereas in 1951 there were seven or eight new marriages per 1,000 persons, by 1989 there were only five new marriages per 1,000 persons.[51] Norway parallels Sweden on divorce, although the rates are a little bit lower. The Norwegians are less liberated than the Swedes.

The Future for Scandinavian Women

The overall picture for women in Sweden and Norway is brighter than for their American counterparts. First, worries over economic assistance, child support, and health are far fewer. Second, since the government is much more family oriented, they can take more time off from work if they need it for family reasons and, consequently, feel less guilt. They are citizens of countries whose governments are proactive in matters of sex discrimination.

A lower COBF in Sweden and Norway than in the United States is more in the realm of social policy than in employment. Generous paid parental leave and the opportunities for women to work part-time while their children are young and to use daycare centers are advantages American women do not enjoy. In the United States, women work a double shift and worry about poor child care, or if they can't afford it, they quit their jobs and stay home with the children when they are young.

Ironically, much of what we have come to admire in Scandinavian social policy that benefits women and families is now threatened. The economics of the global economy and especially that of the Swedish economy dictate large cutbacks. Long-established programs that have helped women are now at risk. Will women lose all they have gained over the past five decades?

NOTES

1. Population Crisis Committee, *Country Rankings of the Status of Women: Poor, Powerless, and Pregnant*, Population Briefing Paper, No. 20, June 1988.

2. World Bank, *World Development Report 1995* (New York: Oxford University Press, 1995), p. 181.

3. Swedish Institute, *Fact Sheets on Sweden*, "Equality Between Men and Women in Sweden," Stockholm, February 1992.

4. Cited in Stephanie Cleverdon, "On the Brink: Three Attempts to Liberate Women," in *Working Papers for a New Society* (Spring 1975).

5. Francine Blau and Marianne Ferber, *The Economics of Women, Men, and Work* (Englewood Cliffs, N.J.: Prentice-Hall, 1992), pp. 300–304.

6. *World Development Report 1995*, p. 219.

7. Swedish Institute, *Current Sweden*, No. 387 (Stockholm: January 1992).

8. *Fact Sheets on Sweden*.

9. Blau and Ferber, citing U.N. International Labor Organization, p. 314.

10. United Nations Development Program, *Human Development Report 1994* (New York: Oxford University Press, 1994), p. 190.

11. Nordic Statistics, Stockholm, Sweden, 1993, p. 265.

12. Blau and Ferber, p. 319.

13. Ibid., pp. 309–310.

14. Blau and Ferber, pp. 294–330.

15. *Fact Sheets on Sweden*.

16. Swedish Statistics, Sweden and the EC, p. 27.

17. Swedish Statistics, Women and Men, pp. 2–3.

18. Linda Haas, "Equal Parenthood and Social Policy: Lessons from a Study of Parental Leave in Sweden," in Janet S. Hyde and Marilyn J. Essex, *Parental Leave and Child Care: Setting a Research and Policy Agenda* (Philadelphia: Temple University Press, 1991), pp. 375–405.

19. Swedish Statistics, Women and Men, pp. 2–3.

20. Ibid.

21. Ibid.

22. Ibid.

23. Ibid., p. 72.

24. Population Crisis Committee, Barefoot, Poor, and Pregnant.

25. Swedish Statistics on Sweden and the EC, p. 19.

26. Swedish Statistics, Women and Men, p. 9.

27. Nordic Statistics, p. 182.

28. Swedish Statistics, Women and Men, p. 10.

29. Swedish Statistics, Sweden and the EC, p. 26.

30. Human Development Report 1994, p. 186.

31. Swedish Statistics, Sweden and the EC, p. 22.

32. Human Development Report 1994, p. 186.

33. Swedish Statistics, Women and Men, p. 12.

34. U.S. Census Bureau study released July 14, 1992.

35. Stephanie Cleverdon, "On the Brink: 3 Attempts to Liberate Women: USSR, Israeli Kibbutz and Sweden."

36. Ralph Smith, *Subtle Revolution* (Washington, DC: Urban Institute, 1978), pp. 141, n. 29.

37. Blau and Ferber, pp. 301–304.

38. Population Crisis Committee.

39. Swedish Statistics, Women and Men, pp. 2–3.

40. Swedish Statistics, Sweden and the EC, p. 20.

41. *Fact Sheets on Sweden,* 1992, Embassy of Sweden.

42. Nordic Statistics, p. 346.

43. Ibid.

44. Norinform, *The Position of Women in Norway* (Ministry of Foreign Affairs: August 1991).

45. Swedish Institute, *Current Sweden,* January 1992.

46. Population Crisis Committee Report.

47. Norinform, Norwegian Ministry of Foreign Affairs, August 1991.

48. Nordic Statistics, p. 87.

49. Ibid., p. 85.

50. Ibid., p. 265.

51. Ibid., p. 69.

7

THE COST OF BEING FEMALE IN FRANCE

Marianne is a physician in her late forties. She grew up in provincial France, the daughter of a small landowner. Her mother earned a Ph.D. in English literature and always worked, first taking American students into her home in the summer and later working for American universities abroad. (Personal Interviews, April 1993)

Marianne was always academically inclined and early developed a fluency in English, spending time both in England and the United States. She decided to study medicine. At no time did she feel medicine was an impossible career for her as a woman, nor did she concern herself with the high cost of a medical education as an American would. In France higher education is very heavily subsidized for those students who qualify.

Marianne married a fellow medical student and began her specialty of pediatrics. When she had her third child, she decided to switch to pathology so as to be able to spend more time at home. Part-time work is much more of an option for French women than for American women.

While her children were young, Marianne had the opportunity to use "les crèches"—daycare for infants and later "les écoles maternelles." Having easy access to subsidized daycare made it possible for her to pursue her career.

When she and her husband spent a year in California on a medical fellowship, they put their three children, then ranging from kindergarten to sixth grade, in public school. The eldest, now a graduate student, still remembers his American year as wonderful, a far less rigid experience than the French system. But Marianne recalls how much less actual schooling they received and how much more parents needed to be available for the outside activities.

Marianne seems content to have opted for the "mommy track" in medicine. Because of her flexible schedule, she also was able to handle the serious caretaking responsibilities when her parents became ill.

A VISIT TO THREE PRESCHOOLS IN MONTMARTRE

In Montmartre the children are singing. A young woman in sandals is leading twenty-five little children in a song with percussion instruments. The children form a circle around her on little chairs and on floormats. She is down on her knees to be at their level. All faces are looking into hers as intently as an orchestra looks to the maestro. (Site visit, April 29, 1993)[1]

It was April in Paris. The chestnut trees were in bloom. Early in the morning, we took the metro to Montmartre and found the preschool on rue de Cloys which we had been invited to visit. Standing outside the preschool (*école maternelle*), we watched mothers, fathers, and grandmothers dropping off their children. There were several interestingly dressed African children and parents. This is a mixed neighborhood of Paris, home to concierges and aristocrats. These were workers' children we were to see, children of the "popular classes," as the French say.

At 8:30 A.M., the director of the preschool, Monsieur Gougelmann, opened the gate and the children raced in across the playground and into the handsome three-year-old building. The aesthetically minded French require that 1 percent of the cost of each preschool be spent on artwork. Mademoiselle Durif, an official in the Ministry of National Education, was to take us to visit three schools. After espresso and cookies, we toured all the classrooms of the school. Each classroom had its own personality. The *écoles* have no fixed curriculum or method of teaching, a rarity for French education which is quite rigid at the higher levels, so the teachers have considerable freedom.

We noticed that the teachers seemed to have no difficulty managing groups of twenty-five or so children. We delighted in the singing of Frère Jacques by little French children, with a touch of spice added from immigrant children named Fatouma and Attila. We saw children playing a variety of musical instruments enthusiastically.

The French love their language, and they love to use it. We observed a strong emphasis on "le français correct" by teachers who enunciated very carefully and drew children into the language with stories and pictures. We saw them teaching very young French and immigrant children to observe, discuss, and reflect in language what they saw on a colorful poster. If parents want to have their children tutored in their native languages, they may use the school facilities after hours to do so. The French do not see the value of bilingual education as we know it because they say that speaking and reading French well is the key to later success and all children must be given a chance to succeed. We observed considerable quiet guidance on the part of the teachers toward socializing the youngsters to the rules of group behavior—taking turns and respecting children who are speaking.

French impressionist artwork was everywhere intermingled with children's paintings in bold-colored poster paint. It was delightful to see the "style" of Picasso and Matisse in the paintings of the children. The children looked very happy, as did most of the teachers. All seemed to be enjoying themselves. We saw no one wandering off mentally or physically.

Mademoiselle Durif next walked with us to another preschool nearby. She introduced us to a lovely lady who was the director. This school was on the lower floor of an apartment building inhabited mostly by retired people who could look down and see the vineyard and the garden which the director and her husband created and maintained. This was also a newly built school, about four years old. Again we were taken to see all the classrooms and were an appreciative audience for some lively musical renditions. This school had a higher percentage of Arab, African, and Asian youngsters.

To give us a fair picture of the preschools in Montmartre, Mademoiselle Durif then took us to an older school built in 1938. The school was more modest than the new ones, but it had its 1 percent devoted to artwork nonetheless. The children here were children of artisans. The teachers are young because they don't have the status to work at the "better schools." The variety in teaching styles was amazing. We saw one class with a teacher who had achieved complete silence and was teaching handwriting to the whole class of about twenty-five children, mostly immigrant. Entering the next classroom, we caught the scent of the plants that created a huge terrarium, filling the room. Along with a wild mix of plants, there were children's paintings and "dress-up" clothes everywhere. Children were busy in small groups all over the room—painting, reading, and discussing. The creativity was marvelous.

Next door was a rundown, forbidding looking school—the *école primaire;* these children would enter after the *maternelle* at age seven.

THE ECONOMIC COBF IN FRANCE

Simone began her working life in Brittany with France Telecom at age eighteen; she was transferred to Paris five years later. She married and had a child. She was able to take off eight weeks when she had her son. When he was two and a half, he started free public preschool, where he stayed until age seven when he began primary school. Simone is forty-eight now and has thirty years of work experience. Her mother did not work. Simone loves being out in the world of work. (Personal Interviews, 1993)

Veronique is also a working mother. She is a waitress. Her six-year-old daughter attends the free public preschool. (Personal Interviews, 1993)

Edith is an eighty-year-old widow. She was a journalist in her working life while she also raised two daughters. At seventy, she and her husband retired to the south of France, but he got bored and moved back to Paris, leaving Edith alone. Recently, she heard that he died in an airplane crash, so now she is a widow. Françoise, her granddaughter, lives in Paris with her parents. She is a translator for a Japanese firm but does not make enough money to live in her own place. (Personal Interviews, 1993)

A higher percentage of French women work for pay than American women—57 percent compared to 51 percent of American women.[2] Seventy-four percent of French mothers of children under the age of three work for pay. One in four French women works part-time.

A plumber's wife works mornings only; and when the école maternelle *is closed on Wednesday, the plumber takes his little girl to work with him.*

The gender gap in pay is smaller in France than in the United States. In the 1994 U.N. *Human Development Report,* the ratio of women's earnings to men's earnings in France was 81 cents on a dollar. This compares well with Sweden at 90 and Norway at 87. French women are doing better than those in the United States who earn 59 cents on a dollar and Japanese women at 51 cents.[3]

French women are just as excluded from the good occupations as American women. The index of segregation for France is 38.4; this represents the percentage of women who would have to change jobs to attain an equal distribution of men and women in all occupations. The figure for the United States is 36.6.[4] In business, one finds 8 percent of employed French women in management, compared to 15 percent of men. When women do attain positions of responsibility, it is in specific fields: communications, human resources, information, finance, and the courts. Only 6 percent of supervisors in industry are female. In the police and military, only 5 percent of employees are female.

Like women all over the world, French women do "women's work." Currently, 45 percent of employed French women are in 20 of the 455 existing professions. Most French women are in the service sector—87 percent of all employed French women as compared to 67 percent of men. In medical and social services, 73 percent of employees are female. In education 61 percent are female.[5]

As for public policy, French women are protected by laws similar to those that protect American women: in 1972, the French passed a law requiring equal remuneration for men and women; and in 1983, they had a law on equality in the employment field between men and women.[6] Since 1980, a French woman cannot be dismissed from her job for pregnancy.

In sum, the economic COBF in France is that women are restricted from the higher paying occupations and jobs reserved for men. However, the pay gap is less in France than in the United States, and more French women work for pay than American women. We believe that the *école maternelle* system dramatically reduces the economic COBF in France.

THE POLITICAL COBF IN FRANCE

Simone Weil was the number two minister in the French government under Balladur. She also served as president of the European Community Parliament in 1979–1982, 1984, and 1989. She led the successful campaign for the legalization of abortion in 1974.

In 1992, there were six female ministers in the French cabinet, a number far greater than in any American administration.

In 1991, Edith Cresson was the first woman to be prime minister of France. It was just too much for French men. She was laughed out of office.

The political COBF in France is the same historic absence from public life that we have had in the United States. French women did not get the vote and the right to run for office until 1945. But French women received equal rights in the 1946 constitution of the Fifth Republic. The Equal Rights Amendment to the U.S. Constitution failed in 1982.

Only 5 percent of the French national legislature is female, matching Greece for the worst country in Europe. There were only 33 women among the 577 deputies in the National Assembly as of February 1993, and 31 of 319 senators in their Senate. As we have seen, female representation in the legislatures of Sweden and Norway is more than one-third. In the United States, since the 1994 election women have increased their share of seats from 5 to 10 percent.

Edith says that even in her generation, her friends became lawyers and judges, but politics is for men!

An American woman writer who has spent half her life in France thinks that university-educated women are highly political and reformist, whereas the majority of French women are politically conservative and pleased with the status quo.

Fifty-three percent of the electorate is female, so there is potential for more women representatives. The number of candidates is growing. In the 1992 election, 1,015 of the 5,169 candidates were women, or 19.6 percent, according to the National Council of French Women.

The Ministry for the Rights of Women

In 1982, a Ministry for the Rights of Women was established as a cabinet-level agency. The first minister was Yvette Roudy. Her ministry published a guide to the rights of women in 1982, which stated that women should not have to accept sexual advances for promotion. French women have tough laws against sexual harassment. In 1991, a sexual harassment law was passed stating that if sexual harassment in the workplace is proven, then the man can go to prison for one year and pay a $16,000 fine.

Under this ministry, France liberalized family law; for example, in 1983, the concept of "head of family" was abolished in tax law. In 1985, legislation strengthened the equal rights of spouses in managing a couple's assets. Children are allowed to take the mother's family name in addition to the father's. In 1988, the social statute for mothers was revised.

The last minister of the Rights of Women, Veronique Neiertz, led a campaign to reduce domestic violence against women. (There were 2 million victims in France in 1993.) She established the National Center for Information on Women's Rights and regional offices to offer help on the poverty of female heads of household and protection for battered women.

A group in the ministry also worked on the problem of women suffering from AIDS. Of 21,487 people with AIDS in France, 3,313 are women. This ministry organized the distribution of condoms. There are now vending machines for condoms on the street in front of pharmacies all over France.

In 1993, the new Balladur government abolished this ministry of the Rights of Women. The official reason was a need for restructuring; the government claims that the work of the ministry continues but is now divided among several other ministries. Nevertheless, the lack of cabinet status has certainly reduced the visibility and effectiveness of its work.

In France, many women join socially oriented associations, often with considerable political influence, such as movements for social advancement of low-income families, consumer protection, and environmental protection. As more French women become involved in groups such as these, we may expect more of them to enter the formal political arena.

THE SOCIAL COBF IN FRANCE

Victor Hugo said that the eighteenth century proclaimed the rights of man and the nineteenth century proclaimed the rights of women. Maybe he had George Sand in mind.[7]

George Sand had an affair with Chopin in the 1830s and scandalized Paris by wearing trousers. She believed that women should have civil rights, which under French law they lost at the time of marriage. She believed that conjugal equality was the basis of happiness.

In the twentieth century, the topic of women's rights was brought up again by Simone de Beauvoir who wrote the classic The Second Sex *in 1949, inspiring the second wave of the women's movement. "Women are not born, they are made," she wrote.*

In the 1990s, Catherine is approaching her thirtieth birthday with some trepidation. She is worried about never meeting the right man and settling down to have a family. She is from Alsace, the region of France bordering Germany. (Personal Interviews, 1991–1995)

Now that Catherine is working in her career as a librarian, she is becoming restless about the opportunities in France. A year of living in the United States and many travels abroad have convinced her of the stodginess of the French bureaucracy.

Catherine is a strong feminist and often feels thwarted by the occupational segregation in her field. She is very creative and is frustrated by bureaucratic resistance to new ideas and methods. Her mother does not work and offered her no encouragement in her career. She is much closer to her father.

Historically, France has been progressive on women's issues. In 1881, it was decreed that women could have bank accounts and make withdrawals. In 1907, married women were permitted to keep their wages. In 1908, married women ceased to be under their husbands' guardianship. In 1965, the civil code was amended to provide for greater equality between spouses. In 1970, it was mandated that husband and wife share parental authority.

French women have fewer children today: in 1965, each French couple had on average 2.83 children; in 1990, they had only 1.78. But French women still have more children than German women: in 1965, German couples had 2.51 children and in 1990 they had 1.41. German women are not encouraged to work, and they still have fewer children, to the disappointment of the pro-natalist Germans. The fertility rates of French women and American women are similar. In 1988, Americans had two children per woman on average, but the figure is now under two. The only country in Europe that is reproducing itself is Ireland.

It is not uncommon for French women to have children outside of marriage. Thirty-two percent of births in France are out of wedlock, compared to 26 percent in Norway and 27 percent in the United States. This is in great contrast to Sweden where 52 percent of women give birth outside of marriage. It is also in sharp contrast to Germany where only 15 percent of births are out of wedlock and Japan with only 1 percent.[8]

French women marry less frequently now; marriage rates have fallen since 1973. French women, when they do marry, marry late; the number of women who marry before the age of 20 has fallen 75 percent in ten years.

Divorce has increased dramatically in France. There are 1.3 million divorced women in France today. Divorce rates tripled from 1970 to 1985. Thirty-one percent of French marriages end in divorce, a figure that still is considerably lower than the rate in the United States at 48 percent, Sweden at 44, and Norway at 40.[9] However, divorce is less frequent in France because fewer people marry in France. So the lower statistic may be misleading.

More French women stay single these days. The number of people living alone doubled from 1968 to 1996. In the 1990 census, there were 6 million single people in a country with about 56 million people. In 1975 there were 3.2 million, and in 1982 there were 4.8 million. Today, one in ten persons lives alone. Twenty-seven percent of principal residences have only one occupant, and 63 percent of these are women. This trend of women living alone was first observed in 1982, when it was a case of mostly older women, widows over 75. But now the people living alone are young, ages 20 to 35: 11 percent of this age group lives alone compared to 8 percent in 1982.

There is a tremendous amount of cohabitation in France. In 1968, only one in thirty-five couples living together was not married; in 1990, one in eight couples was cohabiting. In rural areas, it is only one in ten.

Irene is 28 and works in a travel agency. She lives with her boyfriend Pierre who is an auto mechanic. They have no plans to marry. Her mother is married, but does not care that Irene is not. (Personal Interview, 1993)

Monique is from Madagascar, a former French colony. She studied law in Paris and fell in love with a French man. They live together and have two children. Monique does not have a work permit, and so she cleans houses. (Personal Interview, 1993)

Even though France is a Catholic country, French women have had the right to abortion since 1974. Because of universal health care, no controversy exists over poor women's rights to abortion as there does in the United States. The French invented RU-486, the "abortion pill," and, as we have said, abortion is legal in France. Yet many doctors and hospitals refuse to perform abortions. Most abortions are performed in private clinics because the waiting line in the public clinics is so long. Many women go to the Netherlands rather than wait.

The French are more receptive to working mothers than the Germans. Jeanne Fagnani, a French sociologist, conducted a study at the National Center of Scientific Research on the topic of whether or not French women have fewer children now because they are working for pay. The natalists in France are pressuring women to stay home and have children. Fagnani compared French and German women and found the reverse to be true. German women are more likely to stay home but have fewer children; French women are more likely to work for pay and have more children. Paradoxically, it is having more children that drives women into the workforce. She claims that German women are made to feel guilty if they work for pay and use child care. Such a woman is called a crow for leaving her babies to others to care for. Fagnani claims that French women have broken away from the traditional model of the good mother. Germany is often cited as a successful economic model, but it seems that German women envy French women their careers.

French women work a second shift just as American working women do.

> *Housework? No, my husband doesn't know how to do anything. Trained by her parents to design kitchens, Madame Rodier is proud to say that she has only one child. (Personal Interviews, 1993)*

Seventy percent of French women surveyed said that their husbands participate in household tasks if they insist. French men prefer child care (83 percent of women say their husbands would volunteer for this) and doing errands (66 percent volunteer) to cleaning house.

Has there been a feminization of poverty in France? No, it seems not. Instead of women living alone with their out-of-wedlock children, in France the wife has a breadwinner living with her and probably is a breadwinner herself. Even if she is alone with her children, she has free preschool and health care. It has been the lack of these two public services, along with poor pay, that caused the feminization of poverty in the United States. France spends 29 percent of its gross domestic production on social welfare expenditures, compared to the United States, which spends only 14 percent.[10]

French Social Policy

The French government helps French families balance work and family. Working people in France, like most working people in Western Europe, have more time off with pay than American working people, which enables women and men to take care of their families. France has ten mandated public holidays and thirty mandated days of annual leave, according to the Organization for Economic Cooperation and Development.[11] French women have had paid maternity leave since 1928, whereas American women just got unpaid leave in 1993.[12]

French women also have good-quality, subsidized infant care centers called *crèches* for infants and toddlers. This system is subsidized by the national government but is run locally. They are colorful, well-designed centers. For example, in a French town of 30,000, there is one municipal *crèche*. It takes children from the age of six months on any day of the week, even Sunday, and for all day or just for a few hours. This social service is available until the child is three years old. Twenty percent of all children under the age of three in France are in nurseries.

In addition, the municipal government pays for guardians, whom we would probably call child care providers. They are licensed and inspected regularly. For example, a couple that runs a small convenience grocery store in the above-mentioned town takes their little boy to a woman who cares for only two children. They pay only a small fee for food.

But the most important French policy for reducing the COBF is that the French national government has financed preschools for decades. This family-friendly policy was enacted because the French needed women's labor, at least until the 1970s. French women are great users of this child care. The town of 30,000 has seven *écoles maternelles* serving over 900 children divided into thirty-five classes.

The French preschools that we described earlier in the chapter serve children from the age of three to six.[13] Children are eligible at twenty-seven months, but often there are not enough spaces for children under three. At age seven (there is now a movement to lower this school-entering age to six), the children go to elementary school. In France, 100 percent of the four to six year olds, 95 percent of the three to four year olds, and 34 percent of the two to three year olds are in these preschools.

Teachers in the French preschools have the same training and receive the same pay as elementary school teachers. The goal is to give value to preschool teachers. In France, 97 percent of preschool teachers are women compared to 99 percent in the United States. The teachers have a baccalaureate degree: they must pass a national test to graduate from the lycée. Then they have two years of teacher training and have the same pay scale of teachers at the primary level. "We are running pre-elementary schools, not nursery schools. Our teachers are not glorified babysitters; they are educators, like primary and secondary school teachers, and so they are paid on the same scale," says a preschool inspector in Paris.[14] Most American preschool teachers are unlicensed, and there is no required training for staff. On average, an American preschool teacher makes about $9,000, compared to $30,000 made by workers in tobacco factories, a telling statement of our priorities.[15] Interestingly, in China, although 100 percent of nursery and kindergarten teachers are women, they earn almost as much as doctors and university professors.

The child-to-teacher ratio in France on average is twenty-four to one, plus an assistant. This ratio would be considered too high in the United States where our preschoolers have a ratio of fifteen-to-one, but it seems to work in France.

The French finance the *écoles maternelles* out of general tax revenues. These schools are part of the publicly funded national education system. This system is more egalitarian than the decentralized American system, which is largely funded by local property taxes. Where you live in the United States is the chief determinant of educational quality. The French government also provides family allowances for each child.

In the United States we have a hodge-podge of subsidies for child care. The income tax system provides tax breaks and tax credits for households and businesses for child care services. In addition, some child care is financed for the poor, out of general revenues, in the form of the Head Start program and in subsidies for child care for women on welfare who are trying to get off the dole. Moreover, some of our social security taxes go to states to provide child care for the poor. But child care in America is not part of the school system, and even if it were, it would not be equally financed because of the property-based school tax.

The Effect of Subsidized Child Care on French Women

A higher percentage of French women than American women work for pay; 75 percent in France compared to 58 percent in the United States. In France, 74 percent of mothers with children under age three work. Whether or not they are working for pay, nearly 100 percent of French women send their four to six year olds to preschool. In the United States, 60 percent of women with children under six work for pay. Does the *école maternelle* make it possible for French women to work, whereas the lack of child care prevents many American women from working?

French women earn 79 percent of what French men earn on average, compared to American women who earn 70 percent of what American men earn on average. Does having quality child care available enable French women to achieve more on the job and to advance more in their careers? Does the lack of worry about child care enable French women to choose the career they really want instead of the occupation that is compatible with childrearing, as is often the case in America?

Implications for the United States

According to the Children's Defense Fund, 10 million American children are in the care of someone other than their parents: 38 percent of them are in child care centers, 27 percent in the care of relatives, 20 percent in family daycare homes, and almost 6 percent are with an unrelated caregiver in the child's home.[16]

Child care in America is either high quality and expensive, or merely custodial and still expensive. Most preschool children who are not being cared for by their mothers are in another woman's home, or are in their own home being cared for by a nonrelative. The kind of development and socialization the children receive is not known. Should we in the United States have a preschool, child care system like that of the French? Would it be good for children, for women, and for society?

As for children, we know that in the United States one child in five lives in poverty. Millions of children are in unlicensed care, probably not getting instruction and socialization. Moreover, trained caregivers are in short supply, and their wages are low. There is a 40 percent turnover in child care centers and a 60 percent turnover in family daycare. This cannot be good for the children. Head Start only serves one-third of poor children and then only part-day, part-year, and part of the preschool years (three and four year olds). We now know how important good quality child care is for young children. It can prevent abuse, delinquency, school dropout, and poverty and crime in later years.

As for women, having quality, affordable child care would enable any woman who wanted to have a career, or who needed to work, to do so. In a society as rich as ours, perhaps women have a right to child care. So that all women can choose the kind of life they want to lead, shouldn't we reduce the constraint that society imposes on them by not providing more help with childrearing?

The lack of child care is clearly a barrier to women's legal right to equal economic opportunity. Fifty-nine percent of women with children under six work outside the home, and many more would if it weren't for the lack of quality, affordable child care. This compares with 12 percent in 1950.[17] Child care would be of great help to female-headed families. Furthermore, as of the 1980s, 70 percent of the adult poor are women. If we provided child care, these women would have a better chance to get themselves and their children out of poverty, as well as off welfare.

As for society, providing quality child care for all families would help ensure that the next generation of citizens and employees would be educated, skilled, and socialized. For each dollar invested in quality preschool, we save five dollars later on in welfare and prison costs. Society would also get the benefit of women's talents if more women could offer them in the marketplace. The lack of child care is costing America unnecessary losses.

Can We Afford It?

Barbara Bergmann explains that when we use the phrase "afford it," we are failing to distinguish between two meanings of "afford."[18] In one sense, we say, "I cannot afford to buy a $250,000 house." Here we mean that it would be either impossible or imprudent, given our income. In another sense, we say, "I cannot afford to buy a $250 pair of shoes." Now we mean that we have insufficient desire for the shoes to pay that price. Bergmann estimates that it would cost $40 billion a year to have a high-quality, free preschool system, as the French have. Given what we have paid for the Savings and Loan bailout and what we pay for Stealth bombers and Seawolf submarines, we clearly *can* afford a preschool child care system in the first sense of the phrase. Therefore, we must have insufficient desire to pay for quality child care. It is a question of priorities.[19]

We provided child care in World War II when the Lanham Act authorized the federal government to give matching funds to employers to set up on-site nurseries for women employees. We almost got it in 1971 before the massive influx of women and mothers into the paid labor force. Now we really need it.

THE EDUCATIONAL COBF IN FRANCE

Sylvie is 22 years old; it seems she has been studying and taking exams her whole life. She wants to enter the field of public administration. She feels the most prestigious school is probably closed to her. That is the ENA which grooms the future leaders of France. It is strongly class-based.

Sylvie's father is a businessman and her mother teaches at an école *maternelle. They have encouraged Sylvie and her two younger sisters to succeed. The family is close and frequently takes ski trips together, or goes to Spain to visit Sylvie's father's family.*

Sylvie is good at languages; she speaks German, English, and Spanish. She is extremely interested in politics and social causes. She would like to find interesting work or pursue graduate studies, but the French system is very closed and she is not sure that she'll make it into the schools she needs to attend to achieve her goals.

While she waits to hear the results of the national exams she took in Paris, she has found a part-time job on a local newspaper. She supplements the little she earns there with an assembly-line job at a canning factory. She has not experienced any gender discrimination at work or at school, and she sees that her mother has managed a career and a family, so she expects to do the same thing.

In France, success in the education system is passing a number of exams. Exams are not gender-biased; in fact, more than half of the baccalaureate candidates are female. But women are pressured to study women's subjects, such as education and health. This is reflected later in the occupational segregation we have described.

French women have made great advances at the university level. In the last thirty years, the number of women obtaining university education has increased sevenfold. More than half of college students are women. But they are still not in the math and science fields. Furthermore, the overwhelming majority of professors are male, and in a system that is very depersonalized, it is extremely difficult for women to find mentors.

THE HEALTH COBF IN FRANCE

French women live, on average, almost three years longer than American women, according to the National Institute of Statistical and Economic Studies (the French equivalent of the U.S. Census Bureau). In 1991, French women lived on average to 81.1 years; this compared to 78.3 years for

American women.[20] There is less difference between the two countries among the men: French men live, on average, to 72.9 years and American men to 71.5.

Do French women live relatively longer than their men because they are freed from the role conflict, stress, and strain of the traditional ideal of the good mother who also works for pay? The French woman works for pay, and she has children. French society does not seem to disapprove.

THE COBF IN FRANCE

Looking both at the statistics and our interviews with many women, we may conclude that the COBF in France is less than the COBF in the United States. We speculate that some of the answer lies in French history.

The republican ideal of the French Revolution led to the education of women in France. In time, women were accepted at the university, and they became professors, doctors, lawyers, and journalists. The culture in France is strongly republican, that is, strictly secular, even anticlerical, with a clear separation of church and state. There are no fundamentalist Christians in France trying to get women back in their place. French culture does not make women feel guilty for putting their children in daycare centers and working for pay.

At this writing, France is struggling with the problem of maintaining its high level of social services while reducing its growing deficit. Many critics say that the French government went overboard in granting exceptionally early retirement to some workers and overly generous subsidies to the unemployed and the elderly. If the political leaders can convince the French people of the necessity to curb some entitlements and raise eligibility requirements for some benefits, the economy can weather this crisis and France can meet the economic standards of the European Union. If not, the protests of the winter of 1995 can harm the social fabric for years to come.

We would not like to see a reversal of what we have characterized as enlightened family policy. The major difference in the lives of French women and children as opposed to American women and children is that the French have a far greater sense of security. Their health and well-being have been protected from the vagaries of the market economy by government programs that place a high priority on families. American women deserve the same protection.

NOTES

1. Authors' visit to three *écoles maternelles* accompanied by Mademoiselle Durif, inspector from the Office of the Director of Schools, Ministry of National Education, April 29, 1993.

2. Morley Gunderson, "Male-Female Wage Differentials and Policy Responses," *Journal of Economic Literature* 27 (March 1989): 46.

3. U.N. Development Program, *Human Development Report 1994* (New York: Oxford University Press, 1994), p. 190.

4. Francine Blau and Marianne Ferber, *The Economics of Women, Men, and Work* (Englewood Cliffs, N.J.: Prentice-Hall, 1992).

5. Information provided by the Embassy of France, Washington, D.C.

6. Alice Cook, "International Comparisons: Problems and Research in the Industrialized World," in Koziara, Moskow, and Tanner, eds., *Working Women: Past*Present*Future*, Industrial Relations Research Association Series (Washington, D.C.: Bureau of National Affairs, 1987), p. 347.

7. Priollaud, Nicole, ed., *La Femme au 19e Siècle* (Paris: Liana Levi, Sylvie Messinger, 1983).

8. U.N. Development Program, *Human Development Report 1993*, p. 192 (data for 1985–1989).

9. U.N. Development Program, *Human Development Report 1993*, p. 192 (data for 1987–1990).

10. Francine Blau and Marianne Ferber, *The Economics of Women, Men, and Work* (Englewood Cliffs, N.J.: Prentice-Hall, 1992), p. 318.

11. Marianne Ferber and Brigid O'Farrell, eds., *Work and Family: Policies for a Changing Work Force* (Washington, D.C.: National Academy Press, 1991), p. 160.

12. Ibid., p. 161.

13. Gail Richardson and Elizabeth Marx, *A Welcome for Every Child: How France Achieves Quality in Child Care: Practical Ideas for the US*, the French-American Foundation, Report of the Child Care Study Panel, 1989. (Two of the panel members were Barbara Bergmann of American University and Hillary Rodham Clinton.)

14. Quoted in *Money* magazine, June 1993, p. 79.

15. Children's Defense Fund, *The State of America's Children 1992*, Washington, D.C.

16. Ibid.

17. *Institute for Women's Policy Research*, "Are Mommies Dropping Out of the Labor Force? No," Washington, D.C., 1992.

18. Barbara R. Bergmann, "Economic Issues in Child Care Policy," paper written for the International Conference on Child Care Health, sponsored by the Centers for Disease Control, 1992.

19. Lucinda M. Finley, "Legal Aspects of Child Care: The Policy Debate over the Appropriate Amount of Public Responsibility," pp. 125–161, in Janet Shibley Hyde and Marilyn J. Essex, eds., *Parental Leave and Child Care: Setting a Research and Policy Agenda* (Philadelphia: Temple University Press, 1991).

20. *The American Woman 1992–93*, p. 216.

8

THE COST OF BEING FEMALE IN CHINA

As a little girl, Lu Wei went into the countryside during the Cultural Revolution. Her father, a military man, had fought in Korea. Wei says that she would never have known what the life of a peasant was like if she had not lived in the countryside. Today she works in the Department of American and Oceanian Affairs of the China Association for International Friendly Contact in Beijing. She is married and has one child. She has been to the United States for a four-month business stay. Her mother is a member of a democratic party in China. (Personal Interview, December 1991)[1]

Tian Ling teaches politics at Beijing University. She wants to get a Ph.D. in education at the University of Hong Kong. If she is not accepted, she wants to have a child.[2] She and her husband, Liang Zhihua, lived with his parents for the first several years of their marriage. Only last year did they get their own place, a small apartment.[3]

Ban Hui's mother lives in Xi'an. In response to the new economic reforms, she has opened a small shop selling children's clothes. In one year of hard work, and with the help of her retired husband, she has achieved her goal of making enough money to buy a two-story, multiroom house in the outskirts of town. Now she is working to make money to help her two sons get married; it costs a lot of money for most people to get married in China.[4]

Colin Fu's wife works in Shanghai at the Bank of China. They got married in 1992. They both think that being "dual income, no kids" (DINK) helps their society. Although this seems like a modern marriage, she does all the cooking.[5]

Ruan Tianjun's wife works in Sichuan Province. He works in Guangzhou (formerly Canton) and is from Sichuan, too. She will move to Guangzhou when she can find a job. Ruan Tianjun says that he and his wife can talk about everything, and that he is very happy with his marriage to her. Ruan Tianjun's cousin is married to a man in Hong Kong. She works for an Australian joint venture in Sichuan, and that is how they met. The government policy is that if they stay married for three years, then she can move to Hong Kong.[6]

China has more than half a billion women. Indeed, more than one in five women in the world are Chinese. Thus, if we care about the status of women, we must care about the status of Chinese women.

In the People's Republic of China, almost all women work because most of the people work on the land and agriculture requires the work of both men and women. In the cities, most Chinese women work for pay because the husband is not paid a family wage. To support a family both parents must work.

Since the 1978 economic reforms and China's opening to the outside world, women have benefited from the booming economy.[7] But if they leave the public sector for the private sector, they risk losing the woman-friendly policies they once enjoyed. For example, if a private firm is struggling to make a profit, it may cut out its daycare center.[8]

The socialist government has done much to raise the status of women. They encouraged women to work for pay in the new economy.[9] The leaders worked to improve the lives of women so that China could control the size of the population, which now is over 1 billion people.[10] What did the Chinese know about the causal links between the status of women and fertility rates that we in the United States do not seem to know in the case of our inner-city poor women?

The social COBF in China has been dramatically reduced by the crucial decline in fertility rates. China is the only developing country that has lowered its fertility rates.

Before the Communist Revolution in 1949, the COBF in China was high. Quite a few women were concubines, and many had their feet bound. Female infanticide was practiced, as was child marriage.

While it is not reasonable to compare women in China to women in developed countries such as the United States, Sweden, and France, it is not the *absolute* condition of women that we are discussing. Rather, it is the condition of women *relative* to men in their own societies. With our COBF measures, we can make comparisons.

THE ECONOMIC COBF IN CHINA

Chen Jian is deputy director of the Cao Yang residential Quarter Subdistrict Office, Putuo District People's Government of Shanghai, Foreign Affairs Office. She is a university graduate and was a section chief by age thirty-nine. Her mother was an accountant. She is married and lived with her husband's parents for seven years. She has a nine-year-old son that her mother-in-law takes care of. She received two months paid maternity leave. (Personal Interview, May 1993)[11]

Li Quian is director of public relations in the External Liaison Department of the Shanghai Securities Exchange. She is a glamorous woman who would not look out of place on Wall Street. The Shanghai Stock Exchange is one of two stock exchanges in China. It is located in the ballroom of the former Astor Hotel of the prerevolutionary days. (Personal Interview, May 1993)

Liu Xian Ping is a section leader of the China Chamber of Commerce. She is an interpreter for an organization that promotes international trade and joint ventures in Guangdong Province. The Ball Corporation of Muncie, Indiana, is producing aluminum cans there. Chinese women drive forklifts in the plant. (Personal Interview, May 1993)

Most Chinese women work either for pay or in agriculture in the countryside. In fact, agriculture employs the labor of 218 million of the 291 million working women in China.[12] For the most part, they do the exhausting work of harvesting rice.

Of the 563 million women in China today, 55 million are in the urban labor force. Thus about 10 percent of Chinese women work for pay in the cities. The participation of women in the paid economy has increased eighty-seven times from 1949 to 1992. This growth was from a low base: in 1949, the year of the Chinese Revolution, less than 8 percent of women worked in the money economy. In the 1958 "Great Leap Forward," 5 million Chinese women moved into the paid labor force.[13] The rate of labor force participation was about 33 percent in 1978 and about 38 percent in 1990. Chinese women hold 45 percent of the paid jobs in the economy, falling just short of a full half-share. This compares well to the United States, where women also hold about 45 percent of the paying jobs.[14]

Why do Chinese women work? The primary reason is to supplement the wages of men in socialist countries who are not paid enough to support a family. In addition, with market reform, some Chinese women are working hard to buy a second-story house, a bride price for their sons, or the new things available on the market now—a television, for example.

Things were different in the 1950s and 1960s. Then the impulse to work was based on socialist ideology to "find true independence through economic independence." The slogans to encourage this kind of behavior were "antifeudalism," "self-liberation," and "be your own master."

There is less occupational segregation by sex in China than in any other country of the world, according to the U.N. International Labor Organization.[15] The standard index of that segregation measures the percentage of women who would have to change occupations in order to have an equal distribution of men and women across occupations. It is 10 percent in China compared to 37 percent in the United States, 42 percent in Sweden, and 38 percent in France. Only 10 percent of women in China would have to change occupations to have an equal distribution of men and women.

China ranks third in the world for employing women in production and transportation and as equipment operators and laborers. Thirty-five percent of these workers are women. Women are forklift drivers. They also work in coal mines. In Shandong Province (where Confucius was born and is probably turning over in his grave),[16] 12,000 women are working at the Yanzhou Coal Mining Bureau, along with 28,000 men. However, many of these women are not actually digging coal in the mines, but rather are doing work on the surface.

Many women are clerks; this is a major occupational category now that China is developing so rapidly. Mr. Qian's wife is a clerk at an exhibition center for machine tools. But men are also clerks, so this is not occupational segregation. Mr. Ruan's male cousin is a clerk in a railroad station in Szechuan.

There is some occupational segregation in the Chinese labor market, however. Many women work in food and textile factories, as is true in other countries. Teaching children is women's work in China. All nursery school and kindergarten teachers are women. Seventy percent of primary school teachers are women. But 50 percent of secondary school teachers are women, and 30 percent of university professors are women.

Women are making progress. The number of women in management has increased by a factor of twenty-five from 1951 to 1991. Women are making inroads into technical positions and now represent 35 percent of technicians. There are many women in medicine: In the neighborhood hospitals, 50 percent of the doctors are women.

The Economic COBF in China today is only 14 cents compared to 33 cents in the United States.[17] Why is it less in China? First, we know that the gender gap in pay is caused mostly by occupational segregation, which is low in China. Second, this socialist country does not have large inequalities in income, as we have in the United States. Nursery school teachers make almost as much as university professors. Nursery school and kindergarten teachers are all women, and they earn 300 yuan ($36.00) a month. University professors earn only 400 yuan ($48.00) a month.

In the first large-scale social science research project on income distribution in China, Griffin and Zhao found that women have been treated more fairly during the new phase of land reform than in the earlier phase. In the People's Commune System in the countryside, men and women worked and were rewarded with work points. But women were given fewer work points than men, for more upper body strength is needed in farming. Since 1978, in the Household Responsibility System, land had been distributed to families by the number of members, regardless of gender. This system treats men and women as equals, regardless of upper body strength.

Griffin and Zhao claim that women are less likely to get wage jobs in rural industry, and if they do, they get paid 14 percent less than men. Thus, the male to female earnings ratio is 86 percent, which is better than what we have in the United States, rural and urban combined.[18]

Griffin and Zhao find that women wage earners in the cities also earn less and that the range of wages for women is compressed compared to that for men.[19]

China's public policies help women combine work and family. In the public sector, the major sector of the economy which is now under market socialism, Chinese women have maternity leave with pay for a year for the first child. They get their salary but not bonuses. The COBF in China in this sense is less than that in the United States.

Chinese women don't have to worry about child care, for there are countrywide nursery schools for one, two, and three year olds. There are kindergartens for children four to seven, and primary school begins at age seven. Again, the COBF in China in this respect is less than that in the United States.

Female white-collar government employees can retire at the age of fifty-five, men at sixty.[20] Retired women often take care of the children of their daughter or son, so that the daughter or daughter-in-law can work.

Economic Reform and Opening to the World

The Chinese have been experimenting with market socialism since 1978.[21] China is encouraging private enterprise and the use of market forces in some areas of the economy. Enterprises are expected to cut costs and produce a profit. Women may be adversely affected by higher layoff rates than men, by the closing of child care centers, and by failure to be hired in the first place because they are seen as too costly. They need maternity leave, and they need to nurse. This seems to support the hypothesis that socialism is more female friendly than market economies. Official policy encourages women to stay home for a ninety-day maternity leave.

As enterprises try to become more efficient, they lay off workers. A recent report stated that 21,000 workers, or 60 percent of all workers, recently dismissed from 1,175 state enterprises were women, of whom three-quarters were under the age of thirty-five with little education or training. Seventy percent of the jobless young people in cities are female.

Table 3
Fertility Rates in Selected Countries, 1992

No. of Births per Woman

Kenya	6.7
Nigeria	6.5
India	4.0
Mexico	3.8
Brazil	3.1
Indonesia	3.0
CHINA	2.5
U.S.	2.0

Source: Shanti R. Conly and Sharon I. Camp, *China's Family Planning Program* (Washington, D.C.: Population Crisis Committee, 1992), p. 7.

Since the 1978 reforms, there has been much mobility in China; people move to the special economic zones for jobs.[22] This means that the mother or mother-in-law is not there to take care of the children of the working wife.

THE SOCIAL COBF IN CHINA

It was not until 1911, with the formation of the Republic of China, that the COBF in China was significantly reduced. It is said that China came out of the Dark Ages for women in the 1920s when the practice of arranged marriages finally declined. By then, footbinding was on the wane under the Kuomintang government.[23] Until 1943, however, rich landlords in rural areas usually had concubines.[24]

The social COBF was greatly reduced by the Chinese communists. The marriage laws were liberalized in 1949, the year the Chinese communists took power, and soon thereafter child marriages, polygamy, and concubinage were legally ended. In 1950, Chinese women gained formal equal legal rights in the constitution. By the end of the 1950s, the communists had largely wiped out the age-old practice of female infanticide in China.

Today Chinese women have an average of 2.5 children (see Table 3). This is less than the world average, which is 3.3 children per woman.[25] China is the first, and thus far, the only developing country to make the transition to lower fertility rates. This is unprecedented in world history. The Chinese communists achieved a dramatic fertility reduction in the 1970s, but it was not enough to control population growth.

In the 1950s and 1960s, the Chinese encouraged women to have children because they were following the Soviet line: "the 'heroic mother' had many children to give power to the nation." Thus, in the late 1960s, women in China had six children on average.

In the 1970s, however, the Chinese began to see that they needed to stabilize their huge population, given the relatively small arable land base.[26] The Chinese have been successful in pulling up 140 million people from absolute poverty since 1949, and they still have 70 million more to pull up.[27] In 1973, family planning was begun as national policy as part of the nation's economic and social development plans.[28] The unprecedented decline of fertility occurred in the 1970s. By 1979, the average number of children per family had plummeted to 2.7. The change was most dramatic in cities, where the average number of children per family fell from 3.3 to 1.4. In rural areas, the change was from 6.3 to 3.1.[29] Overall, fertility rates fell by half in twenty years. According to Zero Population Growth, "China has done more to slow world population growth in the last two decades than every other nation in the world combined."[30]

How was this fertility decline achieved? The Chinese seemed to know what the Population Crisis Committee found out when it conducted its study, "Country Rankings of the Status of Women: Poor, Powerless, and Pregnant"[31]—the higher the status of women, the lower the fertility rates.

Education is strongly correlated with fertility rates. Female literacy in the 1980s was 55 percent, compared to only 30 percent in India which has a much higher fertility rate.

Equal employment opportunities for women relate to fertility rates. The Chinese encouraged women to work for pay. Employed women have fewer children than women not in the labor force. When economic opportunities are available, women tend to move beyond their biological function.

Health care for women is also related to fertility rates. The Chinese government, through the State Family Planning Commission, developed policies on age at marriage, family size, and family planning. The minimum age for marriage was set at eighteen. In the mid-1970s, the government implemented an important policy on family size: the "one couple, two children" policy. This policy was generally acceptable both to families and to society. By the late 1970s, "one child per couple" was not too few for a family. In the family planning programs, the Chinese teach the social impact of individual childbearing decisions.

Wide distribution of free and abundant contraceptives and abortion services are provided in China. Seventy-two percent of couples use contraception (see Table 4). The most important method of birth control is the IUD (41 percent), and the second most common method is tubal ligation (37 percent). In 12 percent of couples, the male has a vasectomy. Only 5 percent of Chinese women use the contraceptive pill. The man uses condoms in less than 4 percent of Chinese couples. Only 16 percent of contraception

Table 4
Family Planning in China

Category	Percentage
Chinese using contraception at all	72
Contraception carried out by women	84
Methods used by women	
IUDs	41
tubal ligation	37
the pill	5
by men	
male vasectomy	12
condoms	4

Source: Shanti Conly and Sharon I. Camp, *Family Planning in China* (Washington, DC: Population Crisis Committee, 1992), p. 30.

is carried out by the men. The birth control revolution is not complete in China, and sterilization is used instead of less radical forms of contraception. Again, we must note an important difference between the cities and the countryside.

The Chinese have a liberal abortion policy; as a result, 10 million abortions are performed each year.[32] Unmarried young women can easily obtain an abortion if they get pregnant. The Chinese do not appear to have a teenage pregnancy problem.

Maternity leave plays a role in China's population policy. As of 1953, Chinese women had fifty-six days of maternity leave at full pay. Maternity leave enables women to keep their jobs. Employed women, then, have fewer children.

Similarly, child care centers play a role in population policy. The government of the People's Republic of China supports child care as part of their birth control policy. Thirty percent of children in China are in child care centers.[33] In a study of nine provinces, it was found that 23 percent of preschool children were in daycare centers: 52 percent in urban areas and 15 percent in rural areas. There are state-owned child care centers and kindergartens. Government departments, schools, and the army organize child care centers. Work units run child care centers. Neighborhoods, villages, and towns have them.

Since China has more than 1 billion people, the reduction of fertility rates to 2.5 children per woman on average is not enough to bring the population into line with the available resources. Therefore, the Chinese have stepped up their population programs. In 1980, the minimum age for females to marry was raised to twenty. In fact, at this time the average age of females at marriage is twenty-three years. In the cities, people don't want

Table 5
Progress in China on Population Policy

Rank by Population, 1960	Estimates for the Year 2000 if Trends Continue
No. 4 Shanghai, 11 million	
	No. 5 Calcutta, India, 16 million
No. 6 Beijing, 7 million	No. 6 Bombay, India, 16 million
	No. 7 Shanghai, China, 15 million
	Lower than top 10 Beijing, China

Source: United Nations Development Program, *Human Development Report, 1990* (New
  York: Oxford University Press, 1990), p. 86.

to marry early, but in the countryside this remains a problem.

In 1980, the New Marriage Law stated "one couple, one child" as official government policy. The main purpose of promoting this policy is to release the population pressure on the national economy. If this policy is disobeyed, fines and other disciplinary measures are commonly imposed. There are incentives to follow the policy: maternity leave and child care for one child. If a couple has only one child, they receive 5 yuan a month (a dollar), which is about 5 percent of the average monthly income in China. This continues until the child is sixteen.

The contribution of Chinese family planning to the alleviation of poverty and human suffering can be seen in the statistics on the ten largest cities in the world. See Table 5 and the following explanation.

In 1960, Shanghai was the fourth largest city in the world with a population of 11 million, and Beijing was the sixth largest with 7 million people. At the current rate of population growth, in the year 2000, Shanghai will have dropped to seventh place and Beijing will have dropped off the list of the top ten cities of the world. Two cities of India which were not on the list in 1960 are now expected to be larger than any in China: Calcutta is expected to be the fifth largest city with 16 million people, and Bombay will be sixth largest with 15 million people. India has the world's second largest population after China: 897 million people in 1993.

China relies heavily on legal sanctions and severe social pressure rather than allowing couples free choice in family planning. For that reason we do not advocate the "one child" policy as it is practiced in China. The pre-1980 program (one couple, two children) is more acceptable. However, both policies can be credited for increasing the life span of the Chinese people. In 1945, the life expectancy of a newborn child was thirty-five years; in 1990, life expectancy had doubled to seventy years.[34] The United

Nations Development Program considers life expectancy to be a sign of the health of the population and a measure of human development.

The population crisis is the main justification for the earlier policy as well as the current one child per couple policy in China. *U.S. News and World Report* states that there is no population crisis.[35] We disagree, as the three previous tables show and argumentation demonstrate. More precisely, what we have learned is that world population is stabilizing (mostly because of Chinese efforts), but further reduction in fertility is needed so that the world's population stabilizes at a lower level. The earth can hold only so many people. In September 1994, the U.N. International Conference on Population and Development in Cairo called for raising the status of women for their own sake, for the sake of all human beings in developing countries, and for global population stabilization at a sustainable level. China is working in this tradition.

Zero Population Growth argues that the most common charges of abuse in China's family planning program do not involve the policy itself, but rather how the policy is implemented.[36] "While experts caution against attributing the recent drops in fertility to coercion, they acknowledge that the tremendous pressure to meet specific demographic targets has led to abuses by some local officials."[37]

There are few female heads of household in China, and generally the people are not sentimental about abortion. If an unmarried girl gets pregnant, she gets an abortion. Teenagers do not bear children. They don't have fundamentalist religions that fight against the right to abortion. Rather, they have an enlightened view about the social impact of the individual's decision to have a child. It is not just the right of individuals to have as many children as they would like. Having a child has an impact on society. Society supports those children in addition to the individual support they receive from their parents.

There is evidence, however, that single parenthood is rising. Because of the boom in the south of China and all along coastal China, men leave the hinterland in search of work and leave the women and children behind.

Married women who live and work in the cities do work the "second shift" at home. This is even harder for them than for Americans because China has a six-day work week (just recently it has been shortened to five). Sunday is the day that Chinese women do housework. They also cook when they get home from work. As noted earlier, child care is less of a problem because it is highly likely that a grandmother lives with the family. The one child policy means there are only eighteen years of childrearing. In Beijing, children can start kindergarten at age two and a half. There are also Children's Palaces in cities like Shanghai where children can go after school and on Saturdays and learn and enjoy music and art, while their mothers work for pay.

THE POLITICAL COBF IN CHINA

In 1949, the constitution of the People's Republic of China declared equal rights for men and women.[38] Women got the vote under the new electoral law. Women obtained the right to inherit property under the new Inheritance Law.

Chinese women have greater representation in their national legislature than do their American counterparts. In 1954, at the first meeting of the National People's Congress, 12 percent of the delegates were women. By 1988, at the seventh meeting of the Congress, 21 percent of the delegates were women, compared to a newly achieved 10 percent in the U.S. House of Representatives.

Family planning in China is a cabinet-level ministry, and it is held by a woman. In contrast, family planning in the United States is part of the Public Health Service and is housed in a small office in suburban Washington. There were three women ministers in the new Chinese government in the Spring of 1993: one for family planning, Peng Peiyan, one for foreign trade, Wu Yi, and one for the chemical industry, Gu Xiu Lian.[39]

The Law on the Protection of Women's Rights and Interests was passed by the National People's Congress and took effect in 1992. This is China's first overall law to guarantee women's rights and interests and to promote women's equality with men.

The All-China Women's Federation is the government organization that oversees activity in this area. There are women's federations at the provincial, county, and city, town, or village levels. In 1991, Shunde County government of Guangdong Province allocated 200,000 yuan to the county's women's federation. Women are becoming the main force in farming, as men go to town to earn a living. According to an old Chinese saying, women hold up half the sky.[40] The Women's Federation is training them to tend half the sky.

The Chinese government signed the U.N. Convention on the Elimination of All Forms of Discrimination Against Women, declared by the 1980 U.N. World Conference on Women held in Copenhagen. Surprisingly, the United States has not signed it.

THE EDUCATIONAL COBF IN CHINA

Education is widely distributed in China and . . . access is generally equitable. . . . This reflects the priority given in China to universal primary education and to widespread secondary education. . . . [However] there is considerable evidence of discrimination against women. Men on average receive 2.3 more years of education than women, and the difference in attainment is larger in the countryside (2.5 years) than in the cities (1.8 years).[41]

Table 6
China's Progress in Combating Maternal Mortality

Country or Region	Maternal Mortality per 100,000 Live Births
Sub-Saharan Africa	610
South Asia	490
All developing countries	350
Middle East + North Africa	200
Latin America + Caribbean	180
East Asia + Pacific	160
Russia	49
CHINA	**44**
Industrial world	24
Japan	16
France	13
United States	8
Norway	4

Source: United Nations, *Human Development Report 1994* and *Women and Politics World-wide*, edited by Barbara Nelson and Najma Chowdhury (New Haven, CT: Yale University Press, 1994).

Literacy is the most important measure of education for developing countries, and China is making good progress in educating women. The educational COBF is worse in China than in the United States where women and men are completing high school and college at roughly equal rates. But the appropriate comparison for China is with other developing countries. Here China does very well.

In primary school, girls constitute only 44 percent of primary school enrollment. In secondary school, girls make up 39 percent. At the college level and higher, women account for only 26 percent of enrollment. Chinese women are more literate than Indian women, however. In the 1980s, female literacy in China was 55 percent compared to 30 percent in India. Currently in urban areas, 78 percent of Chinese women are literate, compared to only 48 percent in rural areas. Female illiteracy is not a problem in cities like Shanghai. From 1949 to 1987, 157 million illiterate people were taught to read and write. However, 70 percent of the remaining illiterates in China are female.

THE HEALTH COBF IN CHINA

More public health work was instituted in rural areas after the formation of the People's Communes in 1958. "Barefoot doctors" (peasant doctors who were commune members) and midwives taught pregnant women prenatal self-care, new delivery methods, and infant care.[42] The result was a great decrease in maternal mortality. According to a report by the World Health Organization, China's record compares extremely well to that of most other developing countries where 1 million or more women die each year from pregnancy-related causes.[43] (See Table 6.)

In conclusion, when you consider China as a developing nation, its record on women is very good. It is closing the gaps between women and men economically, politically, and socially. The Chinese are not that far removed from the feudal society that dominated for five thousand years. In a relatively short time period, they have come a long way toward gender equality.

NOTES

1. Lu Wei, Washington, D.C., interviews, Fall 1991 and Spring 1992. China Association for International Friendly Contact, from Beijing.

2. Tian Ling, written correspondence: Department of Education, University of Hong Kong, Pokfulam Road, Hong Kong, and from June 1 to August 15, 1994: Rm. 309, Apart. 4, Bei San Huan Zhong Lu 36, Beijing, CHINA 100088, June 11, 1994 letter.

3. Zhihua ("Jerry") Liang, Beijing, interviews in May 1993, written correspondence, 1994. China Association for International Friendly Contact, P.O. Box 1094, Beijing, CHINA 100034. Huafanzhai Park, 1 Wenjin Street, Washington, D.C., interviews, Fall 1992. Tel: 401 8694.

4. Hui ("David") Ban, interviews in Xi'an, China, May 1993. Written correspondence 1994, Foreign Affairs Office of Shaanxi Provincial Government, 272 Jie Fang Road, Xi'an, CHINA, 710004. Tel: (029) 710309; Fax: (029) 710961.

5. Colin Fu, Shanghai, interviews in May 1993. Written correspondence 1994: Shanghai People's Association for Friendship with Foreign Countries, 1418 Nanjing Road West, Shanghai, CHINA 200040. Tel: 2565900.

6. Ruan Tianjun, interviews, Guangdong (Canton), China, May 1993, translator for Xie Suishen, Deputy Secretary General, Association for International Friendly Contact of the Guangdong Special Economic Zone, Guangzhou, CHINA.

7. Qin Yongchun, Center for Peace and Development Studies, Beijing, China. Discussions in Washington, D.C., January to May 1990, and in Beijing, May 1993.

8. Lena H. Sun, "A Great Leap Back: Chinese Women Losing Jobs, Status As Ancient Ways Subvert Social Ideal," *Washington Post*, February 16, 1993, pp. A1, A24, A25.

9. Qian Decun, China Association for International Friendly Contact, interviews, Beijing, May 1993.

10. "Family Planning in China," *Pictorial China* No. 154 (Beijing, New Star

Press, 1992).

11. Chen Jian, Deputy Director of the Cao Yang residential Quarter Subdistrict Office, Putuo District People's Government of Shanghai, Foreign Affairs Office. Interview, Shanghai, May 1993.

12. "Chinese Women Are Getting Ahead," pamphlet obtained from Li Jing Yu, Senior Engineer, China Petrochemical Corporation, while she was in Washington, D.C., with her husband, Shen Longhai, Economic Counselor, Embassy of China. Thanks to Li Jing Yu for all the pamphlets she provided me. Note: there are many women engineers in China, unlike in the United States where engineering is dominated by men.

13. Li Min, "Parental Leave and Child Care in China," in *Parental Leave and Child Care*, edited by Janet Shibley and Marilyn Essex (Philadelphia: Temple University Press, 1991).

14. "Chinese Women Are Getting Ahead—After Stepping Out From Home," *Chinese Women Series* (Beijing: China Intercontinental Press, 1995), from Senior Engineer Li Jing Yu, Embassy of China in Washington, D.C.

15. Francine Blau and Marianne Ferber, *The Economics of Women, Men and Work*, 2nd ed. (Englewood Cliffs, N.J.: Prentice-Hall, 1986), p. 309.

16. Chen Jingpan, *Confucius as a Teacher* (Beijing: Foreign Language Press, 1990).

17. Keith Griffin and Zhao Renwei (eds.), *The Distribution of Income in China* (New York: St. Martin's Press, 1993).

18. Ibid., p. 17.

19. Ibid., p. 19.

20. Thanks to Haiyan (Helen) Wang who read this chapter and corrected our statistics on retirement ages for white-collar employees. She is the wife of Ma Xin, first secretary of the Economics Section, Embassy of China, in Washington, D.C.

21. Colin Mackerras, Pradeep Taneja, and Graham Young, *China Since 1978: Reform, Modernization and "Socialism with Chinese Characteristics"* (New York: St. Martin's Press, 1994).

22. *China 1994*, compiled by Qin Shi (Beijing: New Star Publishers, 1994).

23. Mary Daly, "Chinese Footbinding," in *GYN/ECOLOGY: The Meta-ethics of Radical Feminism* (Boston: Beacon Press, 1978, 1990), pp. 134–152.

24. Jung Chang, *Wild Swans: Three Daughters of China* (New York: Harper, 1991). I highly recommend this book. The author's grandmother had been a concubine and her mother a revolutionary communist. She is a writer now living in London.

25. Shanti R. Conly, and Sharon I. Camp, *China's Family Planning Program: Challenging the Myths* (Washington, D.C.: Population Crisis Committee, 1992).

26. Family Planning in China, *Newsletter of the Embassy of the People's Republic of China*, August 24, 1995, No. 17.

27. Shen Longhai, Economic Councilor, Embassy of China, Washington, D.C., stated that this is one of the goals of Chinese policy (Personal interview, December 1995).

28. "Family Planning in China," brochure 154 (Beijing: New Star Press, 1992), given to authors by Li Jing Yu, Senior Engineer, China Petrochemical Corporation, currently accompanying her husband Shen Longhai, Economic Counselor, Embassy of China, Washington, D.C.

29. Conly and Camp, p. 11.

30. *ZPG Backgrounder,* "An Uncompromising Position: China, the UNFPA and U.S. Population Policy," June 1990.

31. Population Crisis Committee, "Country Rankings of the Status of Women: Poor, Powerless, and Pregnant," *Population Briefing Paper No. 20* (June 1988) in Washington, D.C.

32. Conly and Camp, p. 36.

33. Li Min, "Family Leave and Child Care in China," in *Parental Leave and Child Care* (Philadelphia, Penn.: Temple University Press, 1991).

34. "Family Planning in China."

35. "Exploding the Population Myths," *U.S. News and World Report,* September 12, 1994.

36. "Continuing questions in China," the ZPG (Zero Population Growth) *Reporter,* October/November 1993.

37. Ibid.

38. Zhong Lu, "Comments on the Law on the Protection of Women's Rights and Interests of the People's Republic of China," *Women of China* No. 7, July 1992, pp. 4–7.

39. Again I thank Haiyan (Helen) Wang for supplying the name of the minister of the Chemical Industry.

40. Harrison Salisbury, *The New Emperors: China in the Era of Mao and Deng* (New York: Avon, 1992).

41. Griffin and Renwei, pp. 20–21.

42. "Public Health: The 'barefoot doctor' program is one of the world's most comprehensive primary health care networks whose success lies in its decentralization. Trained in preventive and curative medicine, health care, and family planning is provided by villagers for villagers." Zero Population Growth, 1990.

43. Mary Batten, *Sexual Strategies: How Females Choose Their Mates* (New York: G. P. Putnam's Sons, 1991), p. 190.

9

THE IMPACT OF THE INDUSTRIAL REVOLUTION ON THE COST OF BEING FEMALE

The Industrial Revolution had a critical impact on the role of women in the economy and in society.[1] We can see this impact in two phases. Initially, women's economic role was reduced when men left the home for the factories and women stayed behind. Women lost power as men brought home money, and women continued their unpaid labor in the home. Eventually, industrialization increased the real wage so much that it pulled low-income women out of the home and into the workforce, thus expanding their role in economic life. However, given the low-level jobs to which they were assigned, they still had neither economic power nor status.

To understand the impact of industrialization on women, we must first look at their lives before this great historical divide. Since the first Industrial Revolution took place in England, we begin our investigation there.

PREINDUSTRIAL WOMEN'S WORK

In rural England, women tended the household plots, small gardens, orchards, and animals such as chickens and milk cows. They spun and wove wool from the sheep. They made soap and candles and almost everything else their families needed. Some of these products were sold to supply other villages, towns, and cities. Women also did domestic work for merchants, who would sometimes give them raw wool to spin in their spare time in the home. In this way, they could earn cash for rent and taxes. Thus women contributed a large proportion of the family's income as well as supplying subsistence in kind (food, fiber, etc.). This gave them a certain power and status.

In agriculture, crafts, and trade, marriage was often a business partnership in which the wives assisted their husbands in their work. This gave married women a certain economic independence. The wife was expected to pay her own way. Women who could not assist their husbands in their work in eighteenth-century England were expected to get a paying job. Public opinion in this preindustrial period was that women and children "were expected to earn at least sufficient for their own maintenance and men's wages were based on this assumption (just enough for the adult male)."[2]

Urban women worked as assistants to their husbands or fathers who were artisans. The men performed the more skilled tasks, and the women processed raw materials or finished the end product. This was seen as subsidiary and thus less important. Although women's work was useful, it required little training. They were denied apprenticeships and the rank of skilled worker. Yet, they contributed to the family's income, and as long as their husbands did well, they were in a satisfactory position.

A major change occurred in the seventeenth century with an agricultural revolution in rural England that ended the family economy as it was known. The open fields were enclosed and converted to commercial agriculture by the landowning classes. The men who used to farm for a living had to find jobs for pay. The women lost their main sources of support when they lost the family plot. This meant unemployment for women and loss of the subsistence and money income for their families.

Starting in about 1750, the first Industrial Revolution in world history began in England. One form of work after another was removed from the home and re-created in factories with systems of machinery and inanimate power. The first to go was the production of clothing and textiles. Women used to spin and weave at home. Now there were factories to spin and weave.

At first, the workers in these cotton factories were women, because they were seen as more docile by the factory owners and could be paid very little. However, the factories were so productive that they could afford to pay high wages, and soon the jobs were taken by the men. Over time, their unions struggled to get a family wage for the men, so that their wives could stay home and work in the home for them: food preparing, making textiles, sewing.

Some men could not afford to keep their wives at home. These women had to work to help the family survive. Yet they were not paid a living wage since men had an interest in keeping them out of the good, high-paying jobs. The factory owners could threaten men with the idea of hiring women for less.

In 1841, for the first time, the Census in Britain asked for the occupations of women. The majority of women worked in five job categories: (1) domestic servants, (2) factory operatives, (3) needle women, (4) agricultural workers, and (5) those employed in domestic industries. Factory women had the best working conditions: they had the shortest working hours and the highest pay.[3] The other occupations commanded low wages and bad conditions because the supply of women was greater than the demand for them. Many English women became domestic servants to the new middle-class families spawned by industrialization.

Eventually, even wage-earning men were paid enough to let their wives stay at home. Hence was born the modern idea that "in the rearing of children and in home-making, the married woman makes an adequate economic contribution."[4] Throughout most of human history, women had been important participants in production; now they were in a separate sphere. Whereas before the home and the workshop were one, now they were "separate spheres."

For the young, single working woman, industrialization and the spread of the factory system meant economic and social independence from their fathers and families. Many young rural women left home to make a living in the city; other women emigrated to America.

Mary Lou's mother left Ireland as a young girl and went to America to work as a domestic in the home of a rich owner of a woolen mill in Lawrence, Massachusetts, home of the 1912 strike of women mill workers. She married and established her own household, where she worked very hard, raising children, cleaning, sewing, and baking bread every day for the family. (Personal Interviews, 1991–1995)

With the end of the family economy and the rise of the market economy, homes were no longer workshops. For the first time women could devote all their time and energy to the care of their children and their homes. However, living in this separate sphere caused the majority of married women to lose their economic independence.[5]

By 1850, the effects of increased wealth and the exclusion of women from industry and trade were easily discernible.[6] The vigorous businesswoman of the eighteenth century was replaced by the sheltered, dependent, Victorian lady. In the Victorian Age, ladies were placed on pedestals.[7] They were angels in the house and were not to be contaminated by the evil ways of the outside world. This separation of the "ladies" from "women" removed women from the economy and from public life.

Industrialization did not create the subordination of women, but it intensified it as men became dominant in the new market economy. It intensified it by depriving women of their economic independence. Women were subordinated long before the Industrial Revolution.[8] During industrialization, the separation of work from the home meant that men were less dependent on women for production (of their food and clothing), while women became more dependent on men economically (to bring home money for them to buy food and clothing). This is the sexual division of labor between paid and unpaid (domestic) labor. Men controlled technology (the steam engine, spinning and weaving machinery), production in factories, and the marketing of manufactured goods. Through this control, they could exclude women from industry, education, and politics.[9]

A gender pay gap emerged in England, with women earning substantially less than men. In 1881, Sidney Webb, a leading British reformer, argued that women rarely did the same level of work as men even when they were in the same occupation and industry, and that is why they were paid less.[10] In 1892, Millicent Fawcett wrote that equal pay for equal work was not possible as long as men kept women from learning the skills that justify the pay.[11] In 1917, Eleanor Rathbone said that women have different family responsibilities and thus have a different role in the workplace. Women are used only for monotonous work or work otherwise not of interest to men.[12]

In 1918, Millicent Fawcett developed the theory of job segregation by sex and the subsequent crowding of women in low-paying jobs.[13] The theory was formalized by a male, F. Y. Edgeworth, in 1922, who added that men should make more money because they were responsible for their families financially. Industrialization in England delivered whole the theory of women's low pay as being due to occupational segregation caused by (1) male unions, (2) men's financial responsibility for the family, (3) women's willingness to work for less because men subsidized them, and (4) women's lack of training and skills.

Along with the creation of a substantial middle class, industrialization also created the "poor," many of whom were women and children. As long as people lived on the land, they could support themselves. If there was a famine or a drought, people starved, but they were not in true poverty. The "poor" first referred to the wives and children of agricultural or urban day laborers in England. Without access to land and depending on their wages to buy food, this section of the population (male and female alike) constituted the poor if the men didn't find employment or if their pay was very low. These people were called paupers.

Life was tough for women in the eighteenth century: many were widows, deserted women, and even unmarried mothers. Moreover, the low wages paid women caused them to be poor. And if women were the sole support of children, their situation was even more desperate.

In response to the problems associated with this new industrial poverty, the English provided an allowance for the poor financed by local "poor rates"; this was the origin of the modern welfare system. Married women could share in the allowance given to the husband, and single women were given a very small amount of money. The allowance system was needed for unemployed women—women who used to be able to produce enough on the land to be self-sufficient. In this rural society, women were used to supporting themselves and their children.

This allowance was terminated in 1834, with the new English Poor Law, and so the workhouse became the only safety net after that. The end of allowances pushed more women into trying to find day-labor jobs. English ladies formed committees to promote the welfare of poor women, such as the Ladies Committee for Promoting the Education and Employment of the Poor.[14] In one report, the ladies said that "much of the profligacy and misery" among women originated in the want of education and employment.

The Social Effects of Industrialization

Urbanization followed industrialization. Young men and women migrated from rural areas to the cities to look for paying jobs. Away from their parents and traditional society, young men and young women often would live together. At the time it was called concubinage.[15] Free love and illegitimacy also resulted from the Industrial Revolution. These "marriages" were also called "marriages à la parisienne." Traditional rural societies had required people to be financially independent in order to marry. Rural immigrants alone in the big, "bad" cities were free from social control. No family was around to make a man marry the woman he got pregnant. Yet, many free unions in the cities were stable and lasted a lifetime. The powers that be did not legalize the union because there was no property at stake to protect or to transmit. Other unions did not last, and the women were left to raise children alone on low wages.

INDUSTRIALIZATION IN THE UNITED STATES

By the early nineteenth century, the Industrial Revolution had crossed the Atlantic. In Colonial America and in the early national period, most families lived and worked on family farms. Men worked in the fields, and women produced goods such as soap and candles in the home. Women's labor was essential to survival and was valued highly.

Alaphar Cohee was born in 1831, the second of ten children. She married Henry Huffer, had five children, but was widowed at age thirty when he died at Shiloh during the Civil War, c. 1863. She was a midwife in the rural midwest. A rich neighbor had been drafted to the Union Army for the Civil War. He promised to take care of Henry Huffer's wife and five children if he would go in his place. But all Alaphar got from him as a Civil War widow was a "litch of bacon." Each year, Alaphar's brother would butcher a hog and cure the meat for her. She had a rocky garden and stored vegetables in a hole in the ground. She made her own wine. She smoked a clay pipe and sat in front of her kitchen stove. She would roll an ember over on her pipe in order not to waste a match. She would roll narrow strips of newspaper with which she could light her pipe, or the coal oil lamp. (Interview with her descendant, Dorothy, 1992)

Anna Bass was one of the twelve children of Mary Kennedy and Hiram Bass. She married a man named Wright and had five daughters. There was a terrible flood in about 1900. Anna and the five girls took shelter in town. Wright stayed behind to fight the flood. He died of dysentery. Anna rented the farm on shares (sharecropping) and raised the girls in town. She was a strong matriarch. At the age of 75 she just sat down one day after her chores and died. (Interview with her descendant, 1992)

Industrialization first came to New England in the form of textile factories. As in England, the first factory workers were girls—the daughters of the New England farmers. Later, with immigration, the factory jobs were taken over by men and single immigrant girls. The factory system spread to the middle Atlantic states and jumped over the Allegheny Mountains to towns like Cincinnati, Pittsburgh, and Chicago. However, in the Midwest, men and women mostly lived and worked on farms.

In 1860, the leading sectors of the economy were textiles and shoes. With the invention of the sewing machine, women were hired to do sewing work in factories. The flood of immigrants into New York provided the labor force for the burgeoning textile industry.

Minnie was born in Odessa. She met her husband in the United States. He was in the sewing machine business. He installed factories with sewing machines for single girls to work on. Minnie was a full-time housewife. (Personal Interview with a descendant, 1992)

The COBF for a "working girl" was terrible sweatshop conditions, but she gained some economic independence by earning a wage.

Clara Lemlich called for a general strike in Yiddish, the native tongue of the majority of the shirtwaist workers in New York. This inspired the garment workers uprising of 1909–1910, when 18,000 shirtwaist makers walked out of nearly 500 shops in Manhattan and Brooklyn.[16]

The New York Women's Trade Union League organized women into Local 25 of the International Ladies Garment Workers Union. They did not win a union shop, but they won a reduction of hours and time-and-a-half for overtime.

The rise of office work and the service sector offered women economic opportunities in a more pleasant environment than a factory. At first, white, native-born women from middle-class families or families aspiring to be middle class were clerks and typists in offices or sales clerks in department stores. Middle- and upper-class educated women became teachers and social workers.[17] But in the nineteenth and twentieth centuries up to World War II, working girls usually quit paid employment when they got married.

Lenora was born in Latvia. She came to New York as a young girl. She worked for a milliner in Manhattan in the early 1900s. One day she was to deliver a peacock feather to another millinery shop. Somehow she lost it. Her employer docked her pay for the lost feather. That week she earned two cents instead of one dollar. When she married a jeweler, she became a housewife. (Personal Interview with a descendant, 1992)

Many housewives in this period did heavy domestic labor. It was not unusual to have more than six children. There was no mass-produced, cheap bread. There were no washing machines or dryers.

The Industrial Revolution occurred simultaneously with an agricultural revolution in the United States. The use of machinery in agriculture meant that fewer people were needed to grow the food for the nation. The move from the farm to town lowered the COBF in that women's work on the farm was hard and heavy.

Nell Case, born in 1888, granddaughter of Alaphar Cohee Huffer, grew up in the horse and buggy days. She took lessons in china painting and embroidery. She completed the eighth grade. She married a college-educated farmer in the Indiana county of Decatur. He had a hired hand to help in the fields. She had a hired girl to do the cleaning. Nell did have a garden and raised chickens. She had one daughter. In the 1920s, an agricultural depression forced the family to give up farming and move to town. Nell stayed at home. She could not imagine why a woman would want to work for pay. She was a member of the town's Garden Club, the Literary Club, and the Church Circle. (Personal interview with her daughter, Dorothy, 1992)

With the spread of public education, the once male occupation of "schoolmaster" became the female occupation of "school teacher." For educated women, it was the career of choice (if not necessity).

Mae Wright was born in 1884, one of five daughters of Anna. She became a teacher in a rural, one-room school house. She drove an open horse-drawn buggy to school. She attended the state teacher's college and played basketball on the women's team. As a married mother in the 1920s, she continued to teach school as a substitute. Like her mother, she was a matriarch. Her husband worked hard, but she ruled. She was widowed at age 66. She began to travel at an advanced age. She died shortly before her 97th birthday. (Personal Interview with a descendant, 1992)

Emergence of Discrimination in the Service Sector

Claudia Goldin, the first female professor to be granted tenure in Harvard University's Department of Economics, has made a great contribution to quantifying what we call the economic COBF. She attempted to figure out what part of the pay gap was due to discrimination. She argues that wage discrimination emerged when women entered the offices of the nation, not the factories. There was a gender wage gap in the factory, but it was due to a wage premium paid for the brawn of males. It is more difficult to measure productivity in white-collar occupations than in factory work. This put women at a disadvantage. Personnel departments assigned women to low-status and low-paying jobs. The devaluing of women's work is a persistent problem apparent today in the debate over "comparable worth," where jobs are analyzed by skill requirements, danger, dirtiness, and responsibility—regardless of whether the jobs are held by men or women. It is an attempt to get rid of two pay scales, one for women's work and one for men's.

According to Goldin's estimates, during the Industrial Revolution in America, women's earnings on average rose vis-à-vis men's. Because machinery and steam power replaced brute strength and brawn, there was now less differential between the productivity of women and men. The returns to men's greater upper-body strength were lessened by industrialization. From 1820 to the 1850s, the gender pay gap narrowed. Moreover, the economic COBF was less in industry than it had been in agriculture where more brute strength was needed.[18]

From 1850 to 1900, the pay gap remained static, although industry was very much segregated by sex. Few, if any, women were to be found in the iron and steel, machinery, lumber, transportation equipment sectors, which were regarded as "men's work." Women worked mostly in the textile, apparel, boots and shoes, canning, and tobacco sectors. They suffered physically in these factories, but, according to Goldin, they did not suffer from wage discrimination. They earned less simply because they had less experience, having dropped out of factory work to marry and have children.

During the rise of white-collar employment from 1890 to 1930, women's earnings compared favorably to men's. Office work paid good returns to a high school education, which thanks to widespread public education in the United States many women were now getting. The pay gap that did exist could not be attributed to women having less education.

Professor Goldin makes the case that wage discrimination against women did not emerge in the United States until the beginning of the twentieth century. Paradoxically, the gap was closing, but the unfair part of the gap was rising. Recall that in the chapter on the economic COBF, we explained that part of the wage gap is fair, to the extent that men have more experience and more education and training. The part of the gap that cannot be attributed to education or experience is the part attributed to discrimination against women. Goldin maintains that discrimination increased with the rise of white-collar work. In blue-collar work, women could be kept out of high-paying jobs by strength requirements and by unions keeping them out of apprenticeships. This was not the case with white-collar work where men and women were equally capable.

Employers discriminated against women, following society's expectations and stereotyped view of the role of women. They used the following rationales: Women were supposed to stay at home; if they did work for pay, they soon dropped out of the labor force; therefore, there was no reason to train them for higher positions. Moreover, there was a strong belief that men were responsible for the financial support of the family and thus should be paid a family wage or salary. Since they were normally not responsible for family support, women could thus be paid less.

The Economic-Political Connection

The Industrial Revolution marks the transition from the family economy to a market economy. For many women this change resulted in their exclusion from the economy and their concomitant loss of political and social power. Inasmuch as they were excluded from the economy, they lost much control over their lives.[19] Middle-class women became secluded into the separate and private spheres of the household, invisible in public life and decision making.

The Industrial Revolution represents the emerging power of technology and, accordingly, the power of men.[20] Wielding this new technological force gave certain men both economic and political power which they exercised by assigning roles according to gender.[21] This kept women in subordinate positions. In contrast to women, many men were able to get high-value, high-status, and high-paying jobs.

Outside the workplace, in the home environment, men remained in control for they assigned women the essential tasks of housekeeping and childrearing which they neither valued nor respected.

Society has traditionally prized those who provision us with our basic material needs. Since women no longer did this in the home, having been displaced by the male wage earners, their labor became less valued. Some men defined work as that which produced income. The work that women did at home was regarded only as part of their obligation in the family and in some male thinking was deprived of economic value.

Since women were confined in their separate spheres, they involuntarily abdicated their public roles to men. This reinforced the stereotype of men as leaders and rulers, those who made the truly important decisions on war and peace.

As industrialization progressed and economies expanded, political deci-

Table 7
Economic COBF in History

PHASE ONE: The Industrial Revolution

Preindustrial Society (before the late eighteenth century in England and before the
    early nineteenth century in America)

The Family Economy
Men and women function together economically on the farm, in artisan crafts.
All family members work together.

Industrial Society

Wage-Based Economy, Separate Sphere
Men work.
Women stay at home, excluded from paid work.
COBF = total economic dependence.

Evolution of a Middle Class
Husband is the sole provider, breadwinner.
Women work less hard as housewives.
Traditional family.
Economic role of middle-class women, to be consumers.

**PHASE TWO: Industrial Society from the Mid-Nineteenth Century for Some
    Women, from the Mid-Twentieth Century for Other Women**[a]

Women Join Men in the Wage-Based Economy
COSTS: Women still do housework and raise children.
They are still excluded from high-paying, high-status jobs.
BENEFITS: Women move toward economic independence.

Dual-Earner Family (in the U.S. from late 1970s)
Changing economic role of women; help support or completely support
    themselves and family.

---

[a]Phase Two is analyzed in more detail in Chapter 10.

sions assumed far greater importance. Governments in modern societies
formulated policies that had far-reaching implications for economic and
social life. These policies became important in redistributing income, in
legislating wages and hours, working conditions, and health and retirement
benefits. Women were bystanders to these momentous decisions, well outside the circles of power.

The first phase of industrialization (the transition from a family economy
to a market economy) resulted in women's increased economic dependence
on men, and this raised the COBF. In the second phase of industrialization
(see Chapter 10), when women moved into the market economy in greater
numbers, they gained a degree of economic independence, reducing the
COBF slightly (see Table 7).

THE AGE OF ENLIGHTENMENT AND THE POLITICAL EXCLUSION OF WOMEN

The major political event of the Enlightenment[22] occurred in 1789 when the French revolutionaries wrote the "Declaration of the Rights of Man and Citizen," which was to be the preamble of their first constitution.[23] A rebellious French woman, Olympe de Gouge, wrote the "Declaration of the Rights of Woman and Citizen," to be read alongside this document.[24] Who was this woman?

Olympe de Gouge (1748–1793) was born Marie Gouzes. She married an older man at the age of 16. She gave birth to his son. Shortly thereafter her husband died, and she refused to be called his widow. So she gave herself a new name, moved to Paris, and became a political writer. She wrote a play against the French use of black slaves in their colonies.

Women's rights were not made part of the new French constitution. An authority on French women writers, Professor Josette Wisman, argues that the male French revolutionaries did not adopt Olympe de Gouge's Declaration of the Rights of Women because they believed that woman's natural place was in the home. However, in the short period from 1789 to 1792, women broke the barriers to speaking in public. For a brief moment, French women like de Gouge came out into the public and spoke. "More than a century before women had the right to vote, Olympe de Gouge, alone, claimed it," writes Dr. Wisman. In 1904, a Doctor Guillois analyzed de Gouge as a hysteric, an unnatural woman.

In 1792, women in France were granted the rights to divorce and to some control of marital property. (However, these rights were restricted under the Napoleonic Code and completely revoked in early nineteenth-century France.) In 1793, the Jacobins sent Olympe to the guillotine.[25]

The major oversight of the Enlightenment and the French Revolution that followed it is that while people talked of the rights of man, they literally meant males and ignored women as humans.

One year after de Gouge published her call for the rights of women, across the channel in England, Mary Wollstonecraft published her call, entitled "Vindication of the Rights of Women." Like de Gouge, she received only ridicule. At the very moment in history that propertyless men were being included in the body politic, women were excluded.

Mary Wollstonecraft (1759–1797) was too intelligent and too restless to stay with her conventional family in the backwaters of England. Her first project was to run a school for girls. When that did not succeed, she set out to see the world. Her first stop was Bath, England, where she was a governess. She hated the shallow women she worked for. Oddly enough, today, there is a fine oil portrait of Mary Wollstonecraft, in one of the regency row houses in the elegant circus of Bath. She looks a beautiful and passionate woman.

Mary had a mentor named Reverend Dr. Richard Price, who had introduced her to the Enlightenment philosophers Rousseau, Locke, and Hume. Reverend Price took Mary into his home and employed her to write for the *Analytical Review*. He introduced her to a circle of intellectuals that included William Blake, Thomas Paine, Samuel Johnson, and William Godwin. She became part of their Thursday evening gatherings, the only woman in the group.

When the French Revolution broke out, Mary was interested in the education of women and the laws of marriage. She went to France and wrote a pamphlet entitled "Vindication of the Rights of Man."

Mary next tried to extend the Enlightenment argument that men had rights because they were rational, to include women. In her book, *Vindication of the Rights of Women* (published in 1792), she claims that women only appear to be irrational because they are deprived of education. She argued that discrimination against women was bad for all human beings, male and female, and that women must become active in the fight to shape their destiny.[26]

The reaction to her book was intense. She was labeled an unsexed female. The prime minister of Britain, Horace Walpole, called Mary Wollstonecraft "a hyena in petticoats!"

In a fictionalized novel about Mary Wollstonecraft, entitled *Vindication,* author Frances Sherwood writes that "she is a model for what many modern women would like to be—brilliant and taken seriously for her mind and yet ardent and loving."[27]

Women, Abolitionists, and Rights

Almost half a century after de Gouge and Wollstonecraft, the argument over the extension of rights continued in the context of the American abolitionist movement. American women sympathetic to the cause of antislavery learned political skills as they worked to promote the end of slavery. In the process, they were confronted with the fact that women were not supposed to speak in public.

Three women who broke this barrier were Lucretia Mott and the Grimké sisters. They attracted huge audiences because they spoke so passionately and articulately on the issue of slavery. During their lecture tours, they began to recognize their rights as human beings, as reasoners, and as moral agents.

Lucretia Mott was a practicing Quaker minister. In 1833, she was one of four women invited to the founding convention of the American Anti-Slavery

Society, but she was not supposed to speak. She did speak two times, but was not allowed to sign the "Declaration of Sentiments and Purposes."[28] *So she founded the Philadelphia Female Anti-Slavery Society, and her home became an "underground railroad" station for escaping slaves.*

The Grimké sisters, Sara and Angeline, were born to a slave-owning family. In 1836, they left South Carolina and began to lecture in New England about the untold evils of slavery that they had seen first hand. They spoke at female anti-slavery society meetings, but were so eloquent that many men attended their lectures.

Angeline Grimké proclaimed in public, "I want to be identified with the Negro; until he gets his rights, we shall never have ours."[29] She demanded the right to speak in public, to petition, and to write. Sara Grimké wrote *The Equality of the Sexes and the Condition of Women*. It was published in 1838. She says, "Men and women were created equal and they are both moral and accountable human beings."[30]

In 1840, Lucretia Mott was among the women excluded from the World Anti-Slavery Conference in London. This treatment caused women to see the connection between the rights of black slaves to be free and women's own emancipation. Elizabeth Cady Stanton was in London because her husband was an abolitionist attending the meeting. The two excluded women, Mott and Stanton, decided then and there to convene a conference on the rights of women. It was held in Mrs. Stanton's hometown, Seneca Falls, New York, in 1848.

First Women's Rights Conference[31]

The three hundred men and women attending the conference in the Wesleyan Chapel passed "The Declaration of Sentiments and Resolutions." With the U.S. Declaration of Independence as a model, this declaration stated that "all men and women are created equal."[32] The Seneca Falls conference called for equal access to education, the trades, and the professions. They demanded the vote and equality in church, state, and family matters.[33] For the first time, the idea of men and women being equal and not relegated to their distinctive spheres was articulated.[34]

The focus of the declaration was on the institution of marriage and its many injurious effects on women; marriage robbed women of their property rights, making wives economically, as well as morally, dependent on their husbands . . . the laws of separation and divorce were almost entirely based on male supremacy.[35]

The Seneca Falls Declaration argued that as a result of women's inferior status within marriage, they suffered inequalities in educational institutions as well as in the professions. Profitable employment and all avenues to wealth and distinction (medicine, law . . .) were absolutely inaccessible to women. The Declaration concludes its list of grievances with an evocation of women's mental and psychological dependence, which has left them with little confidence and self-respect.[36]

The great black abolitionist Frederick Douglass attended the Seneca Falls conference and wrote an article in his newspaper, *The North Star,* called "The Rights of Women." He stated: "All that distinguishes man as an intelligent and accountable being is equally true of women."[37]

In 1850, the first national convention on women's rights was held in Worcester, Massachusetts. Some nasty men at the back of the room heckled the women speakers. The former black slave woman Sojourner Truth was the only woman who stood up and argued against these men who said that women were inferior to men.

In 1851, at the women's convention in Akron, Ohio, Sojourner Truth established a "militant, fighting spirit" for the women's movement by her dramatic speech.

I have ploughed, and planted, and gathered into barns and no man could head me! And ain't I a woman? I could work as much and eat as much as a man—when I could get it—and bear the lash as well! And ain't I a woman? I have borne thirteen children and seen them most all sold off to slavery, and when I cried out with my mother's grief, none but Jesus heard me! And ain't I a woman?[38]

The refrain "And Ain't I a Woman?" became a frequently quoted slogan in the nineteenth century women's movement.

Women's Rights in Marriage

In England, Harriet Taylor, an advocate of women's rights, took inspiration from these American conventions, calling them "the first collective protest against the aristocracy of sex."[39] She wrote an essay on the inequality of women and men entitled "The Enfranchisement of Women." It was published in the *Westminster Review* in 1851.

Harriet Taylor died in 1859 in Avignon of tuberculosis. John Stuart Mill bought a house there so that he could be near her grave. Two years after her death, in 1861, he wrote "The Subjection of Women," a masterful argument for the rights of women. Then he served for three years in British Parliament and fought for women's right to vote and hold office. In 1869, he published his essay on women. In 1873, the year in which he died, he published his autobiography in which he eulogized Harriet.

Here is Harriet's story. She was born in 1807. In 1826, she married John Taylor, a merchant, and soon had three children by him. In the 1830s, the Taylor household was a main meeting place of Unitarian radicals. Being a wife and mother was only part of her life, and not her favorite part at that. She loved the intellectual life and progressive politics. Harriet certainly had her own ideas, opinions, and projects before she met the philosopher, John Stuart Mill.

John Stuart Mill was a philosophical radical. A utilitarian, he had great hopes for the power of reason and rejected sentiment and received wisdom. A practical example of this belief in reason was Mill's work in disseminating birth control literature. Citing Malthus, Mill argued that through voluntary reduction of the number of children per family, full employment at high wages would be possible. Mill was arrested in 1824 for distributing birth control pamphlets.

In 1830, Harriet Taylor and John Stuart Mill met and began a lifetime of collaboration, writing essays on marriage and divorce. Harriet was against having any laws on marriage. She thought it should be a purely private and voluntary arrangement. Thus began their fourteen-year intellectual and political relationship, during which Harriet remained married to Mr. Taylor and raised their two sons and daughter.

It was extremely difficult to get a divorce in nineteenth-century Britain. Before the Matrimonial Causes Act of 1857, "divorce was possible only by Act of Parliament, a process so expensive and unusual as to place it virtually out of reach of the middle classes."[40] Even after 1857, few people tried to get a divorce because of the scandal of having to declare that adultery was the cause. "The Victorians, with no easy escape from difficult domestic situations, were forced to be more inventive."[41] Few were more inventive than Harriet Taylor, who, for twenty years, arranged to live in a *ménage à trois* with her husband and Mill, companion to both, lover to neither.[42]

Harriet Taylor and Mill worked out their ideas on the condition of women together. Harriet believed that women colluded in their own subordination. But she saw, in the United States, women exercising power through collective action. Collusion was no longer universal, she declared in her essay, "The Enfranchisement of Women."

Although the title refers to women's suffrage, "The Enfranchisement of Women" is about sexual inequality in every aspect of women's lives. Harriet "protested the injustice of treating any individual as inferior simply on the basis of the accident of gender."[43]

For Harriet, the primary cause of the exclusion of women was physical force. In history the strong conquer and subjugate the rest. Male dominance of females is just one example.

She also responded to those who contended that women were excluded from public life because it was not compatible with maternity and running households. This only applied to mothers, she argued, and only while they were mothers. This was no reason to deny women a role in the world for their entire lives. It was an injustice to define women only by motherhood.

There was a common belief that women should be excluded from paid work in order to keep men's wages up. One hears similar arguments today about women taking men's jobs. But Harriet argued that married women should be free to hold jobs. For "women to be truly free of the tyranny of protectionism, they must be allowed to support themselves materially and to contribute on equal terms to the family income."[44] "Let every occupation be open to all."[45] As she said, even if women and men, both working, made only as much as previously the man had made working alone, at least then the woman would be a partner and not a servant.

With amazing insights into the psychology of heterosexual relationships, Harriet Taylor thought that if women did work and were properly paid, there would be less domestic violence.

Harriet insisted that women should be educated for the world, not for men. The subordination of women is "a common problem of humanity . . . enslaved women have bad effects on their masters . . . the liberation of men can only come about with sexual equality."[46] Harriet appealed to men to join forces with women in attaining it.

Although Harriet Taylor felt that the institution of marriage subordinated women, she did marry again when her husband died in 1849.[47] Following their fourteen-year long intellectual and political liaison, she and John Stuart Mill would have seven years of marriage. Harriet and John believed that they could transform the marriage union into a relation of equals, and that men and women could be true companions.

Two years after Harriet's death, Mill wrote "The Subjection of Women," an argument for the rights of women. Then he served for three years in the British Parliament where he fought for women's right to vote and hold office.

Mill said that "all that is most striking and profound [in this essay] belongs to my wife."[48] Mill called on women to act on their own behalf. He was completely committed to the "removal of all forms of discrimination between the sexes."[49] "It is not men who are prime oppressors of women, but the tradition and custom of society."[50]

Mill likened the subjection of women to the subjection of some men to other men throughout history. History was progressive in Mill's mind: step by step, men overcome their barbarity. Men once enslaved other men. Men once made serfs of other men. Slavery was ended in the nineteenth century. Peasants won independence from serfdom in the fourteenth century and land in the French Revolution. The reform bill in England brought the vote to all English men. The liberation of women just had not happened yet, but like the liberation of slaves, serfs, peasants, and propertyless men, it would come. These were the words of a strong male feminist. He truly carried on Harriet's work.

Creation of the Middle-Class Woman

In this early phase of industrialization, women were divided into two groups: those who could afford to stay home and those who had to work (the later phase would draw all women to the labor market). With fewer people needed to produce the goods necessary for daily life, a new middle class came into existence. For that class, the men went out to work, and the women were left to tend their households in relatively greater comfort than before. Middle-class men had new income and wealth and did not need their wives to work for pay. It was a mark of status for men if their wives stayed home.

Most middle-class women did not challenge the idea of a separate sphere. In fact, "privileged women got influence and power from the women's sphere."[51] They could spend their time on the pleasures and joys of child-rearing. They could make a beautiful, warm, and supportive home for their husbands and children.

If they could afford servants, women could use their domestic talents in the community and help the less fortunate. Thus, by the end of the nineteenth century, the reform movement was focused on how to enlarge women's sphere, not how to abolish it.[52] Women were encouraged to devote themselves to social reform or self-improvement. Some of these women thought of themselves as paragons of feminine virtue. "By using femininity as their passport to the public sphere, women came to be typecast in traditional feminine roles."[53]

Jane Addams and the settlement house movement was an extension of women's domestic concerns into the world beyond. The idea was that women were special people and they needed protection. Middle-class women worked to improve the working conditions of lower class women. From the 1920s to the 1960s, much protective legislation for women was passed.

The Rebellion Against the Victorian Stereotype of Woman

In 1898, Charlotte Perkins Gilman protested against the separate sphere for women. In her book, *Women and the Economy: The Economic Factor Between Men and Women as a Factor in Social Evolution,* she angrily wrote:

Men may build a career, enter politics; but a woman could only marry and have children. In prehistoric times, women first became dependent on men for food and support. Thereafter a woman's survival rested on her ability to seduce and hold a husband. Sex became a woman's economic way of life. While men worked to live, women mated to live. Women can achieve freedom only when they gain economic equality with men.[54]

Gilman's *Women and the Economy* was the most important feminist book in the nineteenth century after John Stuart Mill's *The Subjection of Women.*

Many women, unimpressed by the Victorian mystique, continued to struggle for women's rights. The word "feminist" was first used in 1910 in the call for a revolution in all the relations of the sexes, emancipation for women from all the constraints previously imposed on them by virtue of their sex.[55]

In 1913, a feminist alliance of women's groups, headed by Henrietta Rodman, was formed. Their platform stated: "Women want the removal of all social, political and economic and other discriminations which are based on sex and the award of all rights and duties in all fields on the basis of individual capacity alone."[56]

An Equal Rights Amendment to the U.S. Constitution was first proposed in 1913 by Alice Paul's National Women's party, a self-proclaimed feminist group: "Men and women shall have equal rights throughout the U.S. and every place subject to its jurisdiction."

The Cost of Femininity

In the Victorian era, a conflict arose between femininity and feminism. Femininity holds that women are different or should be different from men. The nineteenth-century concept of femininity led to the acceptance of feminine weaknesses as virtues. Women were to humanize men who were out in the barbaric, competitive world. Women were to remain in the house to avoid this contamination. The "angel in the house" was the true woman. The feminine virtues were sexual purity, compassion, and talent for nurturing. Women were the moral guardians of society. The COBF was the denial of women's sexuality and their humanity beyond her maternal functions.

THE DEMOGRAPHIC REVOLUTION: LOWER FERTILITY RATES, SMALLER FAMILIES

Nancy's great-great grandmother, Mary was married to Hiram. After the Civil War, Hiram was the first farmer in his area to have a horse-drawn mechanical reaper. With farm machinery, the pressure to have sons to help with the wheat harvest was greatly relieved. Thus pressure on farm wives to have children was reduced. However, it was too late for Mary. She had twelve children. But her daughter, Anna, had only five children and her granddaughter, Mary Mae, only had one child. Nancy has none. (Personal Interviews, 1992)

Barbara's grandmother came to America at the turn of the century, had thirteen children, and died at the age of fifty. Barbara's mother had five children. Barbara has two. (Personal Interviews, 1992)

Closely related to the Industrial Revolution was the demographic revolution. People began to have fewer children in France in the early nineteenth century, when the French peasants began consciously to limit the size of their families by using traditional methods of birth control.[57] The second society to make the demographic transition was America. Other countries followed these examples. Only one country has reduced family size without first industrializing, and that is China.

The reduction in family size lowered the social and economic COBF. Prior to the nineteenth century, many women died in childbirth, but with industrialization came better health conditions and women's life spans grew longer. Thus women spent less of their lifetime pregnant, nursing, or caring for young children. Infant mortality rates were dramatically reduced with improved public health and sanitation. Women used to have to have six to eight children to ensure that two or three would survive. In the United States, the fertility rate has fallen steadily for one hundred years, greatly reducing the COBF.

In traditional society, fathers wanted sons because they needed their labor on the farm and their support when the parents were too old to work. Since the sons would inherit the farm, the fathers were able to control their children even well into adulthood. This reinforced the economic dominance of the fathers.

The Industrial Revolution decreased the economic benefits of children and increased the costs. Children were no longer needed for their labor on the farm, and they no longer needed to inherit land to make a living. It became necessary to educate children to work in this newly industrializing society, a considerable expense for parents. Public education arose in response to this development.

Men came to see that having fewer children was good for them. It improved the family's standard of living. Families focused more on the quality of life than on the quantity of children they produced. Women's bargaining power increased vis-à-vis their husbands now that they bore fewer children.[58]

The Industrial Revolution eventually made women's lives easier. But in terms of equity, how have women fared relative to men? The Industrial Revolution removed most women from economic life and thus from status and power. It was only when industrialization advanced to the point that fewer people were needed to maintain our material standard of living and when people started working in offices, that women reentered economic life in large numbers. The final stage came when women could contribute more to the family by working for pay than by working in the home. Then a new COBF arose for a majority of women, the "second shift." Table 8 combines our analysis of the social COBF and the COBF in history.

Table 8
Social COBF in History

Marriage	Divorce
Nineteenth century	*Twentieth century*
Women as property No rights after marriage No longer a legal entity	State laws slowly drop restrictions on women owning property
Before 1970s	*After 1970s*
Very difficult to get a divorce Social custom was anti-divorce	Revolution in divorce law No fault divorce More socially acceptable to divorce
Social COBF	*Social COBF*
Legal and economic dependence	Reduced dependence on men's income Does no-fault divorce increase or decrease the social COBF?

Childbearing	Decline in Mortality Rates
Through nineteenth century	*End of nineteenth century*
Women had to have six to eight children to make sure that two or three survived	Women don't have to have as many children—Social and health COBF greatly reduced Fewer women die in childbirth Fewer infants die
Before 1960	*After 1960*
Women worry about unwanted pregnancies	Availability of contraception The Pill—Women can be free of unwanted pregnancies

Childrearing	
Before 1970s	*After 1970s*
Women have total responsibility for raising children	The second wave of the women's movement. Men begin to share Women to work Children in daycare

NOTES

1. The COBF does not begin with the Industrial Revolution but was profoundly changed by it. It is beyond the scope of this chapter to seek the roots of the COBF, but interested readers are referred to Gerda Lerner, *The Creation of Patriarchy* (New York: Oxford University Press, 1986). The reader is also referred to June Stephenson, *Women's Roots: Status and Achievements in Western Civilization* (Napa, Calif.: Diemer, Smith Publishing, 1981. I thank my sister Ann Headlee for giving me this book.

2. Ivy Pinchbeck, *Women Workers and the Industrial Revolution, 1750–1850* (London: Frank Cass and Co., Ltd., 1930; New York: Augustus M. Kelly, 1969), p. 1.

3. Ibid., p. 315.

4. Ibid., p. 313.

5. Ibid., p. 312.

6. Ibid., p. 316.

7. Heidi Hartmann, "Capitalism, Patriarchy, and Job Segregation by Sex," in a series on the Historical Roots of Occupational Segregation, *Signs: Journal of Women in Culture and Society* 1, no. 3, pt. 2 (Spring 1976): 154.

8. See Gerda Lerner's *The Creation of Patriarchy.* She traces the subordination of women to men back to the early years in ancient Mesopotamia, at the dawn of civilization.

9. Some men controlled the machines, and other men worked them. The working men who left home to work in the factories wanted to earn a family wage and have their wives stay home. The men who controlled the machines wanted to have women workers and pay them less.

10. Hartmann, p. 156.

11. Ibid., p. 157.

12. Ibid.

13. Ibid.

14. Pinchbeck, p. 304.

15. Louis A. Tilly and Joan W. Scott, *Women, Work and Family* (New York: Routledge: 1978), p. 96.

16. Karen Shallcross Koziara, Michael H. Moscow, and Lucretia Dewey Tanner, eds., *Working Women: Past, Present and Future,* Industrial Relations Research Association Series (Washington, D.C.: Bureau of National Affairs, 1987), 169.

17. William H. Chafe, *The Paradox of Change: American Women in the 20th Century* (New York: Oxford University Press, 1991), p. 13.

18. This seems to conflict with our account at the beginning of this chapter. The story of women's work in history in the feminist tradition differs from the account of Claudia Goldin, a neo-classical economist. It is beyond the scope of this chapter to integrate the two, but it would be a good research project.

19. Which is not to say that men who worked in factories had much control over their lives either.

20. We simplify because of our focus on gender relations. Further research can be carried out to study the more complex picture of gender if we add class to the analysis. Gerda Lerner is the best example of the integration of gender and class analysis.

21. Even on the farm in traditional American society, perhaps in all agrarian societies, roles were arranged by gender. However, before the Industrial Revolution, women and men worked in the same place; women could care for children while still playing a role in production. The COBF does not begin with industrialization; our study just starts there. It is beyond the scope of the book to trace the sexual division of labor back to the point where it was not oppressive to women. It was necessary for the survival of the human race in the hunting and gathering days. It is no longer necessary, but it persists.

22. Christine de Pisan (born 1364, died after 1429) was an Enlightenment personage before her time. She wrote *The Book of the City of Women (Le Livre de la Cité des Dames)* in 1405 in Paris. She was the first female writer to earn a living from her pen, and she defended the status of women. The Fall 1995 Library of Congress exhibition of manuscripts from the Bibliothèque Nationale in Paris includes *The City of Women,* published before the printing press and thus in the handwritten script. Aided by reason, uprightness, and justice, de Pisan lays the foundation of a city exclusively for women who have served the cause of women (female warriors, politicians, good wives, lovers, and inventors among others). Also see the unpublished manuscript by Veerle A. Nelen, "Dante Alighieri and Christine de Pisan" (Washington, D.C., 1995).

23. Josette A. Wisman, "L'Echec de *La Declaration des droits de la femme d'Olympe de Gouge*" (Washington, D.C.: unpublished manuscript, 1993).

24. Olympe de Gouge, "The Rights of Woman," in *The Portable Enlightenment Reader,* edited by Isaac Kramnick (New York: Penguin Books, 1995).

25. Joan W. Scott, "French Feminists and the Rights of 'Man': Olympe de Gouge's Declarations," *History Workshop* 28 (Autumn 1989): 1–21.

26. Mary Wollstonecraft, *The Vindication of the Rights of Women* (London, 1793).

27. Ibid.

28. Angela Davis, *Women, Race, and Class* (New York: Vintage Books, 1981), p. 37.

29. Ibid., p. 68.

30. Ibid., p. 42.

31. Although this was the first women's rights conference, women thought, read, and wrote from the time of the Middle Ages, as documented by Gerda Lerner in *The Creation of Feminist Consciousness: From the Middle Ages to Eighteen-seventy* (New York: Oxford University Press, 1993).

32. Chafe, p. 5.

33. Ibid., p. 6.

34. Ibid., p. 7.

35. Quoted in Davis, p. 53.

36. Ibid.

37. Ibid., p. 30.

38. Ibid., p. 61.

39. Kate Soper, ed. *The Subjection of Women* by John Stuart Mill, and *Enfranchisement of Women* by Harriet Taylor (London: Virago Books, 1983), p. 7.

40. Phyllis Rose, *Parallel Lives: Five Victorian Marriages* (New York: Vintage, 1983), p. 11.

41. Ibid.

42. Rose, p. 11. Harriet did have children from Taylor.

43. Soper, p. vi.

44. Ibid., p. viii.

45. Harriet Taylor quote in Soper edition, p. 14.

46. Soper, p. xii.

47. Ibid., p. 32.

48. Ibid., p. iii.

49. Ibid., p. ix.

50. Ibid., p. xii.

51. Chafe, p. 9.

52. Ibid., p. 4.

53. Wendy Kaminer, "Feminism's Identity Crisis," *Atlantic Monthly* (October, 1993).

54. Quoted in Chafe, p. 7.

55. Ibid., p. 45.

56. Ibid.

57. Tilly and Scott, p. 91.

58. The mechanism by which this worked should be researched and analyzed in the future.

10

THE COST OF BEING FEMALE
ACROSS THE GENERATIONS

One of the inspirations for this book was the ten-year age difference that separated the authors. We were both college professors; we thought we shared similar backgrounds. But how similar? Did the ten-year gap affect our thinking about the status of women? As we got to know each other better, we began to discuss the historical effect of context on women's experiences and attitudes. We thought about our mothers and grandmothers. We thought about our daughters and granddaughters and generations to come. Was it harder or easier to be a woman in one time period or another? Was the COBF greater or lesser then or now? Which way was it heading? We decided to research generations of women.

We soon found a rich mix of political, economic, and social factors that explained many of the differences we observed on the road to gender equality. As women inched forward in the political arena with their painfully won right to vote, their voices began to be heard in electoral politics. Changing economic patterns, as we saw in the previous chapter, gave women the chance to leave the family circle for the world of work. Social attitudes changed more slowly, gradually becoming more accepting of independent, wage-earning women.

In only one generation between Dorothy and her daughter Nancy, nearly half of all full-time housewives moved into the paid labor force. Dorothy was a full-time mother and homemaker in the 1950s and 1960s. Nancy does not have children but does have a career. Barbara is an example of a full-time housewife in the 1960s who moved into the workplace in the 1970s. Her daughter Jennifer, born in the 1960s, is an unmarried professional.

There were laws that changed the context for these women in major ways—laws mandating equal pay for equal work (1963) and laws outlawing discrimination against women in employment (1964).

There were social changes as well. In the 1970s we witnessed a divorce revolution, a decline in fertility rates, and a decline in the marriage rate. Dorothy and Barbara are married to the men they married when they were young. Nancy divorced but remarried. Jennifer is single.

Ideas about the position of women in society changed in the last generation with the return of the women's movement. We may date the beginning of the modern women's movement in 1967 with the founding of the National Organization of Women. In 1967, Dorothy's youngest child had only two more years of high school left. Barbara was home with the children, but had completed a Ph.D. and had plans for a career down the road. Nancy had just joined the paid labor force as a secondary school teacher. And Jennifer was only four years old. By the time Jennifer was nineteen in 1982, the *New York Times* had declared the 1980s the "postfeminist era." Many younger women would know nothing about the earlier battles for equality.

Education has been women's passport to better jobs. In 1972, the United States passed laws barring discrimination against women in education. Although all four of the women we are writing about have college degrees, the typical American woman has not had the opportunity to get a college education. But even women without college degrees have found expanded employment opportunities as the nature of work has changed.

DOROTHY, A WOMAN OF THE PROUD DECADES, 1940s AND 1950s

Dorothy was born on a farm in 1917. She moved to town at age twelve because the Depression hit agriculture in the 1920s. The family lived in a house that rented for $30 a month. Dorothy and her high school sweetheart went to the high school prom in children's party clothes because no one could afford formal wear. Dorothy went to the state university.

Dorothy married her high school sweetheart when she was twenty-four, just before the Japanese bombed Pearl Harbor in 1941. She worked briefly as an interior decorator until she had Nancy, her first child, in 1943. She had her second child in 1946, while living with her parents since her husband was on duty in the army.

Dorothy's husband began what was to be a successful medical practice. They bought their first home in 1950. "By the end of the 1950s, one-fourth of the population had moved to . . . [suburbia]."[1] Whereas her mother had had to wait until she was forty-seven to own her own home, Dorothy achieved this by the age of thirty-three. She had her third child in 1951. In the baby-boom years after World War II, the birth rate for women having a third child increased twofold, temporarily reversing the trend toward women having two children. "The Proud Decades" are the 1940s, when the Americans led their European allies to victory in World War II, and the 1950s, when the economy produced great prosperity for a great number of Americans.

The majority of women did not work for pay in the 1940s, 1950s, or even 1960s—all of Dorothy's childrearing years. As late as 1960, only 38 percent of American women worked for pay.[2]

By 1967 and the beginning of the modern phase of the women's movement, Dorothy was completing childrearing and starting elder care of her mother and her mother-in-law. If Dorothy had wanted to or had to work, she would have experienced occupational segregation. Dorothy had jobs after college, but they were minor and unsatisfying. Dorothy's friend, for example, worked at a VA hospital and was paid less for her social work skills than the men with whom she worked. At that time, Dorothy says women never questioned these inequalities.

The economic COBF for Dorothy and for most of the women of her age was that they lived and worked in women's separate sphere. They were economically dependent on their husbands and were excluded from economic life.

The pay gap was first measured in 1955 by the Women's Bureau in the U.S. Department of Labor. It found that women who worked full-time, all-year-round, made 64 percent of what men made. The economic COBF was 36 cents for every dollar made by men.

It's important to distinguish between the subjective COBF and the objective COBF. Dorothy chose to be a full-time mother and homemaker, so subjectively there was no economic COBF for her. Objectively, the COBF for women who stayed in their separate sphere was that they did not go out into the world and earn their own status by working. Although they had an important social role in rearing children, they had no economic power.

Dorothy has a good marriage. Her generation had a "cult" of happy marriages. "You were expected to get married and stay married." She was a dutiful wife: after her marriage, she always accommodated her wishes to and supported her husband's career, but without any resentment. She was not competitive with her husband, nor was she frustrated or unhappy. Women accepted the limitations society imposed on them. Dorothy is a partner and friend to her husband. Their marriage vow is "truly until death do us part."

Dorothy raised three children. She had no second shift to work, for she did not work outside the home. Once you had children, it was expected that you would stay home and raise them. Dorothy had twenty-six years of childrearing from 1943 and the birth of her first child to 1969 when her last child went to college. Her generation valued the nuclear family with a father, a mother, and children, all directed primarily by the father's needs, secondarily by the children's needs, and lastly by the mother's conscious needs for a happy family.

One may wonder whether this graceful accommodation is generational, or due to a particularly kind and self-abnegating personality. The golden age of the American economy and society was a happy time for white, middle-class women to enjoy raising a family without financial worries. Certainly, after a decade of economic depression and the sacrifices of World War II, women were glad to raise their children in peace and prosperity.

However, there were also frustrated women in this generation. As Betty Friedan told us in *The Feminine Mystique,* many women felt imprisoned in their homes. Of course, this applies to white, middle-class women who did not have to work. Women of lower incomes and most African-American women never had that option.

Dorothy's generation took parenting and family life seriously. There was lots of caring. They wanted to build a decent home life and neighborhood, and they did. The children were nurtured and were taught discipline and virtue of hard work. Unlike the large numbers of single-parent families we have today, in 1959, 91 percent of children lived in a family headed by a married couple.[3] Dorothy was in the PTA and active in her church. This was an era of quality child care, well-raised children, and devoted child-rearing.

> *Though I've enjoyed a great life with many facets of experience, my main focus and pride were my children. They were my main reason-to-be (along with being [my husband's] . . . wife),—my big accomplishment. (Personal Interview, 1992)*

Dorothy had three years of what we now call the "sandwich generation"—women who care for their children and their parents at the same time. Three years before her last child left home, Dorothy's mother-in-law, a widow in her 80s, moved to a home for the elderly near Dorothy's home. Then her own mother, also a widow in her 80s, moved to town to a different home for the elderly. Dorothy went to see both mothers regularly and phoned them daily. In all, there were fifteen years of elder care, three of which overlapped with her last three years of child care.

Despite all the years of caretaking, women in this generation outlive men, and large numbers of them spend their last years as widows.[4]

Dorothy is a far less demanding housekeeper than her mother was. She employed an Eastern European immigrant woman to help clean the house, but she did the cooking. She also sewed beautiful clothes for her family. Whereas her mother had concentrated on maintaining a spotless home,

Dorothy reduced this COBF for herself. She liberated herself from the need for a spotless home, which takes a lot of time, if not all of one's time.

Dorothy grew up in between the two waves of feminism. She was born three years before women won the right to vote. She was fifty and nearly finished with childrearing when the National Organization of Women was founded in 1967.

On the other hand, Dorothy is savvy about politics. She reads the newspaper and watches the news on TV. She has given money to women political candidates for her state legislature. She cares about what's happening in the country.

In 1935, when Dorothy graduated from public high school, 60 percent of white girls (and only 27 percent of black girls) went to high school.[5] She was smart and benefited from the American commitment to public high schools for both sexes. Her own mother had only completed the eighth grade.

Dorothy was a dutiful daughter and chose to go to the state university from which her father had graduated. She had wanted to go to a private woman's college in the neighboring state. She also had wanted to go to library school in the regional capital, but it was expensive and so she didn't apply.

In 1939, when Dorothy graduated from the public university, only 7 percent of white women had graduated from college (4 percent for black women) as of 1931.[6] In class, Dorothy says, it was noticed and expected that men would receive more attention. Women never questioned these inequalities. Today, we protest the chilly climate of college classrooms.

She had played clarinet in the high school marching band and won prizes in other states. When she went to the state university in 1935, she learned that only men were allowed in the marching band. She accepted that policy. Years later when money was tight and her husband needed a new suit, she sold her clarinet to pay for it, without resentment or anger. (According to *Ms.* magazine, in 1972 the University of Minnesota was the first to admit women to their marching band.)[7]

Amelia Earhart taught aeronautical engineering at the state university that Dorothy attended. She was Dorothy's idol. So was Anne Morrow Lindbergh, who was taught by her husband to fly. (In 1972, women were admitted to the U.S. Navy's pilot training program. In 1984, Betsy Carol was the first woman to pilot a jumbo jet across the Atlantic. In the 1990s a woman became the secretary of the Air Force for the first time.) A short time ago on a commuter flight, Dorothy noticed that the pilot was a woman; she spoke to her and told her that she had known Amelia Earhart.

After she raised her children and while she was doing her elder care, Dorothy started working on a Master's degree in history. Although a very modest woman, she did get some quiet enjoyment from her superior performance in classes in competition with younger students. She was one of the first two women to become members of the state Civil War Society. She was the first woman president of the state Lincoln Society.

In addition to her interest in history, Dorothy is the member of two book clubs and regularly gives book reviews herself. She is also very involved in the music and art of her community. She has had a rich life in the past twenty-four years since her last child turned eighteen. She and her husband travel together a lot. She is richly blessed with many women friends, including her two daughters.

Dorothy has severe and painful arthritis in her neck. She had to give up sewing and drawing. Women live longer than men, but too often they are in pain. For a long time, almost all medical research was focused on men. We now have the Women's Health Initiative at the National Institute of Health to research diseases that particularly affect women.

Sum-up for Dorothy and the 1940s women

- The COBF for Dorothy and her peers was that they lived in a separate sphere, the sphere of the home and the family, the world of women and children. They were economically dependent. Their social status came from their husbands.

- Middle-class women were excluded from economic and political life, but they made a rich world of their own. Subjectively, there was little cost for those who wanted to be there. The value of marriage and maternity to women of this generation was so great that the COBF was paid without much stress and strain. For middle-class women, there was no poverty. There was no double shift as they worked only in the separate sphere, not out in the marketplace. After raising their children, many middle-class white women were able to lead fulfilling lives.

NANCY, A 1960s WOMAN

Nancy was born in 1943 and grew up in suburban America with a mother, Dorothy, who was a full-time housewife, and a father, who was a physician.

Nancy attended a liberal arts college in the early 1960s. She felt the "chilly climate" there. In her first year, fresh out of a successful high school career, Nancy enjoyed a Western civilization class, participated in discussions, and earned an A. By the second semester, however, she felt the social pressure from the young men in her class; they were the aggressive ones who talked and were listened to. As a result, Nancy became less active in class. That semester she earned a C. At the time, Nancy was part of an expanding group of women who were gaining access to higher education. She dropped out of graduate school to marry and worked while her husband went to graduate school. While her husband began his career in business, she became a schoolteacher. They were married for nine years before they separated.

The women's movement in the 1970s made Nancy realize that she did not have to stay married to her first husband. Having freed herself from an unhappy and traditional marriage, she looked beyond school teaching to a nontraditional career. Nancy began to work on a Ph.D. in social science at age thirty-three.

In 1983, Nancy remarried but kept her birth name as a statement that hers was not a traditional marriage. (The first notable woman to keep her maiden name was Lucy Stone, a nineteenth-century suffragette.) In 1974, the passport office began to accept the use of a married woman's birth name.

Nancy is nearly fifty now and has been an assistant professor for six years. It was the male backlash and the encroachment on reproductive rights that rekindled her interest in the women's movement in the 1990s.

When Nancy was twenty-four years old, in 1967, President Johnson prohibited sex discrimination by federal contractors, signaling increased governmental regulation of employment practices.[8] In that same year Nancy had her first job as a high school teacher and earned $5,000. She was married to her first husband at the time. By choosing to teach, Nancy was following the rules of occupational sex stereotyping.

When Nancy was thirty years old in 1973, the Supreme Court outlawed sex-segregated help-wanted ads. At the time, Nancy was teaching in a private, special education elementary school. Also in that year of 1973, AT&T paid a $38 million settlement in a sex and race bias case. Nancy was beginning to get restless in a totally female workplace. In the 1970s through the 1980s, 85 percent of elementary school teachers were women.

The women's liberation movement of the 1970s encouraged women to aspire to occupations that had formerly been off limits to them. Many women, anticipating equal treatment, trained for traditionally male jobs. When Nancy was thirty-two, she decided to leave school teaching and started work for a Ph.D. in social science.

When Nancy was thirty-five years old, in 1978, pay equity became a major issue and women wore buttons emblazoned with "59 cents," referring to the ratio of female to male earnings. The rebirth of feminism challenged traditional sex roles and male privilege. Nancy began to read women's history.

When Nancy was forty-one years old, in 1984, former news anchor Christine Craft won $325,000 from KMBC-TV in Kansas City for demoting her because of her appearance and for not being "deferential" toward men. Nancy learned what happens when a woman doesn't defer to men. This lack of deference harmed her in her professional organization and in the workplace. Even in the professions, many men simply do not listen to women.

In 1992, State Farm Insurance had to pay $200 million to women for refusing to give them sales jobs. This was the largest damages recovery under the 1964 Civil Rights Act. Actually, selling insurance is an occupation into which women made inroads in the 1970s, but court cases take a long time. Nancy has had difficulty finding a permanent, tenure-track position, although by 1992, she had six years of full-time college teaching under her belt.

The sexual revolution of the 1960s took the stigma out of premarital sex for white middle-class women. Yet abortion was illegal, and contraceptives were not readily available. Nancy had to have an illegal abortion in 1966. Abortion was not legalized until 1973 by the Supreme Court decision in *Roe v. Wade.* It is estimated that there are now 1.5 million abortions a year in the United States.[9]

Nancy was the first person in her family's history to divorce. The year her divorce became official, 1979, was the peak year for U.S. divorce rates; 22.8 divorces per year per thousand married women.[10] About 3 million Americans cohabit outside of marriage these days. Nancy lived with a man for eight years before they married.

In her second marriage (and the second for her husband as well), there is a more equal distribution of labor than there was in her first. They do a lot of chores together. Since there are no children, there is not much household work and no child care. They use a professional house cleaning service.

In contrast to her mother's child-centered generation, and like many women of her age cohort, Nancy has chosen not to have children.

This generation of women, having experienced the women's movement, had always planned to support themselves. They were not, on the whole, as greatly harmed by midlife divorce as were women a generation earlier.

Most of these 1960s women did have children and were in their child-raising period when "super mom" was the ideal: super mom could raise her children, keep her house, and have a career. Only later would they realize this was a second shift which their husbands did not have to work. The social COBF for most women of this cohort was the second shift.

Nancy is a 1960s woman. She voted for the first time in 1964, the first year in which more women than men voted for president. In 1967, Nancy protested the war in Vietnam. She was affected by the civil rights movement and the War on Poverty. She taught two years in a large inner-city public high school.

In the early 1970s, "countless Americans were debating feminist issues: the ERA, childcare, abortion, open marriage, the sexual revolution, greater sharing of household responsibilities. The women's movement was unified, vigorous, enthusiastic, and energetic. It had political sophistication."[11]

At age twenty-nine, in 1972, Nancy was a founding subscriber to *Ms.* magazine. She read Kate Millett's *Sexual Politics,* Shulamith Firestone's *The Dialectics of Sex,* Germaine Greer's *The Female Eunuch,* and Phyllis Chesler's *Women and Madness.* Feminism for Nancy was rebellion against her first husband and her traditional marriage. "The personal is political." She read Doris Lessing's *The Golden Notebook,* which gave her the confidence to leave her husband.

The American Association of University Women celebrated its centennial in 1981. Nancy received a doctoral fellowship from the AAUW in 1982. With this financial help, along with other financial help from the university, her father, and her husband, Nancy earned a Ph.D. at age forty-three. She was lucky to have a woman as a mentor who taught her how to do social science research.

At age thirty-seven, Nancy was part of the first gender voting gap in the 1980 election. This is the first time it was recorded that men and women voted differently. Ronald Reagan was elected president with 8 to 10 percent fewer female than male votes.

She was also part of the 1991 protest against the Persian Gulf War. According to *Ms.* magazine, this was the biggest-ever gender gap in the public opinion polls. She gave a teach-in at a local university against the war.

Nancy became active again in the women's movement following the attack on abortion rights. In 1986 and 1989, she participated in NOW's March for Women's Lives in Washington. In 1992, she joined NOW's March for Reproductive Rights along with 750,000 other people at the largest demonstration ever in Washington. Nancy contributes to NOW's educational and legal fund to work against Operation Rescue. On this issue, Nancy and her mother are in agreement. Dorothy believes in women's right to abortion and is a longtime supporter of her state's Planned Parenthood.

Sum-Up for Nancy and the 1960s Women

- Despite some inroads into male occupations, occupational segregation still exists as does the pay gap. Nancy feels that she lost ten years in her career while she was in a traditional marriage and a traditional female occupation.

- Women were still forced to choose between career and family. If they had children, they had the extra burden of the second shift.

- Women were still largely excluded from national politics and political discourse.

Some of these women have a measure of economic and social independence because of their education and employment. On balance, this generation of women has made progress, but much injustice and many inequities remain.

BARBARA, A 1950s WOMAN

Barbara was born in 1933. She was brought up in a middle-class environment and went to public schools in a small industrial city in New England.

Barbara attended an Ivy League women's college whose faculty was predominantly female. At that time, women were not accepted at the male Ivy League schools. Her college had a reputation for feminism. By the 1950s, however, the mood had changed. In the speech given (by a man) at her graduation, Barbara was told that paid work was only something women did to help their husbands through law or medical school and until they had babies.

She married before she graduated from college. Marriage for her mother had been freedom from a life of hard work in a large first-generation immigrant family. Marriage for Barbara meant independence from her family but not true independence. Women of this generation typically went from their fathers' home to their husbands' home.

Barbara and some of her friends tried to break into the world of publishing in the 1950s but without success. Most ended up working for women's publications or serving as secretaries and researchers for mainstream publishers.

When her husband started to move dramatically ahead in his career, Barbara had to figure out how to balance her comparatively unimportant career and family with his "fast-track" work schedule. She started working on a Ph.D., so that she could be a college professor with a flexible schedule. She rejected the idea of becoming a lawyer as incompatible with family needs.

Once she decided to become a college teacher, Barbara attended graduate schools, beginning very slowly in an evening program. She started at night and later switched to a day program, but as a part-time student. She was pregnant when she was taking her coursework. There were only two other women in her program. No mentor stepped forward to show her the ropes. There was a "chilly climate" for women in the classrooms of higher education. But she got her Ph.D. before the age of forty when her children were seven and eleven.

She had her first child in 1960. She had her second and last child in 1963. She earned her Ph.D. in 1970. Barbara is an associate professor at a women's college. Her husband's earning power far surpasses hers. Without his income, she would never have been able to send two children to college and graduate school.

Women were excluded from some of the leading law schools and medical schools through the late 1940s and early 1950s. Women of this generation had difficulty getting credentials for the occupations they wanted. Once they had the credentials, they often could not find work. Supreme Court

Justice Sandra Day O'Connor graduated from Stanford Law School but was unable to get any job interviews.

After 1964, women could sue if they were excluded from employment because of their sex. In 1977, NBC agreed to pay $1.7 million for back pay and training programs for women.[12] In 1978, a women's group at the *New York Times* settled a discrimination suit begun in 1972 for $350,000.[13] Only after the 1970s did women make inroads into book editing. By the late 1970s and early 1980s, two-thirds of the workforce in the publishing industry was female.[14] But these advances came too late for Barbara and her friends.

Women need to find careers that can be balanced with family life. Barbara had to quit her job at a women's magazine because it conflicted with her husband's schedule. Barbara dropped out of the labor force for ten years to rear her children. She also moved from city to city as her husband's career dictated. Job moves like these interrupt wives' work history.

Often women are offered only part-time jobs. When her children were safely in school, ages eleven and seven, Barbara looked for a job. She wanted a full-time, tenure-track teaching position, but all she could find were part-time, adjunct positions. Finally, six years later, she found a full-time job, when her children were teenagers, seventeen and thirteen.

Marriage is a political experience. Phyllis Rose suggests that "marriage is shifting tides of power between a man and a woman joined for life." Her book, *Parallel Lives,* presents marriage as the management of power between men and women, working out the balance between the relative importance and the priority of desires, between the two partners.[15] Many of Barbara's generation saw marriage this way.

Barbara saw her friends' midlife divorces as an unfair social COBF. The men of this generation had the advantage of these women's youth. A COBF is that women are only attractive and desirable to men when they are young. Phyllis Rose wrote that "when divorce is possible, people no longer need to conform themselves to the discipline of the marital relationship."[16] Barbara's generation suffered from the sexual double standard. Many women she knew were harmed by midlife divorce because they were not prepared to support themselves economically. These were women who took their identity from their husbands; they were known as "somebody's wife." This was particularly damaging to foreign service wives who accompanied their husbands abroad but who were prohibited from working. They contributed to their husbands' success by being gracious hostesses, but they lost their pension rights when they divorced. These women won a class-action lawsuit in the 1980s restoring their pension rights.

Unlike previous generations, Barbara's did have the benefit of modern birth control. Her grandmother died at age fifty after having thirteen children. Her mother had five children. In 1965, the Supreme Court in *Griswold v. Connecticut* stated that married couples had a right to privacy that included the right to use contraceptive devices. By 1985, 68 percent of couples in the United States used some form of contraception.

Barbara lived and worked in a separate sphere, raising children full time for ten years. In this way, her life was like Dorothy's. But, like Dorothy's daughter, Barbara also experienced the COBF when she went to work for pay; she was still responsible for the children and the house. She worked a second shift for eleven years, although she did have some household help. She has some elder care responsibilities. She does have a woman to help with housecleaning.

In her thirties, when she had young children, Barbara lived through, and was interested in, the early politics of the women's movement. When Barbara was thirty-one and caring for two preschoolers, Congress passed the 1964 Civil Rights Act, Title VII, prohibiting discrimination in employment by sex.

When Barbara was thirty-four and caring for one preschooler aged four and a school-aged child of eight, the National Organization of Women was formed to get the Equal Employment Opportunity Commission to enforce Title VII.

When Barbara was thirty-six and was caring for two school-aged children, the Women's Equity Action League formed as a breakaway group from NOW over the issues of abortion and lesbianism. This group focused on employment issues for women. Barbara was involved with this group on employment discrimination cases before she went back to work. She also did volunteer work at the library of her children's schools and taught U.S. history to teenage expectant mothers.

When Barbara was thirty-seven, she earned her Ph.D. Two years later, the 1972 Education Amendments to the Civil Rights Act of 1964 were enacted, prohibiting educational institutions from discrimination against women. This led to the opening up of men's colleges to women.

When Barbara was thirty-nine in 1972, Congress sent the Equal Rights Amendment to the states for ratification and the National Women's Political Caucus challenged the Democratic and Republican parties on the lack of women delegates to their national conventions. Back in 1968, only thirteen Democratic women and seventeen Republican women were delegates; in 1972, forty Democratic women and thirty Republican women were delegates.[17]

In her 40s, Barbara lived through the heyday of the second wave of the women's movement as a mother of school-aged children. By the end of the wave, she had completed twenty-one years of childrearing (1960 to 1981). When Barbara was forty-four, the Congresswomen's Caucus was formed by fifteen women representatives in the House. When she was forty-eight, they admitted men and changed the name to the Congressional Caucus on Women's Issues. Later, in 1981, the Caucus introduced the Economic Equity Act on survival issues, pensions, child care, and insurance—setting the agenda for the 1980s.

When Barbara was forty-five, Congress extended the ratification deadline for the Equal Rights Amendment to 1982. When Barbara was forty-nine, the Equal Rights Amendment failed to get three-quarters of the states to ratify; obtaining only thirty-five of the thirty-eight states needed for ratification. Barbara published an article in her professional journal on why the ERA failed.

The political COBF is that women are excluded from public life. Barbara un-excluded herself and protested such exclusion by her involvement in the events of her time. She got herself a Ph.D. in political science. She has been researching and writing about women in public life throughout her professional career.

As to the educational COBF, Barbara's mother had only completed the eighth grade, but Barbara earned a Ph.D. Many of Barbara's peers put their husbands through law school and medical school, subordinating their own desires. Well after their husbands were launched on their careers, many of her friends also returned to school for graduate degrees.

Barbara has lost family and friends to breast cancer. It seems to be the scourge of her generation. She feels that women's health has not been given much attention until recently.

Sum-Up for Barbara and the 1950s Women

- What is the COBF if you stay in the traditional gender role? Barbara had ten years in the separate sphere. She was economically dependent on her husband and was excluded from the world of work and politics.
- Then she had eleven years of the second shift when she went to work for pay, but she was still responsible for the children and the house. This meant more work and less leisure. She had twenty-one years of childrearing. Which held the higher COBF for her: the separate sphere or the second shift?
- She was excluded from her first professional goal in the 1950s, publishing. She did achieve her goal of becoming a college professor.
- Going to school part-time and being exposed to the "chilly climate" in the classroom worked against her on the job market. She never had a female professor to mentor her during her Ph.D. coursework. She entered the field late and may not make it to the top rank. Many of her friends never realized their aspirations. Some had four or five children to raise, and unlike Barbara, their husbands were not sympathetic to their career goals.

Barbara has economic security. She benefited from great educational opportunities. She raised a family and has a career. She has gone further than most women of her generation. She has some economic and social independence as a result of her education and employment.

However, she is rightly angry at the injustice of the COBF. She is concerned for her daughter's generation which has entered the workplace with most of the barriers down, but a workplace that she sees as still structured according to male preferences.

JENNIFER, A WOMAN OF THE "POSTFEMINIST" ERA

Jennifer was born in 1963, the year before Title VII of the Civil Rights Act prohibited sex discrimination in employment. In the year of her birth, her mother, Barbara, was working on a Ph.D. However, family responsibilities always had priority, and her mother stayed home for ten years with Jennifer and her older brother. Jennifer was a little girl in the prosperous 1960s.

In the 1970s, during the second wave of the women's movement, Jennifer had a working mother. When Jennifer was eight, her mother returned to work part-time. When Jennifer was thirteen, her mother was working full time. Jennifer grew up with no sense that girls and boys might have different career paths.

However, in the 1980s, the spirit of the times had changed. Jennifer graduated from high school in 1981 a year before the *New York Times* announced the beginning of the postfeminist era. She attended college during the early 1980s, the beginning of what Susan Faludi called the "backlash" against women. On the other hand, the issues of date rape and sexual harassment in the classroom made a moderate feminist of Jennifer—although by then, feminist was a dirty word.

After college, Jennifer worked for two years for a small organization headed by a man and staffed by women. Opportunities for advancement were limited. In her spare time, Jennifer did volunteer work in the Hispanic community. She also had time for sports and other recreation.

She then went to law school, where she saw sexism on the part of both men and women. For three years she has been working in a private law firm learning litigation. She doesn't like what she sees. The men lawyers don't listen to the women lawyers. Women lawyers with children work late at night and on weekends. They bow to male standards, she feels.

Jennifer is thirty now, single, and wondering whether she can ever have a personal life or whether she must sacrifice it to her career.

Jennifer has made inroads into a "masculine" career. In 1970, only 5 percent of lawyers were women; by 1989, 22 percent were.[18] Estimates today are approaching 30 percent and are rising. Many law schools today have nearly 50 percent female enrollment. Jennifer is in the vanguard of these developments. The COBF has been somewhat reduced for her in that she was able to enter the legal profession.

Jennifer has role models to aspire to that earlier generations of women did not have, including for example, her mother Barbara, the college professor. In 1977, the first woman U.S. attorney, Virginia Dill McCarthy of

Indiana, was appointed.[19] Janet Reno became our first woman attorney general in 1993. And now we have our second woman on the Supreme Court, Ruth Bader Ginsburg.

There is a little less occupational segregation now, but it takes a more subtle form—such as segregation within occupations and "glass ceilings." Now that Jennifer has been practicing law for three years, she notes that the number of women partners in her firm is low. The pace of work is intense. Decisions to travel are made at the last minute. She observes that women lawyers with children are working late nights and weekends, and travel frequently. It looks to her that she must choose between career and family, a choice men don't seem to have to make. She is on a partner-track, but the hierarchical style of the firm makes her angry; "It's so macho," she says. "Men don't listen to the women partners."

The economic COBF for young, unmarried, educated women has been reduced at last. The earnings ratio that was stuck at 66 percent for so many decades is starting to rise for these women. Their ratio is about 71 percent.[20]

Jennifer would like to leave the male world of private corporate litigation and move into public law or city planning. She has done some *pro bono* work, which she finds more satisfying than her conventional work. She likes helping individuals; money is secondary to feeling useful. The number of young lawyers leaving the private practice of law is evidence that this feeling is widespread, she feels.

Jennifer is liberated from some of the constraints of her mother's generation. She doesn't feel she must have her hair done at the beauty shop. She doesn't have to cook every night. Moreover, there has been a sexual revolution between mother and daughter's eras, and thus, there is less need to marry. But she is unhappy being single.

What's wrong with being single? In 1986, *Newsweek* and other magazines wrote about a Harvard–Yale study showing that women who are college-educated and over thirty are not likely to find a husband. Susan Faludi, author of *Backlash,* states that she had not been worrying about marriage, but when she read about the study she felt glum and grouchy. She found that the numbers were actually wrong. But Faludi's protest is against "the morality tale implicit in the research story: if you put off marriage for a career, you face the COST of not being likely to "find" a husband." "Why is it men that get to choose which women marry and which women do not?" she asked. Is it the social custom or practice based on the fact that men earn large incomes and can make the commitment to support the woman and not vice versa? Why does a woman have to be chosen? Does a woman really have to seduce and keep a man? Jennifer says that she "just can't act dumb. If you challenge men, they are put off."

It is harder for women to develop self-esteem and self-confidence. Jennifer hopes that the next generation of women will have less of a problem with this. Here it is the 1990s, and Gloria Steinem has written a book on self-esteem and the need for a revolution from within. Jennifer says that she knows she should be smarter. This is the self-esteem problem. But she also says that she just can't play dumb with men. This is the femininity problem, so well documented by Susan Brownmiller in her book by that name. It is paradoxical that Jennifer has to worry about being too smart and not smart enough.

Jennifer does, however, make more money than her mother. In fact, she makes a lot more money than either Barbara or Nancy.

Many young professionals of this cohort have substantial incomes and can pay for child care. Where are the child care centers and preschool education for the children of such a couple? It is more of a problem of supply than price. Where is the social support for the dual-career family?

In earlier generations when women stayed home, they often had good support systems—grandmothers living in the household or nearby. People were less mobile and tended to stay close to where they were born. Most people worked within "coming home to lunch" distance from their places of employment. Today, average commuting time in large metro areas is two hours a day. Most people do not have close relatives at hand for routine or emergency duty. Yet society has not created the institutions that would replace the network of family and friends.

There has been a wave of antifeminism. The New Right questions the achievement of the second wave of the women's movement.[21] The pro-family movement has taken on feminism as its number one target. They are advocates of the traditional family and women's role in it. They exhort women to be proud to be housewives and mothers. But economic forces make this no longer possible for the average American woman.

When Jennifer was seventeen, in 1980, the U.S. Congress failed to ratify the U.N. Convention for the Elimination of All Forms of Discrimination against Women, which was adopted in Copenhagen. It was ratified by France, China, and Sweden.

The struggle over abortion has heated up: from "Operation Rescue" to the shooting of Dr. David Gunn outside an abortion clinic in Florida in March 1993 by an anti-abortion advocate.

The struggle over sex education continues. When Joycelyn Elders was nominated as surgeon general, she had a hard time at her hearings before the Senate Labor and Human Resources Committee because she is an advocate of sex education and the distribution of condoms in school clinics (summer 1993). Later she was forced to resign for her comments on masturbation upon being asked by the press to state her views.

Has the backlash increased the COBF for Jennifer and her cohorts? Objectively, the evidence is ambiguous. Subjectively, the women are ambivalent. In a recent *Time/CNN* poll, only 29 percent of women consider themselves feminists, but 39 percent say that the women's movement has improved their lives! In addition, 82 percent of women say that women have more freedom than their mothers did, but only 50 percent say that they enjoy their lives more than their mothers did.[22] Freedom is one thing, enjoyment is another. Subjectively, women of this cohort may feel more stress and strain over their roles as women and as human beings. There has been a certain stalling in the advancement of women. However, objectively it must be said that the COBF for Jennifer and her cohorts is less than it is for Barbara and Nancy's generations.

Jennifer went to a girls' high school and then to a co-ed college, unlike her mother, Barbara, who went to a women's college and who teaches in a women's college. She did not personally experience sexism or discrimination.

Jennifer felt that being female helped her get accepted into law school. However, the women she met there were often in law school just to find a husband. Half of the students in law school are women now. The educational COBF for Jennifer and her cohorts is that they are no longer excluded from professional school.

Sum-Up for Jennifer and the 1980s Women

- Although there are still high levels of occupational segregation and a pay gap, highly educated women like Jennifer can make inroads into men's occupations.
- There is still no solution in sight to the second shift problem. Husbands help very little with childrearing and housework, although more men are showing an interest in family life and are willing to participate in the necessary tasks.
- These days feminism, like liberalism, has a bad name. This attitude results in a high subjective cost for these women for the social pressure is back to get married and stay quiet.
- On the plus side, these women do not have the problem of a late start as earlier generations did; almost all fields are open to them.

Objectively, this generation has the most opportunity to participate in the world of work and politics. Subjectively, there is great stress and strain because the gender role revolution is apparently unfinished. Social institutions have not changed to support these new women.

THE COBF ACROSS THE GENERATIONS

Barbara, Nancy, and Jennifer are members of the first three age cohorts of white, middle-class women to join the workforce in the United States. In 1958, when Barbara was the only one of the three in the workforce, only 38 percent of women were working for pay in the United States. She was unusual. Dorothy was more typical in that she did not work for pay once she had children. In 1980, when Nancy was preparing to enter the labor market for college teachers, 51 percent of women in the United States were working for pay. All three of the women who worked for pay encountered occupational segregation. This is in some ways not so different from the separate "feminine" sphere of Dorothy.

The index of occupational segregation reveals what percentage of women must change occupations in order for men and women to be equally distributed across all occupations. Research suggests that Equal Employment Opportunity legislation increased the likelihood of a woman holding a male-dominated job, such as university professor or lawyer. From the time Barbara left the workforce until her daughter Jennifer entered it, the index of segregation fell 17 percentage points, from roughly 74 to 57.

The percentage of college and university teachers who are women rose from 29 in 1970 (when Barbara was about to get her Ph.D. to prepare herself for college teaching) to 39 in 1989 (when Nancy was beginning her career in college teaching).[23]

Another form that occupational segregation takes is that women are more likely to work part-time and, if college teachers, to be on nontenure tracks. According to the American Association of University Professors, many more women than men are on nontenure tracks.

Women may make it into a profession like college teaching, but they don't move up to the top ranks as fast as men, if ever. According to the American Association of University Professors,[24] from the time period when Barbara began as an assistant professor to fifteen years later when Nancy began, the percentage of women who are full professor increased only three points, from 10 to 13 percent.

The wage gap is not an economic COBF for Dorothy as she does not work for pay. In 1955, for the first time, the Women's Bureau of the U.S. Department of Labor calculated the wage gap between men and women. The median annual earnings for year-round, full-time workers was $2,719 for women and $4,252 for men, and so women made 64 cents for each dollar earned by a man. In 1955, Barbara was working at a women's magazine. This was before the Equal Pay Act of 1963, which made it illegal to pay a woman less if she was doing the same job as a man.

By 1990, when Jennifer was working for pay, women earned 72 cents per a man's dollar: Women made on average $19,822, and men $26,678. Jennifer makes a lot more money than either Barbara or Nancy, and therefore she is more economically independent. The 1964 Equal Employment Opportunity legislation passed when Jennifer was one year old and reduced the COBF by eight cents.

Actually, the COBF for Jennifer is even less because if we look at the pay gap for young women (aged 25 to 35), the gap has closed even more. Back when Nancy was between twenty-five and thirty-five years old, the gap for young women was 35 cents; now that Jennifer is in the 25- to 35-year-old range, the gap is down to 26 cents.[25]

The COBF for Barbara who had children is greater than the COBF for Nancy who did not have children. Studies show that women with children make 72 cents for a dollar made by a male with children and women with no children make 91 cents for a dollar made by a male with no children.[26]

In 1974, when Barbara began teaching in college, Nancy Gordon found that, controlling for years of experience and for the number of publications, women college professors earned 10 percent less than men college professors.[27] This book began with the current story of Alice Brick who got a 10 percent raise when it was found that she was being unfairly rewarded for her experience and her publications. Thanks to the movement for pay equity on college campuses, this COBF is decreasing.[28]

Dorothy was not excluded from an excellent education. She studied Latin for four years in her public school in the Midwest. She was fortunate to have the opportunity to earn a B.A. at a state university. But she was atypical for her generation.

When Barbara and Nancy came of age, women were excluded from the professions to a large degree. The only higher education generally available to women at that time was the Ph.D. In 1971–1972, only half as many women as men obtained professional degrees such as the Ph.D.[29] The number of women getting the Ph.D. degree doubled from 1973 to 1988. In 1973, just two years after Barbara got her Ph.D, 18 percent of all Ph.D. degrees went to women. In 1988, just two years after Nancy got her Ph.D., 35 percent of Ph.D. degrees went to women.[30]

In 1972, the equal educational opportunity legislation was passed. The professions opened up to women so that by Jennifer's generation, in 1988, twice as many women got professional degrees as got the Ph.D.[31]

Dorothy did not work a second shift because she did not work a first shift. When Barbara returned to the world of work for pay, she did work a second shift. Her husband was unusually successful and could pay for help with domestic chores, but still, childrearing was a second shift for Barbara for eight years. Nancy has pretty much avoided the second shift by not having children. She and her husband are of the 1960s generation and have a less conventional division of labor in the household. As a single woman on a fast track, the second shift does not have much relevance for Jennifer's life.

Objectively, the COBF is lower now than a generation ago because women have moved out of the separate sphere of the home into economic life. Dorothy did not have this choice. Barbara, Nancy, and Jennifer are working women. It's easier now to be a lawyer, a university professor, a businesswoman, or a physician. The pay gap is less for Jennifer than for Barbara and Nancy.

Women are now freer to move beyond their socially assigned roles. They have more of a chance to develop themselves as human beings in economic or political life and in artistic or scientific life. To the extent that women are having fewer children, the COBF has been reduced. Having children reinforces women's dependence. Jennifer has reproductive rights that Nancy did not have.

There is more political consciousness now about the rights of women as human beings. These rights are still contested, but they are defended. In 1992, the "Year of the Woman," more women were elected to Congress and state and local governments in America than ever before. (Many of these "freshman" women lost in 1994, but the number of women in the House remained constant as they were replaced by Republican women. The number of women in the Senate actually increased!) The Clinton administration has set a record for appointing women to important posts. There were no women on the Supreme Court when Dorothy was young. Now there are two.

There has been a great reduction of the educational COBF. There are more women than men in college now. Women have made inroads in graduate school, law school, medical school, and business school. As for health, the National Institutes of Health have begun to focus research on women's health issues.

On the other hand, the subjective COBF is higher now in certain ways than it was a generation ago, essentially because society has not changed to reflect the increase in women's labor force participation. Women have moved into the workplace, but men have not moved into childrearing and housework. The COBF has increased because women work a second shift. As one woman who works for a child advocacy group said, "Americans pretend that women don't work and that's how they can rationalize the lack of quality child care facilities in the United States." The COBF has increased because many women have to work and have to worry about their children due to lack of universal, quality, affordable child care. The subjective COBF emerged because women's new opportunities produced new psychological strains.

A second reason why the cost is higher now is that the COBF increases when a woman questions her role as a woman. The COBF was not great for women who stayed in their separate spheres. Dorothy did not question her role as a woman and thus felt little stress and strain. The COBF was increased for Barbara as she worked on her career and combined it with childrearing. The COBF was increased for Nancy because she tried to break into a male-dominated occupation. The COBF for Jennifer in this sense is the highest: she walked right into the male world of law. When a woman today tries to combine productive activity in economic life with her social role of raising children and keeping a home, a role conflict emerges. This is a psychological COBF.

In some ways, the COBF is the same now as it was a generation ago because women still have less control over their lives than men. The patterns of their lives tend to be more reactive than proactive. Women still have less power to make decisions. They have less bargaining power in marriage, especially if they have children. And even if they don't have children, they can rarely make as much money as men can. Men are still dominant socially. Men still control politics, corporate life, the media, and the law.

It is not possible to add up the economic, political, social, educational, and health costs of being female, and thus we cannot have a unitary COBF. In the conclusion, we quantify the costs of being female in a five-part index.

Across the generations, women have, for the most part, lived by male rules. What impact have men had on women's lives? Clear patterns of dependency emerge from our study.

When middle-class women stayed at home and were the center of family life, they were totally dependent on their husbands for their economic security. Moreover, they were dependent on them for a perspective on the world outside the household. Their political judgments, particularly voting, most often reflected their husbands' opinions. They were generally less educated than their husbands and deferred to them on most matters, except for everyday household management.

The transitional generation, the generation of middle-class women who came of age in the 1950s, served as a bridge for their younger sisters and daughters. They were as qualified as men, but their husbands' careers always came first. They used their considerable organizational skills in all sorts of volunteer activities—running auctions, bazaars and charity events. They knew they could have competed in the working world, but they could not gain entry. We undoubtedly lost many potential judges, research scientists, and corporate executives as a result. These women were very much dependent on their husbands for economic support, and their social roles were clearly delineated as wives and mothers.

Women in the 1960s and 1970s, more liberated than their older sisters sexually, did not feel the need to marry immediately. Some decided not to have children, and to pursue their own careers instead. They did not want to be dependent on men; they wanted independence. These yearnings for independence set in motion many divorces based on women's desires to assert themselves as individuals outside marriage.

In the 1980s and 1990s, men's roles and expectations had also shifted. If women were able to support themselves and, in many instances, take "men's" jobs as a consequence of affirmative action initiatives, then why did men have to play the role of provider? Males' commitment to being the economic mainstay of a partnership or family unit was on the wane. If women wanted equality, they could forget protection.

On the other hand, we note some movement that should have an impact

Table 9
The COBF across the Generations

Barbara's grandmother *came to America at the close of nineteenth century*	Barbara's mother *continued big-family lifestyle. Left NYC for suburbs*	Barbara *career and family*	Barbara's daughter *dilemma of career and family*
(1) Worked in husband's store	Lived in separate sphere	Not trained for a career	Trained for a career, glass ceiling
(2) No women in Congress	One woman in Congress	Handful of women in Congress	5 percent of Congress are women
(3) 13 children, no contraceptives	5 children, 35 years childrearing; no contraceptives	2 children, prime childrearing	Pressures associated with choosing between or balancing career and family Economy may necessitate dual incomes Quality and expense of available childcare an issue
(4) Immigrant, literate	8th grade	Ph.D.	J.D.
(5) Died at 50	Died at 68	Exercise Nutrition Safer childbearing Two sisters died of breast cancer	Has personal trainer Has own exercise machinery

Note: (1) Economic COBF, (2) Political COBF, (3) Social COBF, (4) Educational COBF, (5) Health COBF.

on everyone's lives in the twenty-first century. That is an increasing realization among men, now working and competing with women in the same occupational environment, that the rules of the workplace are not congenial to family life. Men, as well as women, are asking for government and business to adopt policies that make it possible to lead more balanced lives—family leave with pay, longer maternity leaves, on-site daycare centers, shorter work weeks, and more flexible work schedules.

To sum up our view on the COBF over the generations, we created Table 9 about one of our interviewees, Barbara. We bring together the economic, political, social, education, and health COBF for Barbara's grandmother, her mother, herself, and her daughter.

NOTES

1. John Patrick Diggins, *The Proud Decades: America in War and Peace, 1941–1960* (New York: W. W. Norton, 1988), p. 183.

2. Morley Gunderson, "Male-Female Wage Differentials and Policy Responses," *Journal of Economic Literature* 27 (March 1989): 47.

3. Marian Wright Edelson, *The Measure of Our Success: A Letter to My Children and Yours*, p. 88.

4. If women survive childbirth, they outlive men. Further research is needed to determine when maternal mortality decreased enough for the life expectancy rate of women to exceed that of men. Bangladesh is a country today where so many women die in childbirth that their life expectancy is less than that of men.

5. Claudia Goldin, *Understanding the Gender Gap: An Economic History of American Women*, (New York: Oxford University Press, 1990), pp. 144–145.

6. Ibid.

7. *Ms.*, 20 years of the U.S. Women's Movement, 1972 to 1992.

8. Barbara F. Reskin and Patricia A. Roos, *Job Queues, Gender Queues: Explaining Women's Inroads into Male Occupations* (Philadelphia: Temple University Press, 1990), pp. 54, 301.

9. Irwin Garfinkel and Sara S. McLanahan, *Single Women and Their Children*, p. 159, citing *Family Planning Perspectives* 4, no. 1 (1982).

10. Victor Fuchs, "Sex Differences in Economic Well-being," *Science* (April 1986): 18.

11. William Chafe, *The Paradox of Change: American Women in the 20th century* (New York: Oxford University Press, 1991), pp. 210–211.

12. *Ms.*, 20th anniversary issue.

13. Ibid.

14. Reskin and Roos.

15. Phyllis Rose, *Parallel Lives: Five Victorian Marriages* (New York: Vintage Books, 1983).

16. Ibid., p. 19.

17. Chafe, p. 216.

18. Francine D. Blau and Marianne A. Ferber, *The Economics of Women, Men, and Work*, 2nd ed. (Englewood Cliffs, N.J.: Prentice-Hall, 1992), p. 124.

19. *Ms.*, 20th anniversary issue.

20. Fuchs, p. 18.

21. See Tanya Mellich, *The Republican War Against Women: An Insider's Report from Behind the Lines* (New York: Bantam Books, 1996).

22. "NOW's 25th anniversary," *Washington Post*, January 11, 1992.

23. Blau and Ferber.

24. Cited in ibid., p. 125.

25. June O'Neill, "Women and Wages," *The American Enterprise* (November–December 1990): 24–33.

26. Ibid.

27. Nancy Gordon, "Faculty Salaries: Is Their Discrimination by Sex, Race, and Discipline?" *American Economic Review* (1974).

28. Mary Gray, "Achieving Pay Equity on Campus," (American Association of University Professors, 1992).

29. Ronald G. Ehrenberg, "The Flow of New Doctorates," *Journal of Economic Literature* (1992).

30. Ibid.

31. Ibid.

CONCLUSION: REDUCING THE COST OF BEING FEMALE IN THE TWENTY-FIRST CENTURY

This book has explored the costs of being female. We have reviewed data gathered in dozens of studies which have illustrated these costs. Women have earned less, experienced more social inequities as a result of marriage, divorce, and their responsibilities for child care, have been excluded from politics and policy-making, and until recently have been denied equal opportunity in education and equal expenditures in health research.

There is a long history of treating women differently from men and, accordingly, rewarding them differently. We can trace this treatment back to earliest civilization. To this day, patterns of male domination and female subordination persist in different degrees throughout industrial and developing societies. Feminists have sounded alarm bells to alert contemporary societies to the injustices they are perpetuating.

Even though much discrimination is grounded in superstition and no longer has any relevance to modern life, gender remains an unconscious factor in organizing today's society. Why, as late as the second half of the twentieth century, were women forced to leave their jobs when they were pregnant? What kind of mind-set ordered that pregnant women were not to be seen in public? What belief systems refused to permit women to be ordained as ministers or rabbis? Why were women not considered as candidates for university presidents until the 1970s? Why have women continued to be paid less than men? Why have banks systematically denied credit to prospective female householders?

These questions disturb us because women have paid a price for policies and practices that have been accepted in a context where overwhelming numbers of women work and are the sole support of their families. Children then become the unfortunate victims of this discrimination. And the impact on society is devastating.

As we reviewed the data, and as women told us their stories, we had two strong reactions. First, we were horrified to realize how many inequities women had accepted for centuries, and second, we were gratified to see that there has been progress: the availability of education and training for women; more attention to women's health problems; the expansion of jobs and careers open to them; and the increasing numbers of women entering public life. It seems that we are on the road to equality, or at least to fair treatment.

Many obstacles remain. As with any cure, there are troublesome side effects. As women of this generation walk through doors closed to their mothers and grandmothers and enter law schools and law firms, medical schools and medical practice, become letter carriers and bus and truck drivers, police officers and fire fighters, airline pilots and military officers, they now encounter problems in advancing. These problems are so rampant that a new term for them has entered the vocabulary—the glass ceiling.

As we discussed in Chapter 9, the Industrial Revolution separated work and family, placing full responsibility on the woman for housework and child care. This division persists today. During and after the world wars, as women entered the workforce in great numbers, they continued to do their "housework" as well as their paid work. We conclude from our narratives and statistical studies that if women are engaged in work outside the home, the burdens of running that home ought to be shared by men.

The economics of modern life, leading to the two-income family (sometimes the three- or four-income family), is not conducive to childrearing or a tranquil life. We have observed other systems which work better, at least for motherhood and child care—for example the Scandinavian maternity/paternity leave guarantee and the French preschools. However, these initiatives occur within cultures in which women are not considered equal in professional or corporate life.

QUANTIFYING OUR FINDINGS

In the Introduction to the book, we proposed constructing a COBF index. We wanted to chart the costs that result from unequal gender relations. Table 10 presents five indices, one for each dimension of the cost of being female. In the first part of the table, we use the indices to compare the COBF across five countries; in the second part of the table, to compare the COBF in the United States across three time periods. We realize that the categories of our indices are not commensurate. There is no common

Table 10
The COBF Index

	Wage Gap[a] (1)	Representation Gap[b] (1)	Social COBF[c] (3)	Health COBF[d] (4)	Educational Gap[e] (5)
United States	59	10	2.0	13	110
France	81	6	1.8	13	97
Sweden	90	33	2.0	7	110
Norway	87	39	1.9	4	113
China	77	21	2.3	44	42
United States Today	71	10	2.0	13	30
United States After WW II	64	1	2.5	207	11
United States Before WW I	46	0	5.0	608	6

a Female earnings as percentage of male, 1990–1992.

b Percentage of seats occupied by women, 1992.

c Total fertility rate: children per woman, 1992.

d Maternal mortality rates per 100,000 live births, 1988.

e Ratio of female to male graduates from college, 1991; percent of females graduating college, 1945, 1900.

Sources: (1) Economic COBF: UNDP, *Human Development Report 1994* (New York: Oxford University Press, 1994), p. 185. China statistics from *Women in China*, Beijing, January 1996; The Women's Bureau, Division of Statistical and Economic Analysis, December 1993, "Comparison of Median Earnings of Year-Round Full-Time Workers, by Sex, 1955–1992"; Claudia Goldin, *Understanding the Gender Gap: An Economic History of American Women* (New York: Oxford University Press, 1990), p. 60. (2) Political COBF: Barbara Nelson and Najma Chowdhury, eds., *Women and Politics Worldwide* (New Haven, Conn.: Yale University Press, 1994). (3) Social COBF: UNDP, *Human Development Report 1994*, pp. 201, 174; Bureau of the Census, *Historical Statistics of the United States, Colonial Times to 1970, Bicentennial Edition, Part I* (Washington, D.C.: Government Printing Office, 1975), p. 50; Jeremy Atack and Fred Bateman, *To Their Own Soil: Agriculture and the Antebellum North* (Ames, Iowa: Iowa State University, 1987), p. 63. (4) Health COBF: UNDP, *Human Development Report 1994*, p. 189; U.S. Bureau of the Census, *Historical Statistics of the United States*, p. 57. (5) Education COBF: Nelson and Chowdhury; Goldin. 145.

metric between, say, loss of a vote and gain of employment or of state-provided child care. Since there can be no single composite measure of the COBF, we have to describe the COBF in its five separate dimensions. First, we must consider each dimension's index individually, and then we must consider them like a five-part package.

The economic COBF was initially easy to quantify because the difference in pay earned by women and men has been well documented in the post–World War II era. Since the "unfair" part of the earnings gap, that part explained by discrimination (see Chapter 1 for a fuller explanation), is difficult to estimate, and few studies have attempted to do it, we use the whole gender earnings gap as a proxy for the unfair part. There is a long history of using proxies in historical social science research, but the proxy provides only a suggestion of the discrimination that exists in the pay gap. It is not an exact measure of the unfair part of that gap.

We estimate the political COBF by using the percentage of representatives in the lower houses of the national legislature who are female. This serves as a proxy for the level of female participation in politics in general.

Since women have historically borne the burden of childbearing and rearing, we selected total fertility for our measure of the social COBF. This is a proxy for a very complicated and evolving social phenomenon. The health COBF is related to the biological fact that women bear children, and we measure it by maternal mortality rates. The index is the number of mothers who died in childbirth per 100,000 live births. This is strictly a female health cost and has been of concern over the centuries. It is a good proxy for the overall health of women.

As a measure of the educational COBF, we use the proportion of college graduates who are women for our international comparisons. However, to make comparisons with the past, we had to use another data set. So few women went to college in the nineteenth century that the ratios would not have been very useful anyway. Moreover, the only numbers we found were the percentage of white women graduating from college.

Here is a guide to reading Table 10, the COBF index. Let us start with the United States and read that row across the table. What it says is that the economic cost of being female in the United States today is that women earn only 59 percent of what men earn; the political COBF is that only 10 percent of our representatives in the House are female when half the population is female; the social COBF is that American women have primary responsibility for rearing 2 children on average; the health COBF is that 13 mothers die in childbirth per 100,000 live births; and the educational COBF is actually not a cost, but a benefit in that the ratio of female to male college graduates is 110. This means that more women than men are graduating from college in the United States.

Why do we have two different statistics for the economic COBF in the United States, 71 and 59? Throughout this volume we have used statistics from the Women's Bureau of the U.S. Department of Labor. Using their method and their sample, the economic COBF in 1992 is that women on average earn 71 percent of what men earn. To make cross country comparisons, the United National Development Program uses another method and sample. They find that the economic COBF in the United States is 59 percent.

Now let's use the COBF index to see how countries compare in the status of women. Read down the first column of the table to see how the economic COBF compares in the four countries we have included. The economic COBF is lowest in Sweden where women earn 90 percent of what men earn. Norway is close behind at 87 percent, and in France the figure is 81 percent. The United States, with only 59 percent, is in the worst position.

Scandinavia is also very good, relatively speaking, on the political COBF. In Norway, 39 percent of the legislature is female, and in Sweden, 33 percent. American women do a little better than the French with 10 percent female elected representatives compared to only 6 percent in France. Although 21 percent of the Chinese legislature is female, the system is not democratic, and the legislature does not have the power of European or U.S. legislatures.

In the health COBF, Scandinavia scores relatively better than the United States and France. In Norway, only 4 women die in childbirth for every 100,000 live births; in Sweden 7 die. In the United States and France, 13 women die per 100,000 live deliveries. In China, 44 die.

Finally, in the educational COBF, the indices of 113 for Norway, and 110 for the United States and for Sweden mean that more women than men are graduating from college in these countries. In France women are getting just under their share of spaces in higher education at an index of 97. In China, the index of women to men in higher education is 42. For a developing country, they score relatively well.

Let us now examine the COBF index across time periods. Table 10 shows the five indices for three points in American history. Let's begin with the economic COBF index. As you can see in the first column, the economic COBF has declined slightly over time. When the wage gap was first measured by the Women's Bureau in 1955, women earned on average 63.9 percent of what men earned. By the time the Women's Bureau made its calculations for the year 1992, women were earning 70.6 percent of what men earned. (This figure differs from the U.N. figure of 59 percent because it uses a different method and different sample). Claudia Goldin estimates that the earnings ratio in manufacturing in 1885 was between 46 and 51 percent.

The political COBF, though high, has fallen somewhat. Until 1917 when Jeannette Rankin became the first woman elected to the U.S. House of Representatives, there were no women representatives in our lower house. As late as 1955, only 1 percent of the House was female, and by 1994 it was only 10 percent. If this body is to be truly representative, the figure should be at least 50 percent.

The social COBF has declined in the United States. Before World War I, as far back as 1860, on farms in the Midwest, women had on average five children. The index declines to 2.5 children per woman on average in 1945, a reduction of 50 percent. The index is 2 children per woman in 1992.

Great progress has been made in reducing the health COBF in the United States. In 1915, 608 women died in childbirth per 100,000 live births. As late as 1945, that index was 207 women's deaths. Even in 1992, 13 women died in childbirth per 100,000 live births.

The educational COBF in the United States has also been reduced. In 1900, only 6 percent of white women in the population graduated from college; 11 percent in 1930; and in 1960, 30 percent.

As the declining indices show, progress has been made on all five dimensions of the COBF. Yet discrimination against women persists in employment as evidenced by the economic COBF index. Although women now have the education and have increased their work experience, they earn only 71 percent of what men earn. And there is still discrimination against women in politics, with only 10 percent of our democratically elected lower house being female.

POLICY RECOMMENDATIONS

1. Promote child care and universal preschools. The most important thing we could do to reduce the COBF in the United States today would be to subsidize child care. A universal program could be financed by a sliding scale for parents of differing incomes, by employers' contributions, and by local, state, and federal tax dollars. This investment would pay off in increased productivity for today's workers and would produce better workers and citizens for the future. Financing an expanded child care system could be budget neutral because affordable child care would allow more women to work and thus add to tax revenues.

We should raise the status of child care providers by requiring, as the French do, high standards of education and training. We believe that quality personnel results in quality care and education and that working in the area of child care should be valued and rewarded.

2. Eliminate discrimination against women in employment by enforcing Title VII of the Civil Rights Act of 1964. Although we have equal pay and equal employment opportunity laws on the books, they are not enforced energetically. The Equal Employment Opportunity Commission needs more resources in order to help people sue if they are victims of discrimination. This agency enforces the 1963 Equal Pay Act and Title VII of the 1964 Civil Rights Act, which prohibits discrimination against women in employment for firms that employ more than fifteen people. Since the Civil Rights Act of 1991, women may sue for punitive damages for intentional discrimination.

3. Legislate paid family leave for men and women. As early as 1920 when the Women's Bureau was founded, one of its first tasks was to try to obtain maternity leave for women workers. Finally in 1993, the U.S. Congress passed and the president signed the Family and Medical Leave Act providing for six weeks of unpaid leave. The United States was the last of the twenty-four OECD (Organization for Economic Cooperation and Development) countries to provide for family leave. But it is unpaid leave, and thus not many people can afford to take advantage of it.

According to economist Heidi Hartmann, in testimony before a congressional committee in 1991, paid family leave would cost business less than $200 million a year, compared to the over $600 million a year that women lose when they have a child and do not have the right to return to their jobs.

4. Provide public support for family planning. We believe in the reproductive rights of women. We need to provide all women, rich and poor, with methods of family planning, contraception, and the right to abortion if necessary, but hopefully avoided. The U.S. government is now supporting family planning for women in developing countries. We need to do more in our own country. Title X for family planning needs more funding.

5. Legislate public financing of elections. Men have traditionally had the edge in raising money for campaigns. This is beginning to change as women develop campaign skills, but we believe it would be fairer for everyone to put limits on campaign spending and to finance campaigns from public funds. We believe that this would lower the political costs of being female by eroding the "old-boy" network. Public financing would level the playing field and open politics to women, minorities, and other challengers. It would also benefit everyone to shorten the campaign season.

6. Reform the tax system and social security. The social security and the federal income tax systems were set up for the traditional family of the "breadwinner father" and the "homemaker mother." We should change the income tax system by taxing individuals, not couples. Joint returns discriminate against working wives. Sweden has already done away with joint returns and taxes each person individually. We should change the social security system to reflect the economic emergence of women. Everyone should have his or her own pension as in Sweden, and not have to depend on a spouse's pension.

In addition, we recommend recognizing the value of "homework," the hours women work in caregiving, through some form of tax relief.

7. Promote mathematics and science education for girls and women. Although American women attend colleges in greater numbers than men, they tend to avoid math and science courses and stay within the traditional areas of study for women—the humanities and fine arts. This is one reason why women earn less than men. We believe girls and women should be encouraged to pursue studies in math and science from a very early age on to the university level. Under the Women's Education Equity Act, the federal government is obligated to fund programs designed to further this goal. However, these programs are notoriously underfunded.

8. Promote women's health. The Women's Health Initiative promises to be very helpful to women, but we must keep up the pressure for increased research on diseases specific to women, as well as on women's experiences with the diseases of both men and women, for example, heart disease and arthritis. Procedures like mammograms should be accessible to all women who need them. We should reduce the costs of childbearing by providing reproductive health services to all women.

The link between poverty and poor health has been proved in both industrialized and developing economies. Since more women than men are poor, women's health suffers. We propose universal health care as a benefit to women, children, and society generally.

9. Give incentives to the private sector to offer family friendly policies. When it benefits business, business will provide. We want government at all levels to give tax breaks, subsidies—whatever it takes—to encourage firms to provide child care on the premises, paid maternity and paternity leave, and flexible work schedules that permit employees to take care of family obligations. We believe productivity will increase as a result.

10. Encourage the private sector to help reentry into the workplace. In the postindustrial society, many people will have several jobs in their working lives and often more than one career. Women and men who take time out to retrain or reeducate themselves, or to handle family responsibilities, should be accepted as serious workers when they return. We do not expect them to reenter as though no time had passed, but to reenter without penalty or stigma.

We recommend these policies because sexism is costly and unjust. Gender discrimination prevents half of our population from moving up as far as their talents will bring them and deprives the nation of the best use of its human capital. Two-thirds of the net additions to the workforce in the year 2000 will be women and minorities. If we paid women better, we would have less poverty among female heads of household and fewer women on welfare. Furthermore, utilizing the talents of women gives us a comparative advantage relative to Japan where women do not play as important a role in the workforce as they do in the United States. Finally, as a matter of simple justice, fairness, and human decency, we should eliminate discrimination against women.

APPENDIX: THE WOMEN IN THE NARRATIVES

In preparation for this book, we interviewed more than seventy women in the past five years. To protect the privacy of some of the interviewees, we have changed their names. Other women whom we interviewed hold public positions, and so we have used their real names.

Our sample is representative by age, class, and race. We talked to women whose ages range from 18 to 95; African American and white, from the working, middle, and upper middle classes; who are letter carriers, factory workers, lawyers, doctors, and members of Congress.

UNITED STATES

Alice Brick, college professor

Caroline, desktop publishing operator

Shantel, mail carrier

Mary Lou, retired secretary

Meg, physician

Berdie, machine operator

Cindy, forklift operator

Debbie, manager

Juanita, piece worker on an assembly line

Linda, state government employee

Rose, police officer in a rural county

Agnes, Ph.D. in economics

Pat, former employee of Veterans Administration

Mary, doctor's wife

Mary Ann, college professor

Kim, nursing student

Maria, student

Debbie, secretary, single

Monica, M.A. in economics

Dorothy, doctor's wife

Barbara, college professor

Nancy, college professor

Jennifer, lawyer

Dianne L. Wade, captain and pilot for Midwest Express Airlines

Dr. Vivian Pinn, director of the Women's Health Initiative at the National Institutes of Health

Frances Davidson, nutritionist for the Agency for International Development

Dr. Eleanor Sorrentino, psychiatrist

Elinor Lander Horwitz, editor, *Outlook* magazine, American Association of University Women magazine

Leslie Gladstone, Congressional Research Service, senior legislative analyst

Julie Timmons, Women's Campaign Fund

Karin Johanson, EMILY's List

Representative Constance A. Morella (R-Md.)

Representative Barbara Rose Collins (D-Mich.)

Mary Boergers, former member of the Maryland State Senate, 1994 gubernatorial candidate in Maryland

Carol Berman, advocate and member of governing board for Zero to Three (Child Development Group)

Dr. Susan Bertram Eisner, assistant professor of education and co-director, Onica Prall Lab School, Hood College

Doris Ablard, Head Start consultant

Dr. Edith Corliss, retired physicist, National Bureau of Standards

Natalie Leibowitz, retired pension fund administrator

NORWAY

Sverre Mauritzen, Conservative member of Parliament active on family issues

Annelise Hoeth, minority leader for Conservatives in Parliament

Kjellborg Lunde, Socialist member of Parliament active on women's issues

Marit Orheim Mauritzen, owner of a resort hotel in Norway, active in hotel owners association

Arni Hole, member of National Science Board and representative to the European Union on science issues

Fride Ege-Hendricksen, director of Women's Studies at the University of Oslo

SWEDEN

Lillemor Sillen, communications director for the Swedish equivalent of our EEOC

Peter Maripuu, young husband who is on paternity leave to raise his child

Bo Johnson, retired shipping executive

Birgitta, retired librarian

FRANCE

Marianne, physician

Simone, French Telecom employee

Veronique, dress shop owner

Edith, journalist

Catherine, librarian

Irene, travel agent

Monique, cleaning woman

Sylvie, student

M. Michel Forget, chief of French education in North America, French Embassy, Washington, D.C.

Mme. E. Durand, deputy secretary of education

Mlle. M. Durif, regional director of Les Ecoles Maternelles in Paris

Three principals and several teachers at three *écoles maternelles*

Families of former students and friends

CHINA

Wang Haiyan, Embassy of China, Washington, D.C.

Li Jing Yu, Embassy of China, Washington, D.C.

Lu Wei, Chinese Association for International Friendly Contact, Beijing

Tian Ling, Chinese graduate student in Hong Kong

Chen Jian, Civil Service, Municipal Government of Shanghai

Li Quian, Public Relations, Stock Exchange, Shanghai

Liu Xia Ping, China Chamber of Commerce, Guangzhou

Li Li, Chinese Association for International Friendly Contact, Beijing

SELECTED BIBLIOGRAPHY

Adelman, Clifford. *Women at Thirtysomething: Paradoxes of Attainment.* 2nd ed. Washington, D.C.: U.S. Department of Education, 1992.

———. *Lessons of a Generation.* San Francisco: Jossey-Bass, 1994.

American Association of University Women Report. *How Schools Shortchange Girls.* Washington, D.C., 1992.

Barrett, Nancy. "Women." In *Human Capital and America's Future: An Economic Strategy for the '90s.* Edited by David W. Hornbeck and Lester M. Salamon. Baltimore: Johns Hopkins University Press, 1991.

Batten, Mary. *Sexual Strategies: How Females Choose Their Mates.* New York: G. P. Putnam's Sons, 1992.

Becker, Gary. *Economics of Discrimination.* 2nd ed. Chicago: University of Chicago Press, 1971.

Beller, Andrea H. "Changes in the Sex Composition of U.S. Occupations, 1960–1981." *Journal of Human Resources* 20, no. 2 (1985).

Bergmann, Barbara. *The Economic Emergence of Women.* New York: Basic Books, 1986.

Bickel, Janet. "Women in Medical School." *The American Woman 1990–91: A Status Report.* New York: W. W. Norton, 1990.

Blau, Francine, and Marianne Ferber. *The Economics of Women, Men and Work.* 2nd ed. Englewood Cliffs, N.J.: Prentice-Hall, 1992.

———, and Andrea Beller. "Trends in Earning Differentials by Gender, 1971–1981." *Industrial and Labor Relations Review* 41, no. 4 (July 1988).

Blinder, Alan S. "Wage Discrimination: Reduced Form and Structural Estimates." *Journal of Human Resources* 8, no. 4 (1973).

Buek, Alexandra Polyzoides, and Jeffrey H. Orleans. "Sex Discrimination—A Bar to a Democratic Education: Overview of Title IX of the Education Amendments of 1972." *Connecticut Law Review* 6, no. 1 (Fall 1973): 1–27.

Burrell, Barbara. *A Woman's Place Is in the House: Campaigning for Congress in the Feminist Era.* Ann Arbor: University of Michigan Press, 1994.

Chafe, William. *The Paradox of Change: American Women in the 20th Century.* New York: Oxford University Press, 1991.

Congressional Research Service. "An Estimate of the Loss in Potential Gross National Product Due to Existing Employment, Productivity, and Wage Differentials between White and Nonwhite Workers in the United States." Washington, D.C.: Library of Congress, 1979.

Conly, Shanti R., and Sharon I. Camp. *China's Family Planning Program: Challenging the Myths.* Washington, D.C.: Population Crisis Committee, 1992.

Conway, M. Margaret, David W. Ahern, and Gertrude A. Steuernagel. *Women and Public Policy.* Washington, D.C.: Congressional Quarterly Press, 1995.

Corcoran, Mary, and Greg J. Duncan. "Work History, Labor Force Attachment, and Earnings Differences between the Races and Sexes." *Journal of Human Resources* (Winter 1979).

Darcy, Robert, Susan Welch, and Janet Clark. *Women, Elections and Representation.* New York: Longman, 1987.

Dubois, Ellen Carol. *Feminism and Suffrage.* Ithaca, N.Y.: Cornell University Press, 1978.

Duke, Lois Lovelace, ed. *Women in Politics: Outsiders or Insiders?* Englewood Cliffs, N.J.: Prentice-Hall, 1993.

Elshtain, Jean Bethke. *Public Man, Private Woman in Social and Political Thought.* Princeton, N.J.: Princeton University Press, 1981.

Faludi, Susan. *Backlash: The Undeclared War Against American Women.* New York: Crown, 1991.

Feminist Majority Foundation. *Empowering Women in Business.* Washington, D.C.: 1991.

Ferber, Marianne, and Brigid O'Farrell, eds. *Work and Family: Policies for a Changing Work Force.* Washington, D.C.: National Academy Press, for the National Research Council and financed by the Women's Bureau, 1991.

Ferraro, Susan. "The Anguished Politics of Breast Cancer." *The New York Times Magazine,* August 15, 1993, pp. 25–62.

Folbre, Nancy. *Who Pays for the Kids? Gender and the Structures of Constraint.* New York: Routledge, 1994.

———. "Of Patriarchy Born: The Political Economy of Fertility Decisions," *Feminist Studies* 9, no. 2 (Summer 1983).

Fuchs, Victor. *Women's Quest for Economic Equality.* Cambridge, Mass.: Harvard University Press, 1988.

———. "Sex Differences in Economic Well-Being." *Science,* April 1986.

Fulenwider, Claire Knoche. *Feminism in American Politics: A Study of Ideological Influence.* New York: Praeger, 1980.

Garfinkel, Irwin, and Sara S. McLanahan. *Single Mothers and Their Children: A New American Dilemma.* Washington, D.C.: Urban Institute, 1986.

Gilligan, Carol. *In a Different Voice.* Cambridge, Mass.: Harvard University Press, 1982.

Goldin, Claudia. *Understanding the Gender Gap: An Economic History of American Women.* New York: Oxford University Press, 1990.

Gordon, Nancy, Thomas E. Morton, and Ina Braden. "Faculty Salaries: Is There Discrimination by Sex, Race, and Discipline?" *American Economic Review* 64, no. 3 (June 1974).

Griffin, Keith, and Zhao Renwei, eds. *The Distribution of Income in China.* New York: St. Martin's Press, 1993.

Hall, Roberta M., and Bernice Sandler. "The Classroom Climate: A Chilly One for Women?" *Project on the Status and Education of Women.* Washington, D.C.: Association of American Colleges, 1982.

Harlan, Sharon, and Ronnie Steinberg, eds. *Job Training for Women: The Promise and Limits of Public Policies.* Philadelphia: Temple University Press, 1989.

Hartmann, Heidi. "The Family as the Locus of Gender, Class, and Political Struggle: The Example of Housework." *Signs: Journal of Women in Culture and Society* 6, no. 3 (1981).

———. "Internal Labor Markets and Gender: A Case Study of Promotion." *Gender in the Workplace.* Washington, D.C.: Brookings Institution, 1987.

Herndl, Diane Price. *Invalid Women.* Chapel Hill: University of North Carolina Press, 1993.

Hersch, Joni. "The Impact of Non-market Work on Market Wages." *American Economic Review* (May 1991).

Himmelfarb, Gertrude. *Marriage and Morals Among the Victorians.* New York: Vintage Press, 1987.

Hochschild, Arlie. *The Second Shift.* New York: Avon Books, 1989.

Hrdy, Sarah Blaffer. *The Woman That Never Evolved.* Cambridge, Mass.: Harvard University Press, 1981.

Kaminer, Wendy. "Crashing the Locker Room." *The Atlantic Monthly,* July 1992.

———. "Feminism's Identity Crisis." *The Atlantic Monthly* (October 1993).

Katzenstein, Mary, and Carol Mueller, eds. *The Women's Movement of the United States and Western Europe.* Philadelphia: Temple University Press, 1987.

Lindgren, J. Ralph, and Nadine Taub. *The Law of Sex Discrimination.* St. Paul, Minn.: West Publishing, 1988.

Lovenduski, Joni, and Pippa Norris, eds. *Gender and Party Politics.* New York: Sage, 1993.

Massey, Sharon. "Co-Ed Schools Are Studying All Girl Classes." *The Wall Street Journal,* September 10, 1993.

Mathews, Donald G., and Jane Sherron De Hart. *Sex, Gender and the Politics of ERA.* New York and Oxford: Oxford University Press, 1994.

Nelson, Barbara J., and Najma Chowdhury, eds. *Women and Politics Worldwide.* New Haven, Conn. and London: Yale University Press, 1994.

Neuman, Elena. "Cancer: The Issue Feminists Forgot." *Insight* (February 9, 1992): 7–13.

The New Our Bodies, Ourselves. New York: Touchstone, 1992.

Office of Research on Women's Health. *National Institutes of Health: Opportunities for Research on Women's Health.* (September 1992). National Institutes of Health, Bethesda, MD.

O'Neill, June O. "Women and Wages." *American Enterprise* (November–December 1990).

Population Crisis Committee. *Country Rankings of the Status of Women: Poor, Powerless, and Pregnant.* Population Briefing Paper No. 20 (June 1988).

Population Bulletin 40, no. 2. Population Reference Bureau, Inc., April 1975.

Ravitch, Diane. *The Troubled Crusade: American Education 1945–80.* New York: Basic Books, 1983.

Reskin, Barbara, and Patricia Roos. *Job Queues, Gender Queues: Explaining Women's Inroads into Male Occupations.* Philadelphia: Temple University Press, 1990.

Ries, Paula, and Anne J. Stone, eds. *The American Woman 1992–93, A Status Report.* New York and London: W. W. Norton, 1992.

Rinehart, Sue Tolleson. *Gender Consciousness and Politics.* New York: Routledge, 1992.

Rose, Phyllis. *Parallel Lives: Five Victorian Marriages.* New York: Vintage Press, 1984.

Rosenberg, Rosalind. *Divided Lives.* New York: Hill and Wang, 1992.

Saltzman, Amy. "Trouble at the Top. Why the 'Glass Ceiling' is Changing Women's Work Lives." *U.S. News and World Report,* June 17, 1991.

Schor, Juliet B. *The Overworked American: The Unexpected Decline of Leisure.* New York: Basic Books, 1991.

Shibley, Janet, and Marilyn Essex, eds. *Parental Leave and Child Care.* Philadelphia: Temple University Press, 1991.

Smith, Ralph, ed. *The Subtle Revolution: Women at Work.* Washington, D.C.: Urban Institute, 1979.

Sommers, Christina Hoff. *Who Stole Feminism?* New York: Simon and Schuster, 1994.

Sorensen, Elaine. *Exploring the Reasons Behind the Narrowing of the Gender Gap in Earnings.* Washington, D.C.: Urban Institute, 1991.

Sturnick, Judith A., Jane E. Milley, and Catherine A. Tisinger, eds. *Women at the Helm: Pathfinding Presidents at State Colleges and Universities.* American Association of State Colleges and Universities, 1991.

Turk, Michele. "The Neglected Sex." *American Health* (December 1993): 54–57.

Ulrich, Laurel Thatcher. *A Midwife's Tale.* New York: Vintage, 1991.

United Nations Development Program. *Human Development Report 1994.* New York: Oxford University Press, 1994.

United States Department of Labor. *A Report on the Glass Ceiling Initiative.* Washington, D.C.: 1991.

Weitzman, Lenore. *The Divorce Revolution: The Unexpected Social and Economic Consequences for Women and Children in America.* New York: Free Press, Macmillan, 1985.

Wollstonecraft, Mary. *Vindication of the Rights of Woman.* Harmondsworth, England: Penguin Books, 1982. (Originally published 1792.)

Women's Bureau, U.S. Department of Labor. *1993 Handbook on Women Workers: Trends and Issues.* Washington, D.C., 1993.

Women's Research and Education Institute. *The American Woman 1994–95: Where We Stand.* Edited by Cynthia Costello and Anne J. Stone. New York: W. W. Norton, 1994.

Woody, Thomas. *A History of Women's Education in the United States*. New York: Octagon Books, 1929.

World Development Report 1993. *Investing in Health*. New York: Oxford University Press, 1993.

INDEX

About the Authors

SUE HEADLEE is Assistant Professor of Economic Policy in the Washington Semester Program with The American University. Dr. Headlee has written and researched on issues related to this work and is the author of *The Political Economy of the Family Farm: The Agrarian Roots of American Capitalism* (Praeger, 1991).

MARGERY ELFIN is Professor of Political Science and Chair of the Department of History and Political Science at Hood College in Frederick, Maryland. Dr. Elfin has published in the areas of political science and politics.

ISBN 0-275-95536-2

9 780275 955366

90000>

EAN

HARDCOVER BAR CODE

8/16